The Public Legitimacy of Minority Claims

Problems involving minorities still constitute a significant challenge for public policies in countries such as those on the territories of the former Soviet Union and Yugoslavia. Relatively unassimilated, but in most cases not enjoying administrative autonomy, their lifeworlds being to a great extent culturally "non-transparent" to the general public, the minority groups in Central and Eastern Europe face problems that are quite different from those of minorities in Western Europe and North America.

This book presents a study of public policies concerning the national, ethnic, and religious minorities in the countries of Central and Eastern Europe. It explores the opportunities available for applying the model of deliberative democracy to the domain of designing and realizing minority policies. It examines the possibility that minority groups can influence – and ideally even pre-decide – minority policies by legitimizing claims concerning their needs and rights in a way that leaves democratic public opinion no choice but to support them. Adopting a novel approach to the public legitimization of minority claims, it proposes that the general public's evaluation of the credibility of minority claims should focus on the *procedural* qualities of the intra-group discourses through which these claims are articulated and substantiated.

This text will be of key interest to students and scholars of public policy, minority politics, the politics of Eastern Europe, political theory and comparative politics.

Plamen Makariev is Professor in the Faculty of Philosophy, Sofia University, Bulgaria.

Routledge Studies in Governance and Public Policy

The Public Legitimacy of Minority Claims

A Central/Eastern European perspective

Plamen Makariev

Routledge
Taylor & Francis Group

LONDON AND NEW YORK

First published 2017 by Routledge

2 Park Square, Milton Park, Abingdon, Oxfordshire OX14 4RN
52 Vanderbilt Avenue, New York, NY 10017

Routledge is an imprint of the Taylor & Francis Group, an informa business

First issued in paperback 2018

British Library Cataloguing-in-Publication Data
A catalogue record for this book is available from the British Library

Library of Congress Cataloging-in-Publication Data
Names: Makariev, Plamen.
Title: The public legitimacy of minority claims : a Central/Eastern European perspective / Plamen Makariev.
Description: Abingdon ; New York, NY : Routledge, 2017. |
Series: Routledge studies in governance and public policy ; 27 |
Includes bibliographical references and index.
Identifiers: LCCN 2016015759| ISBN 9781138183742 (hardback) |
ISBN 9781315645667 (ebook)
Subjects: LCSH: Minorities–Government policy–Europe, Central. |
Minorities–Government policy–Europe, Eastern. | Minorities–Legal status, laws, etc.–Europe, Central. | Minorities–Legal status, laws, etc.–Europe, Eastern. | Minorities–Political activity–Europe, Central. | Minorities–Political activity–Europe, Eastern. | Deliberative democracy–Europe, Central. | Deliberative democracy–Europe, Eastern.
Classification: LCC JN96.A38 M557 2017 | DDC 323.10943–dc23
LC record available at https://lccn.loc.gov/2016015759

ISBN: 978-1-138-18374-2 (hbk)
ISBN: 978-0-367-17355-5 (pbk)

Typeset in Times New Roman
by Wearset Ltd, Boldon, Tyne and Wear

Contents

Preface

This study focuses on minority issues that are specific to the ethnic, religious, and national minorities in the countries of Central and Eastern Europe. Within the context of the current refugee crisis and the unprecedented wave of immigration to Western Europe, the issues related to the minority groups already present in these countries tend to pale in comparison, and the need to create measures to address them tends to lose its sense of urgency under the pretense that their resolution can be postponed for "calmer times." This subject can nonetheless be viewed from an entirely different angle, for it is conceivable that the immigrant crisis could lead to an exacerbation of the xenophobic and nationalistic tendencies that exist in the political life of the countries in Europe. It is very unlikely that people who harbor xenophobic or nationalistic sentiments would selectively direct their hatred of "Others" toward one group over another – that is, that they would make a distinction between "good" and "bad" minorities. The more likely scenario is that both public policies and mainstream citizen attitudes towards cultural differences would develop in ways that add fuel to the already volatile problems of traditional minorities in this particular region. The events that recently took place in Eastern Ukraine serve as an example of what such processes could possibly lead to.

This study is guided by two main principles to ensure that the standards for quality research are met. One calls for unwavering consideration of the diversity, complexity, and dynamics of minority issues. In the course of his decades-long experience in this field, the author of this study has encountered numerous examples of inept theoretical approaches and political decisions that resulted from underestimating the challenges presented by the interconnectedness of the effects of disparate factors on various minority-related problems. The second principle mandates searching for theoretical solutions that could facilitate the development and implementation of self-consistent public policies.

The two quality principles that the author has chosen to apply may at first glance appear to be mutually exclusive. However, the present discussion resides upon the presumption that it is possible to reconcile (or "resolve" in Hegelian terms) this contradiction, but only insofar as one crucial condition is observed – namely, that policy challenges related to minority issues are approached from a philosophical frame of reference that can help make sense of the confusing jumble of divergent, yet interdependent processes and events that take place in this study's area of focus. The study may thus be regarded as bringing together policy studies and political philosophy in an effort to attain the goals of the investigation.

The author of this book, Professor Plamen Makariev, has more than 20 years of experience in the fields of policy studies and political philosophy. He is the co-founder and was the first director of the Intercultural Studies Master's Degree Program at Sofia University (1995). In addition, he has taught as a part-time instructor at the Higher Islamic Institute in Sofia; authored the research mono-graphs *Multiculturalism between Toleration and Recognition* (2008) and *Minority Policies and Deliberative Democracy* (2009); conducted research on minority educational policies on the Balkans as a fellow of the International Policy Fellowships Program of the Open Society Institute, Budapest (2001); wrote a study on the role of religions in the public sphere in the capacity of a fellow of the Fulbright Program (2012); and worked as a coordinator for South-eastern Europe at the Center for the Study of Culture and Values in Washington, DC. Professor Makariev has also served as a member of the National Consulta-tive Board for Minority Education (2004–2012) at the Ministry of Education and Science in Bulgaria and participated in the development of the National Strategy for Educational Integration (2015).

Introduction

Why the communicative empowerment of minorities?

Should minority policies conform to the interests of their "target groups"? They obviously should in a democratic political system. However, when such policies are determined exclusively by the will of those in power – and representative democracy, by and large, hinders minority representation in government – members of minority communities are in a disadvantaged position that is, indeed, incompatible with the principles of democracy.

Historically, minority protection has been exercised primarily through the promotion of human rights, and modern democratic legislation provides a number of safeguards designed to prevent the exercise of arbitrary power by authorities in respect to minority groups. One such safeguard is the notion of universal human rights, which protect persons belonging to minorities from unequal treatment and focus on the fight against discrimination. Nevertheless, the protection of individual rights as such is not sufficient to ensure the repro-duction of the cultural identity of a minority group across time.[1] The latter is usually considered to involve the exercising of cultural rights, which are col-lective or group specific, and, unlike universal rights, do not enjoy general approval in either scholarly literature, politics, or the eyes of the public. Fears have been voiced that the recognition and protection of such rights may in fact lead to the violation of the cultural and, hence, political integrity of the societies concerned (see Jones 2010; Bisaz 2012; Jovanović 2012).

It is because of such fears that not all democratic legislation contains provi-sions on cultural rights; moreover, even where such provisions exist, they are usually worded in a way that lacks a sense of imperativeness. This also holds true for the relevant international instruments concerning minority rights. An example of this is provided by the *Framework Convention for the Protection of National Minorities* (1995), which includes a number of articles that contain such phrases as "as far as possible,"[2] "if those persons so request and where such a request corresponds to a real need,"[3] "taking into account their specific con-ditions,"[4] and "when there is a sufficient demand for such indications."[5]

Real-life examples and commonsense demonstrate that the application of legal norms concerning cultural identity may produce very different effects in differing circumstances. In some cases, the existence of media outlets owned and/ or operated by representatives of a particular minority community may help the identity of that community develop into an important positive factor in the public life of the country. It may help, for example, to raise the social status of the community, as well as the self-confidence of its members, so that they feel like fully-fledged citizens. In other circumstances, however, the operation of minority-oriented media outlets may lead to the self-segregation of the minority groups whose interests they ostensibly serve, and to a confrontation between those groups and society at large. In a similar fashion, if place names that are traditional for a substantial minority population of a particular area in a given country are added to the official names of towns, villages, or rivers, such as on signposts, this may be regarded as an acknowledgment of the worth of the minority's identity and have a positive effect on relations between the community and society. But in another country, or even in another region of the same country, such multiculturalist tolerance may create tension between ethnic groups, provoke outbursts of nationalism, and in general prove to be counterproductive. Everything depends on the specific circumstances, which may vary from place to place.

This study proceeds from the position that the mechanisms used to align minority policies with the interests of the minorities themselves should be consistent with the multiplicity, complexity, and dynamics of the problems related to the interactions of minority groups with society in general. The hypothesis that this study seeks to test is whether or not another instrument may be added to already existing mechanisms of this type in order to make them more effective. More specifically, can the *public legitimization of minority claims* be convincing enough to garner the support of the public in a given country? The task of the research presented below is to identify the reasons why minority claims concerning public policies often "fall on deaf ears" and to propose ways in which to cope with this challenge.

If the authorities in a given country are sufficiently sensitive to the public legitimization of norms and policies and configure their actions accordingly – that is, if conditions exist that enable civil society to exercise what Jürgen Habermas (1996, 371) calls "communicative power" – then minority policies could be adjusted to meet the real needs of the communities concerned in ways significantly more flexible and context-relevant than relying solely on the indiscriminate application of the system of human rights. This would also make it possible to maintain a balance between the interests of such communities and the interests of society as a whole.

This is, of course, not the only means that minority groups may use to influence the policies that address their needs. A similar effect may be achieved through their direct empowerment – that is, by ensuring, in one form or another, their representation in the legislative and executive branches of government. This, too, is a way of protecting the interests of such communities that can make public policy more sensitive to the "nuances" of minority issues that arise from the complex nature of these issues as well as from their dependence on a diverse and mutable social context.

Although such – political – empowerment has been applied in a number of democratic societies for decades, my view is that the outcomes of such practices have not been encouraging. One of the following chapters is devoted specifically to the relations obtaining between political power and minority policies. After reflecting on several models of minority participation in the exercise of political power that have been implemented to one extent or another in various countries, I have arrived at the conclusion that the conflation of cultural and power-based relations is highly problematic. The influence exercised in this way by minority groups over relevant policies either has been ineffective, or has led to the self-segregation of these communities and confrontation with society.

I explain why and how this happens in Chapter 3. At this point I will only note that I have ample reasons for choosing to explore possible mechanisms for influencing minority policies "from below." Such an influence can be exerted in two ways, the first being *participatory democracy*. For instance, citizens can bring pressure to bear on policymaking through the use of various means for legitimizing public causes, including such actions as street protests (the Occupy and Anti-Globalization movements), chaining themselves to railway tracks, breaking down the doors of fur farms and letting the animals free, and so forth. Another form of participatory democracy consists of government officials delegating decision-making authority to citizens (see Wampler 2008, 62). This most often occurs at the local government level, where civil society organizations become "agents of participatory democracy" (Bell and O'Rourke 2007, 294). They can play this role by, for example, discussing the development plans of the community in dialogue with local authorities, implementing citizen monitoring programs, and creating channels for citizens and civic groups to provide feedback to members of the local government. It stands to reason that not only does such interaction between civil society and authorities put participatory democracy into action, it can also be used to reconcile public policy with the various cultural needs of minority communities.

The second way in which to put pressure on minority policies from below involves *deliberative democracy*, particularly the legitimization of minority claims, which may be described in Habermasian terms as the *communicative empowerment of minorities*. By participating in public debates, representatives of minorities can, if certain conditions are met – and these conditions are precisely the subject matter of my research – challenge "the pre-existing assumptions held by members of the larger society about what is right and fair for these groups" (Kymlicka 2002, 292). My study will focus on empowering minorities in this manner.

It is clearly no easy task to convince public opinion in a given country that the reproduction of the identity of a particular minority group over time, or the proper realization of that minority's identity, requires a particular set of conditions to be in place, and that this can only be ensured through adequate minority policies. This is especially true if attaining this goal must rely upon the representatives of the minority itself, who do not have the same material and intellectual resources at their disposal as the state. The communicative empowerment of minorities is possible under particular conditions that are not in place everywhere in the world. This is the reason why my study is limited to the situation in Central and Eastern Europe, for, as I will demonstrate later, this is one of the regions where the conditions in question exist to one extent or another.

This study will thus focus on the issues of minority groups that are typical for Central and Eastern Europe – relatively large and autochthonous groups that have been exposed to dynamic historical changes in the recent past. These changes have involved the redistribution of territories among existing countries as well as the formation of new states, which in some cases "created" minorities out of the populations of certain regions and, more generally, generated feelings of insecurity and of being threatened in all the groups involved. This includes, for instance, a constant suspicion of hidden agendas behind seemingly innocuous claims to a minimal level of cultural rights, such as the right to mother-tongue instruction in municipal and state-owned schools.

For such reasons, the discussion below will deal not with racial and immigrant groups, but rather with issues pertaining to national, ethnic, and religious minorities. I will pay particular attention to the Roma communities that are present in significant numbers in several countries of the region. In respect to the specificity of the region, it is also important to note that I base my study on the information available concerning the educational levels attained by minority populations in the countries of Central and Eastern Europe, their experiences in participating in public communication, the overall level of development of the public sphere in these countries, the extent to which civil society is capable of influencing the policies of the authorities, and the technical capacities of the media of public communication, especially the internet. When taken together, all of these factors – the particular cultural traits of the minority groups in this part of Europe, their capacity for the self-reflective reproduction of their identities over time, their ability to participate in the public sphere, as well as the level of democratic development of the societies in which they live – highlight a vast range of problems and the need for solutions. With this in mind, it seems that the communicative empowerment of minority groups may be the most effective instrument for fine-tuning public policies so that they can be harmonized with the multiplicity and "fluidity" of the issues and needs of the communities in question.

Overview

I start off Chapter 1, entitled *Minority identities*, with a couple of definitions that are necessary in order to justify the ultimate aim of the communicative empowerment of minorities: the fully-fledged reproduction of their identities over time. I point out what I shall mean further by "minority," "culture," "community," "identity group." The chapter's main subject is the controversy between two paradigms in cultural identity theory: the essentialist and the constructionist ones.[6] I propose a number of arguments in favor of the constructionist alternative. This is important for the further elaboration of the concept of communicative empowerment of minorities because their claims, which are subject to public legitimization, pertain primarily to the need for minority policies to provide favorable conditions in order to ensure that the identities of these communities are preserved and flourish over the long term. Special attention is paid to the problem of the legitimacy of identity construction and reconstruction, which emerges when these activities are regarded as instrumentally rational (*zweckrational*, in the sense of Weber 1978). I interpret the constructionist paradigm in the light of Jürgen Habermas's (1984) theory of communicative action, which allows me to identify the conditions whose fulfillment would make the active management of cultural identities morally justifiable.

Chapter 2, *The complexity of minority issues*, seeks to substantiate one of the basic theses of this study – namely, that minority issues are so diverse, complex, and dynamic that they cannot be dealt with solely by applying traditional mechanisms of aligning public policies with the interests and needs of minority communities; i.e., mechanisms such as the observance of universal and collective, or group-specific rights, etc. Without pretending to be comprehensive, this chapter examines three types of factors that influence relations between minority groups and society at large, as well as relations within minority groups themselves. These factors are *cultural differences*, *group solidarity*, and *social and political tensions*. A typical mistake made when analyzing and designing minority policies is to misinterpret the effect of one of these three factors as being the effect of another factor (this misinterpretation may be due to simple confusion or may be the result of manipulative influences); another mistake often encountered is to completely ignore the role of one or more of these factors.[7]

The section on cultural differences examines the problems of self-segregation and assimilation of minority communities, as well as of intercultural interaction. The self-segregation of minority groups is explained as being mainly the result of their activists and leaders taking an essentialist approach to their cultural identities. In this explanation I build on the identity theories of Charles Taylor (1994) and Will Kymlicka (1995). More specifically, in the case of minorities in the countries of Central and Eastern Europe, self-segregation is also related to a *sui generis* "post-traumatic syndrome" caused by national, ethnic and/or religious conflicts experienced by these minorities in the past.

As far as the issues arising from intercultural interactions are concerned, they are viewed as a result of the circumstantially inevitable close cohabitation of people who have a different perception of cultural context (Hall 1976), and hold different views on power, in-group solidarity, uncertainty, assertiveness and cooperation (Hofstede 1991), the delineation between formal and personal relationships (Trompenaars and Hampden-Turner 1997), and so forth.

The section on group solidarity deals with in-group–out-group relations as a source of tension in the interactions between ethnic or religious communities. This tension only serves to magnify the already existing cultural differences. When a particular cultural trait plays the role of an in-group–out-group difference marker, it may be perceived by the other side in a negative light, even if it is completely innocuous in itself, and thus often serves as a reason for discrimination against those possessing the trait. The analysis of the antagonizing role of group solidarity in relations between minorities and society at large is generally based on the social identity theory associated primarily with the research of Henri Tajfel (see Tajfel 1978).

The final section in Chapter 2 is devoted to the role of social and political factors in minority issues. This section makes the case that there is a principle difference between cultural and social issues. The argumentation refers to dichotomies such as community/society (Tönnies 2001), mechanical solidarity/ organic solidarity (Durkheim 1997), recognition/redistribution (Fraser and Honneth 2003), and identity groups/interest groups (Gutmann 2003), which refer to modern societies. I claim that it is both cognitively incorrect and practically counterproductive to represent all cultural issues as essentially social ones, and vice versa – that is, to deny the original specificity of the former or the latter based on principle. It is also just as wrong and counterproductive to misidentify specific cultural conflicts as social ones, or vice versa. Hence, I propose two main criteria for distinguishing between these two types of issues. In my opinion, the "dividing line" can be drawn between behavior driven entirely by rational motives, and behavior determined, in a more or less mediated way, by contingent circumstances. Furthermore, a distinction can be made between two types of interpersonal relations: relations guided by the interests of the persons involved, and relations determined by the identities of the persons involved (here I am referring to Gutmann's typology which distinguishes between "interest groups" and "identity groups").

Chapter 3, *Political power and minority policies*, the final chapter in Part I of this book, is devoted to the models of direct minority participation in the exercise of political power. As mentioned above, this is another way to make minority policies more sensitive to the needs and interests of minority communities as this approach takes into account their diversity and dynamics. This chapter presents a series of critical arguments against the models of *socialist internationalism* (see, for example, Kanev 1998), of *consociational democracy* (in the sense of Lijphart 1977), and of the *politics of presence* (Phillips 1995). The last section in the chapter offers a more general critique of the conflation of power relations and community bonds. It reveals the risks posed by combining the right to a legitimate use of force, which is one of the characteristics of political power, with exclusive solidarity, which is characteristic of identity groups. Along these same lines, a critique is also made of the so-called "Bulgarian ethnic model," that is, the participation in political life of a party (the Movement for Rights and Freedoms, DPS[8]) that is, in essence, an ethnic (Turkish) one, but uses universalist (liberal) rhetoric, proclaiming – in its statutes and, generally, in its doctrine – that its objective is to protect the rights and freedoms of all Bulgarian citizens, regardless of ethnic and religious background.

The first three chapters that make up Part I of this study seek to justify the following objective: to elaborate a methodology for the public legitimization of minority claims. This is achieved by revealing the complexity and dynamic nature of the needs and interests of minority groups, which are dependent on a number of diverse circumstances. The main premise here is that even with the best intentions, minority policies cannot be "tweaked" to keep pace with such dynamic diversity if only the *rights* of minorities are being taken into consideration. Minority policies also need to be more sensitive (and more "fine-tuned") to the needs and interests of minority groups, and this may be achieved by taking their claims into consideration as well. These claims, however, should be publicly legitimized in a way that makes them convincing enough to gain the support of the public.

The five chapters in Part II examine the conditions necessary for legitimizing minority claims in the eyes of the public, or, to put it briefly, for the communicative empowerment of minorities. The main obstacles to the realization of such a dialogue are first identified, and then the ways in which they may be overcome are mapped out.

More specifically, Chapter 4, *Communicative power*, sketches out some of the main tenets of the theory of the public sphere. In reviewing the forms of public legitimization of norms and practices, it places emphasis on two things. One is the distinction of public legitimacy proper from merely de facto public legitimacy. I have in mind the difference between two types of justification of norms and policies: justification that is consistent with the moral beliefs of the target group at which it is directed, and justification that motivates people to accept as legitimate the norms and policies that conflict with their own moral views. To make this distinction, I refer to some criteria which, *mutatis mutandis*, are used by Jürgen Habermas (1991) in *The Structural Transformation of the Public Sphere*,[9] then in some of his works on discourse ethics, and, recently, on the theory of deliberative democracy. The other emphasis is on the plurality of the public sphere – that is, the obvious fragmentation of the public sphere into different publics that approach public legitimization in different ways; consequently, this leads to situations in which what is legitimate for some may not be considered legitimate by others. Keeping in mind the concept of communicative empowerment of minorities, this plurality is a problem because it calls into question the possibility that minority groups and public opinion in a given country may find a "common language" when it comes to assessing the legitimacy of particular minority claims.

Chapter 5, *Legitimacy and public deliberation*, presents a specific methodology for public legitimization – namely, that of public deliberation. In my opinion, public deliberation offers the most appropriate and trustworthy means available for justifying minority claims in the eyes of the public. The procedure of reaching an agreement on publicly important issues in a fair way, which is a characteristic of this methodology, contains – or, at least, is meant to contain – guarantees that the communication between the parties to the debate will not be manipulative. This chapter pays special attention to the model of deliberative democracy as developed by Jürgen Habermas since this is where the concept of the "communicative power" of civil society was elaborated. Some critiques of the public-deliberative paradigm, particularly the critique made from the standpoint of "agonistic pluralism" (Mouffe 1999), are also examined.

Chapter 6, *The internet as a medium for public deliberation*, explores the capacities of the internet to serve as a public deliberation environment. Online communication is especially important for the communicative empowerment of minorities in that it enables individuals and groups to influence public opinion even if they do not have political power or significant material resources; furthermore, their participation in public communication does not even have to be organized, coordinated, or directed by somebody. If what determines the outcome of a debate is "the unforced force of the better argument," to quote one of the main tenets of the theory of public deliberation, then the internet is the perfect platform for the public legitimization of minority claims. This chapter also includes several case studies of, generally speaking, successful internet forums for public deliberation.

Chapter 7, *Is intercultural public deliberation possible?*, presents the problem which, to my mind, is the main obstacle to the public legitimization of minority claims. This problem stems from the cultural "non-transparency" of minority groups' lifeworlds to the general public. Typically, minority claims are justified by stressing the need to ensure adequate conditions for the reproduction of the cultural identity of the respective group over time. But if the "addressees" of such messages do not share that identity, how can they know that it is these, and not other conditions, that are necessary for the identity in question to "flourish"? In other words, how can an outside observer be sure that a given minority claim is an expression of a genuine cultural need of the group and not simply an instrument that its leaders are using in an effort to manipulate public opinion to selfish ends, or an expression of false consciousness, or a product of some sort of in-group rivalry, and so forth?

I also examine several attempts of authors working in the public-deliberative paradigm to find an answer to the following question: how can rational communication possibly overcome the "barrier" of cultural non-transparency? Critical comments are offered on the texts of Jürgen Habermas (1996), John Rawls (1997), James Bohman (2000), Jorge Valadez (2001), Michael Rabinder James (2004), and Monique Deveaux (2006).

In Chapter 8, *The communicative empowerment of minority groups*, I formulate and substantiate my proposal for a solution to the problem in question; a solution that would enable the legitimization of minority claims in a manner that is convincing enough to sway public opinion. This would also constitute the communicative empowerment of minorities which, in turn, would open up possibilities for designing and implementing flexible minority policies that take into consideration the whole gamut of diverse and ever-changing problems associated with life in minority communities.

I believe the solution lies in binding the legitimacy of minority demands to none other than the *procedural correctness* of the debates within the communities themselves, through which those demands are formulated. In other words, if in a given case the debate follows a procedure that guarantees that all parties concerned have the opportunity to defend their positions in an adequate way, then it ought to be clear to an outside observer that the decision reached represents the true state of affairs – that is, it has not been manipulated. Or, more specifically, that the thus-formulated minority claims take into account the genuine cultural needs of the community concerned and, in this sense, are legitimate. The procedural correctness of a debate can be evaluated from all points of view; one does not need to be competent on the subject of the debate – in this particular case, to share the identity of those whose needs are discussed.

What follows is that the above-mentioned debates within minority groups should be conducted in the format of public deliberation. However, a serious problem arises at this point. How can the interests of society at large – a society undoubtedly among the parties affected by minority policies – be represented in such debates? If its interests are not represented, then the debates in question will deteriorate into what some authors call "enclave deliberations" (see Sunstein 2002), with all of the flaws of "groupthink" (see Janis 1982). This question is discussed in the final section of Chapter 8.

Methodology

Finally, I would like to share a few words about the methodology of this study. As must have become clear by now, my methodology is based on the Habermasian version of the theory of public deliberation and the model of deliberative democracy. The proceduralist approach to the legitimatization of both moral and legal norms that is a distinctive feature of this paradigm is a method that I have chosen to also apply to the public legitimization of minority claims. I rely strictly on this approach to find opportunities for rational dialogue between minority communities and the mainstream public that span the "barrier" of cultural differences. Put in the terms of *Between Facts and Norms* (Habermas 1996), this solution to the problem may be described as ensuring communicative continuity between the *lifeworld* of a minority community, the intra-group *ethical-political discourse* through which its self-understanding is articulated, and the *moral discourse* that ultimately legitimizes norms and practices in the eyes of the public and within society at large.

Overall, I have tried to achieve methodological continuity between the different levels of abstraction of my research – from policy analysis to philosophical reflection, and vice versa. I have been guided by the conviction, derived from decades of work on minority issues, that finding the solution to a number of real-life paradoxes of minority policies is impossible without reviewing the paradoxes within an adequate conceptual frame of reference in which they make sense. And the choice of such a frame of reference is precisely a matter of philosophical consideration.

Demographic data about the countries of Central and Eastern Europe

For the reader's convenience, in this Introduction I have included data on the ethnic and religious composition of the population of the countries in Central and Eastern Europe. These figures provide only a rough idea of the minority populations in this part of the continent as it should be noted that not every ethnic or religious community in a country can be considered a minority group. As I already mentioned in the Overview, Chapter 1 contains a definition of the term "minority," which will inform the further content of my study, and – to get ahead of myself – I would like to clarify that according to this definition an ethnic or religious community must meet a number of criteria in order to be considered a "minority" group. Providing such a specific definition is not a matter of semantic perfectionism, but reflects the fact that a minority status infers the existence of considerable issues that are particular to the lives of minority communities. A democratic society creates policies specifically to address such issues; it is these minority policies that are the main focus of my study.

In this book, I discuss three types of minorities: religious, ethnic, and national. The status of national minorities is a contentious issue. It is widely accepted that some minorities share a cultural identity with the mainstream population of another country (some scholars use the term "kin-state" to denote the role of a neighboring country in relation to the particular minority group). Some examples of this type of relationship include the Turks in Bulgaria, the Hungarians in Serbia, Slovakia and Romania, and the Russians in the Baltic countries. It is arguable, though, whether or not the fact that there is a shared identity between a particular minority and the majority population of a neighboring (or even a non-neighboring) country can give the "kin-state" grounds to claim the right to exercise certain protection over that particular minority despite the fact that the members of this group are citizens of another sovereign country. Such an interpretation of the term national minority can be found, for example, in the well-known international document, *The Bolzano Recommendations on National Minorities in Inter-State Relations* (OSCE High Commissioner on National Minorities 2008). According to another interpretation, national minorities are all numerically significant autochthonous minority groups in a given country. An illustration of this interpretation is the Estonian *Law on Cultural Autonomy for National Minorities* of 1993 (see Lagerspetz 2014). Then there are those countries – such as Bulgaria, for example – that do not recognize whatsoever the existence of national minorities within its territories.

The data on the population size of ethnic and religious minorities are derived from official population censuses, which is why, in some cases, these data are starkly different from the de facto numbers. It is not uncommon for a part of the population included in a census to refuse to declare their ethnic identity, and, consequently, some communities are represented in the final results by a relative share of the overall population of the country that is far from the actual situation. In the case of the Roma people, there is another tendency that also "distorts" the picture – a large number of the members of this group tend to identify themselves as members of another group; for example, in Bulgaria, depending on their religious affiliation, some Roma identify themselves as Bulgarians, and others as Turks. This is why in some cases I have supplemented the official findings of population censuses by expert assessments that quote more realistic figures, albeit without purporting to be exact.

Albania, source, www.instat.gov.al/en/census/census-2011.aspx
Out of the country's population of 2,800,138, according to the results of the 2011 census, 82.58% identified themselves as Albanians, 0.87% as Greeks, 0.3% as Roma, 0.3% as Aromanians, and 0.2% as Macedonians. The number of the respondents who chose not to answer the question about ethnic affiliation was unusually high – 14%. A possible explanation is that four ethnic Macedonian organizations in Albania appealed to the people of their ethnic group to boycott the census. In 2003, these organizations conducted an unofficial census among their community. As a result they claimed that the Macedonian minority numbered between 120,000 and 350,000 – a number that is not comparable with the 5000 of the 2011 census.

Concerning religion, the distribution was: Muslims 70%, Catholics 10.03%, Orthodox 6.75%, Bektashi 2.09%

Bosnia and Herzegovina, source: www.popis2013.ba/index.php/en/
The census was conducted in 2013, but up to the time of completion of this book no official results have been published. As far as the total population of the country is concerned, it numbers 3,791,622 of whom 2,371,603 reside in the Federation of Bosnia and Herzegovina, 1,326,991 in Republika Srpska, and 93,028 in the Brcko District.

Some preliminary results were published by the European Parliamentary Research Service (http://epthinktank.eu/2014/01/27/bosnia-2013-census/). According to them, 48.4% declared themselves as Bosniaks, 32.7% as Serbs and 14.6% as Croats.

The distribution according to faith is: Muslim – 40%, Orthodox – 31%, Roman Catholic – 15%, other – 14%.

Bulgaria, source: www.nsi.bg/census2011
According to the results of the 2011 census, the total population is 7,364,570, of whom 77% are Bulgarians, 8% Turks, and 4.4% Roma. A big part of the Roma population identified themselves either as Bulgarians, or as Turks, depending on their religion. Unofficially, their number is estimated to be between 700,000 and 800,000.

Concerning religion, 59.4% identified themselves as Orthodox, 7.41% as Muslims/Sunni, 0.37% as Muslims/Shia, 0.66% as Catholics and 0.87% as Protestants.

A special case is the community of the Bulgarian Muslims, or the so-called "Pomaks" – descendants of ethnic Bulgarians who converted to Islam during the Ottoman rule. Some (probably most) identified as Bulgarians by ethnicity and Muslims by religion, but significant numbers as Turks.

Croatia, source: www.dzs.hr/Eng/censuses/census2011
The census was conducted in 2011 and the total population was 4,284,889.

According to ethnicity: Croats – 90.42%, Serbs – 4.36%, Bosniaks – 0.73%, Roma – 0.4%, and Hungarians – 0.33%.
According to religion: Catholics 86,28%, Orthodox 4,44%, Muslims 1,47%.

Czech Republic, source: www.czech.cz/en/About-CZ/Facts-about-the-Czech-Republic/Census
Population, according to the 2011 census: 10,562,214.
Ethnicity: Czechs – 63.7%, Moravians – 4.9%, Silesians – 0.1%; Slovaks – 1.4%; Roma – under 0.1% (unofficially their number is estimated at about 220,000). About 26% of the population boycotted the "nationality" question.
The only sizable religious community is the Catholics – 10.3%.

Estonia, source: www.stat.ee/phc2011
Census conducted in 2011. Population: 1,294,455.
Ethnicity: Estonians – 68.7%, Russians – 24.8%, Ukrainians – 1.7%, Belarusians and Finns – less than 1% each.
Major religious communities: Orthodox 16%, Lutherans 10%.

Hungary, source: www.ksh.hu/nepszamlalas/?lang=en
Census conducted in 2011. Population: 9,982,000.
Ethnicity: Hungarian – 85.6%, Roma – 3.2%, German – 1.9%, other – 2.6%, unspecified – 14.1%
Religion: 37.2% Roman Catholic, 11.6% Calvinist, 2.2% Lutheran, 1.8% Greek Catholic.

Latvia, source: www.csb.gov.lv/en/statistikas-temas/population-census-30761.html
Census conducted in 2011. Population: 2,074,605.
Ethnicity: Latvians – 62.1%, Russians – 26.9%, Belarusians – 3.3%, Ukrainians – 2.2%, Poles – 2.2%, and Lithuanians – 1.2%
Religion: 24.1% Orthodox, 20.7% Catholics, 20.0% Lutherans.
Language spoken at home: 62.1% Latvian, and 37.2% Russian.

Lithuania, source: http://osp.stat.gov.lt/en/2011-m.-surasymas
Census conducted in 2011. Population: 3,043,429.
Ethnicity: Lithuanians – 84.2%, Poles – 6.6%, and Russians – 5.8%.
Religion: 77.3% Catholic, 4.1% Orthodox.

Macedonia, source: www.stat.gov.mk/OblastOpsto_en.aspx?id=31
Census conducted in 2002. Population: 2,022,547.
Ethnicity: Macedonians – 64.2%, Albanians – 25.2%, Turks – 3.9%, Roma – 2.7%, Serbs – 1.8%, and Aromanians (Vlachs) – 0.5%.
Religion: 64.78% Orthodox, 33.33% Muslim.

Montenegro, source: www.monstat.org/eng/page.php?id=57&pageid=57
Census conducted in 2011. Population: 620,029.
Ethnicity: Montenegrins – 45%, Serbs – 28.7%, Bosniaks – 8.6%, Muslims – 3.3%, Albanians – 4.9%, and Roma – 0.8%.
Religion: 74.24% Orthodox, 17.74% Muslim, 3.54% Catholic.

Poland, source: http://stat.gov.pl/en/topics/population/census-2011-results
Census conducted in 2011. Population: 38,562,189.

Ethnicity: Polish – 96.9%, Silesian – 1.1%, German – 0.2%, Ukrainian – 0.1%.

Religion: 87.2% Catholic (includes Roman Catholic 86.9% and Greek Catholic, Armenian Catholic, and Byzantine-Slavic Catholic), 1.3% Orthodox, 0.4% Protestant.

Romania, source: www.recensamantromania.ro/en/
Census conducted in 2011. Population: 20,121,641.

Ethnicity: Romanians – 88.9%, Hungarians – 6.5%, Roma – 3.3%.

Religion: 86.5% Orthodox, 4.6% Roman-Catholic, 3.2% Reformed, 1.9% Pentecostal.

Mother tongue: 90.9% Romanian, 6.7% Hungarian, 1.3% Romani.

Serbia, source: http://popis2011.stat.rs/?lang=en
Census conducted in 2011. Population: 7,186,862.

Ethnicity: Serbs – 83.32%, Hungarians – 3.53%, Roma – 2.05%, Bosniaks – 2.02%, Albanians – 5809, under 0.01% (boycott in three municipalities with predominantly ethnic Albanian population).

Religion: 84.5% Orthodox, 5% Roman Catholics, 3% Muslim, 1% Protestant.

Slovakia, source: http://slovak.statistics.sk/wps/portal/ext/themes/demography/census
Census conducted in 2011. Population: 5,397,036.

Ethnicity: Slovaks – 80.7%, Hungarians – 8.5%, Roma – 2%.

Unofficially, the number of the Roma is estimated (for a variety of reasons) to be between 1% and 10% of the population. A realistic estimation places them in the region of 300,000 (about 5.6%).

Religion: 62% Roman Catholics, 6.9% Protestants, 4.1% Greek Catholic, 2.0% Reformed Christian Church, and 0.9% Orthodox.

Slovenia, source: www.stat.si/popis2011/eng/Default.aspx?lang=eng
In 2011 a register-based census was conducted according to which the population of the country was 2,050,189. No data about the ethnic and the religious affiliation of the population were available.

According to the census of 2002, the population numbered 1,964,036.

Ethnicity: Slovenians – 83.1%, Serbs – 2%, Croats – 1.8%, Bosniaks – 1.1%, Muslims – 0.5% (as the two latter terms were generally considered to be synonyms, the ethnic group in question actually numbered 1.6%).

Religion: 57.8% Roman Catholic, 2.4% Muslim, 2.2% Orthodox.

Notes

1 By "reproduction of a cultural identity across time" I mean the mode in which such an identity exists. If we regard cultural identity as the self-understanding of an individual or of a group, we cannot assume that it exists as a thing. Its being should rather be conceived of as the multifaceted unfolding of activities and interactions through which the cultural identity is perpetually renewing itself and yet remaining true to itself.
2 Article 9 (3), on the possibility of persons belonging to national minorities to create and use their own media.
3 Article 10 (2), on the use of the minority language in relations between persons belonging to national minorities and administrative authorities.
4 Article 11 (3), on the display of traditional local names, street names and other topographical indicators in the minority language.
5 Ibid.
6 Some of the authors who work in this field prefer the term "constructivist."
7 The "deconstruction" of minority issues I propose along the above-mentioned three "axes" is analogous to the "intersectionality" paradigm in gender studies. The difference is that I use the more general category of "cultural differences" instead of "gender" and "race," and of "social and political factors" instead of "class"; besides, as a third dimension, I introduce group solidarity in the sense of the "social identity theory." As a whole, I have sought to construct a conceptual frame of reference that helps to reveal the complexity of minority issues on a general level, with a particular focus on the issues of ethnic, religious, and national minorities.
8 "Dvizhenie za Prava i Svobodi" in Bulgarian.
9 First English language edition – 1989.

References

Bell, Christine and Catherine O'Rourke. "The People's Peace? Peace Agreements, Civil Society, and Participatory Democracy." *International Political Science Review* 28, no. 3 (2007): 293–324.

Bisaz, Corsin. *The Concept of Group Rights in International Law. Groups as Contested Right-Holders, Subjects and Legal Persons.* The Raoul Wallenberg Institute of Human Rights Library, vol. 41. Leiden/Boston: Martinus Nijhoff Publishers, 2012.

Bohman, James. *Public Deliberation.* Cambridge, MA: The MIT Press, 2000.

Deveaux, Monique. *Gender and Justice in Multicultural Liberal States.* Oxford: Oxford University Press, 2006.

Durkheim, Emile. *The Division of Labor in Society.* New York: Free Press, 1997.

Framework Convention for the Protection of National Minorities, Strasbourg, 1995.

Fraser, Nancy and Axel Honneth. *Redistribution or Recognition? A Political-Philosophical Exchange*, London and New York: Verso, 2003.

Gutmann, Amy. *Identity in Democracy.* Princeton, NJ: Princeton University Press, 2003.

Habermas, Jürgen. *Theory of Communicative Action.* Boston MA: Beacon Press, 1984.

Habermas, Jürgen. *The Structural Transformation of the Public Sphere: An Inquiry into a Category of Bourgeois Society.* Cambridge, MA: The MIT Press, 1991.

Habermas, Jürgen. *Between Facts and Norms.* Cambridge MA: The MIT Press, 1996.

Hall, Edward. T. *Beyond Culture.* New York: Anchor Books, 1976.

Hofstede, Geert. *Cultures and Organizations: Software of the Mind.* New York: McGraw-Hill, 1991.

James, Michael R. *Deliberative Democracy and the Plural Polity.* Lawrence, KA: University Press of Kansas, 2004.

Janis, Irving L. *Groupthink*, Boston MA: Houghton Mifflin Company, 1982.

Jones, Peter. "Cultures, Group Rights, and Group-Differentiated Rights." In *Multicultur-alism and Moral Conflict*, edited by Maria Dimova-Cookson and Peter Stirk, 38–58. New York: Routledge, 2010.

Jovanović, Miodrag A. *Collective Rights: A Legal Theory*. Cambridge: Cambridge University Press, 2012.

Kanev, Krassimir. "Law and Politics on Ethnic and Religious Minorities." In *Communities and Identities in Bulgaria*, edited by Anna Krasteva, 55–95. Ravenna: Longo Editore, 1998.

Kymlicka, Will. *Multicultural Citizenship. A Liberal Theory of Minority Rights*. Oxford: Clarendon Press, 1995.

Kymlicka, Will. *Contemporary Political Philosophy. An Introduction*. Oxford: Oxford University Press, 2002.

Lagerspetz, Mikko. "Cultural Autonomy of National Minorities in Estonia: The Erosion of a Promise." *Journal of Baltic Studies* 45, no. 4 (2014): 457–465.

Lijphart, Arend. *Democracy in Plural Societies*. New Haven: Yale University Press, 1977.

Mouffe, Chantal. "Deliberative Democracy or Agonistic Pluralism." *Social Research* 66, no 3 (1999): 745–758.

OSCE High Commissioner on National Minorities. *The Bolzano Recommendations on National Minorities in Inter-State Relations*, the Hague, 2008.

Phillips, Anne. *The Politics of Presence*. Oxford: Clarendon Press, 1995.

Rawls, John. "The Idea of Public Reason Revisited." *University of Chicago Law Review* 64, no. 3 (1997): 780–807.

Sunstein, Cass R. "The Law of Group Polarization." *The Journal of Political Philosophy* 10, no 2 (2002): 175–195.

Tajfel, Henri. *The Social Psychology of Minorities*. London: Minority Rights Group, 1978.

Taylor, Charles. "The Politics of Recognition." In *Multiculturalism. Examining the Politics of Recognition*, edited by Amy Gutmann, 25–74. Princeton, NJ: Princeton University Press, 1994.

Tönnies, Ferdinand. *Community and Civil Society*. Cambridge: Cambridge University Press, 2001.

Trompenaars, Fons and Charles Hampden-Turner. *Riding the Waves of Culture: Understanding Diversity in Global Business*. London: Nicholas Brealey Publishing, 1997.

Valadez, Jorge. *Deliberative Democracy, Political Legitimacy and Self-Determination in Multicultural Societies*. Oxford: Westview Press, 2001.

Wampler, Brian. "When Does Participatory Democracy Deepen the Quality of Democracy? Lessons from Brazil." *Comparative Politics* 41, no. 1 (2008): 61–81.

Weber, Max. *Economy and Society. An Outline of Interpretive Sociology*. Berkeley: University of California Press, 1978.

Part I
Identities and policies

1 Minority identities

Minority

Although the term "minority" is of prime importance to this study, I will not attempt to define it here in the comprehensive and reasoned way it deserves, as this would be a task beyond the scope of my research, which has, as we have seen, more specific objectives. That is why, as a starting point, I will resort to the use of the concept of "minority" as it was defined in the latest report of the Office of the United Nations High Commissioner for Human Rights (OHCHR 2010).

The UN report highlights, first and foremost, the fact that any definition of "minority" must take all relevant factors (both objective and subjective) into consideration. On the one hand, it should refer to the characteristics that are common – and beyond their power to change – to all of the members of a minority group, such as shared ethnicity, language, or religion. On the other hand, this definition should reflect the characteristics of their self-identities.

I will now examine the following definition of "minority" that was proposed by Francesco Capotorti (Special Rapporteur to the United Nations Sub-Commission on the Prevention of Discrimination and the Protection of Minorities) in 1977:

> A group numerically inferior to the rest of the population of a State, in a non-dominant position, whose members – being nationals of the State – possess ethnic, religious or linguistic characteristics differing from those of the rest of the population and show, if only implicitly, a sense of solidarity, directed towards preserving their culture, traditions, religion or language.
>
> (OHCHR 2010, 2)

Several points can be made concerning this definition. First, the definition claims that being in "a non-dominant position" is a sufficient enough feature to identify a group as a minority. Whether or not the group in question is a *numerical* minority is not a decisive factor as there are quite a few instances in which a numerical majority is in a socially and politically disadvantaged position. By way of illustration, the OHCHR report cites the case of the indigenous population of the Republic of South Africa under the apartheid regime. There are also other examples, such as the Shia in Iraq under Saddam Hussein and the Sunnis in Syria before the so-called "Arab Spring."

Another point to be made regarding Capotori's definition is that the OHCHR report notes that binding the definition of "minority" to having citizenship of the country in which the group lives makes it too narrow. Indeed, according to widely accepted notions of the minority status of a group, this group may include people who are immigrants to the country in question who have yet to receive citizenship and are unlikely to receive it soon but do not intend to leave the country in the foreseeable future. The so-called *Gastarbeiters* (i.e., migrant workers) in Germany are a case in point.

Without delving into the definition of "minority" any further, I should point out that my study is concerned with the issues of minorities that differ from the rest of the population of a given country as a result of their cultural – in the sense of national, ethnic, and religious – identity.

Identity and culture

To define the term "cultural identity" we first have to clarify the general meaning of identity, as well as that of culture. As in the case of the term "minority" above, here, too, I will narrow my focus to only those aspects of the definition of these two terms – "identity" and "culture" – which I will be using further on in this study.

Identity is viewed in different ways in psychology, sociology, and philosophy. However, it is invariably associated with the specificity (or uniqueness) of the existence of its subject, as well as with the subject's awareness of this specificity. The subject possesses an identity due to the unique combination of her characteristics, but also as a result of the continuity of all of her individual actions (in the case of collective identity, this is also due to the interconnectedness of the members of the group). In other words, "the formation of group identity is a process whereby individuals recognize in each other certain attributes that establish resemblance and affinity" between them (Isin and Wood 1999, 19).

The other term I would like to define here is "culture." Perhaps the most popular and succinct definition of "culture" from an anthropological point of view is "patterns of learned behavior" – meaning that these are not natural, physiologically determined acts performed "instinctively;" rather, they are constructs created during the process of people interacting with their environment and with one another. These constructs were developed over time as human groups went through the process of adapting to their surroundings, which means that the only way individuals belonging to a group can access them is by learning them from other members of the same group. In the words of Terence Turner (1993, 426), "Cultures are the way specific social groups, acting under specific historical and material conditions, have 'made themselves' ... [C]ultures ... are historically contingent products of such collective activity."

To my mind, what is especially important in this formulation is that culture is defined as the way specific social groups have "made themselves" within the context of actual historical circumstances. Thus, Terence Turner presents an unquestionable distinctive feature of culture: that it invariably has a group-specific character that unifies people who belong to the respective cultural community by distinguishing them from all others. In other words, culture is the collective "software of the mind" that distinguishes the members of one group or category of people from another (Hofstede 1991).

Furthermore, if we think of culture as the process of the self-creation of communities within the context of actual historical events, we will foreground its contingent character – the fact that the specific characteristics of a group's way of life cannot be "deduced" from principles; instead, these characteristics must simply be accepted as a given and should be valued by the members of the respective community for what they de facto are, without having to rationalize or justify this stance.

In addition, the definitions of "culture" emphasize the relationship between the forms of behavior which, taken as a whole, distinguish one group from another, as well as the ways in which these forms are interpreted in the respective cultural context:

> Culture is a historically created system of meaning and significance or, what comes to be the same thing, a system of beliefs and practices in terms of which a group of human beings understand, regulate and structure their individual and collective lives. It is a way of both understanding and organizing human life.
>
> (Parekh 2000, 143)

The culture of a given community demarcates what is acceptable from what is unacceptable behavior (i.e., how one is expected to behave, or not to behave, in particular circumstances). This distinction is based on historically established values. The self-creation of a community (if we refer back to Turner's terminology) does not have a mechanical character, that is, it is not simply reproducing such forms of behavior that contribute to the survival of a group in the respective conditions; the self-creation of a community also incorporates the formation of mechanisms for explaining and morally justifying a particular way of life. In other words, a community's self-understanding and self-organization presuppose each other.

At the descriptive level, some scholars have pointed out the following as elements of culture: values, language, religion, standards of behavior in day-to-day life, exemplary intellectual and artistic achievements of members of the community, traditions and rituals, and characteristic patterns of living including styles of architecture and patterns of land use (see, for example, Kidd 2002, 10). Geert Hofstede (1991, 8) classifies these elements into four categories: symbols, heroes, rituals, and values.

Whose identity?

If we are to work with the term "cultural identity," we need to know who the carrier of this identity is. Ranked by degree of their internal cohesion, there are three kinds of "candidates" for this "position": particular types of people (i.e., categories of people), particular groups, or particular communities.

The development of gender studies in the past few decades has shown beyond a doubt that gender differences are not just physiological but also cultural. However, if we assume that there is a female cultural identity, it cannot be attributed to a particular group or community; in other words, what we have here is a category of people. As we will see later, belonging to a community entails maintaining relationships of solidarity among the members of the community, while holding discriminatory attitudes toward all others (see Tönnies 2001, 17). The term "group" is more vague. Many authors use it as a synonym for community when writing about "ethnic groups." The prevalent notion, though, is that "group" is a more general term. A group's members belong to it insofar as they not only share some identical characteristics (as in the case of categories of people), but also common goals, values, and some form of internal organization, be it formal or informal.

The difference between communities and groups in general (the former may also be regarded as a type of group), is that the relationships within a group are not necessarily characterized by solidarity and mutual identification; groups may also be quite disjointed. One may regard as a group, for example, the staff of a company because the staff members tend to share common goals and values regarding their professional activity; however, while they may belong to the same organizational group, they do not have any particular moral commitments to each other, or at least not any that are more binding than the universal moral norms and standards of decent behavior.

In the publications concerning minority policies, the term "community" is used primarily in the sense of *Gemeinschaft* as defined by Ferdinand Tönnies (2001) in his seminal book *Gemeinschaft und Gesellschaft*, published in 1887. In Chapter One, Tönnies introduces the term human "association" (*Verbindung*) signifying a group of people bound by relationships based on mutual affirmation. He distinguishes between two types of associations of people, which he calls "community" (*Gemeinschaft*) and "society" (*Gesellschaft*). The former is conceived of "as having real organic life," and the latter "as a purely mechanical construction, existing in the mind" (Tönnies 2001, 17). The main difference between the two is that "community" is about the kind of coexistence of its members, which is based on mutual trust and feels "familiar, comfortable and exclusive" (i.e., it is "exclusive" in the sense that members of the community are treated differently from non-members). "Society," on the other hand, is about public life, or life "in the outside world," as Tönnies (2001, 18) puts it. "In *Gemeinschaft* we are united from the moment of our birth with our own folk for better or for worse. We go out into *Gesellschaft* as if into a foreign land" (Tönnies 2001, 18). There is "a community of language, custom, belief; but a society for purposes of business, travel, or scientific knowledge" (Tönnies 2001, 18). In other words, "society" simply means "individuals living alongside but independently of one another" (Tönnies 2001, 19).

To quote Tönnies (2001, 19), "Community [*Gemeinschaft*] is old, Society [*Gesellschaft*] is new, both as an entity and as a term." Community is associated with rural life, and Society with "the third estate."[1] The paragraph in Chapter One, devoted to the definition of the two terms, ends with the following conclusion:

> Community means genuine, enduring life together, whereas Society is a transient and superficial thing. Thus *Gemeinschaft* must be understood as a living organism in its own right, while *Gesellschaft* is a mechanical aggregate and artefact.
>
> (Tönnies 2001, 19)

The German sociologist distinguishes between three types of community: "by *blood*," "of *place*," and "of *spirit*" (Tönnies 2001, 27; emphasis in original). According to him (Tönnies 2001, 28), these three types may be described as kinship (referring above all to the nuclear family), neighborhood, and friendship or comradeship. While it is clear in what sense and to what extent kinship meets Tönnies' criteria for community, it is necessary to elucidate his understanding of the other two types of community.

Neighborhood, according to Tönnies (2001, 28; emphasis in original), "is the general character of life together in a *village*." The spatial proximity of its residents and "even the way the holdings run alongside each other, cause the people to meet and get used to each other and to develop intimate acquaintance. It becomes necessary to share work, organization and forms of administration."

Friendship, or comradeship, in the sense of "a community of spirit," includes not just informal ties based on mutual sympathy, but also religious communities and communities that arise from within cultural life. Tönnies views art "as a kind of priestly activity, for everything that is good, noble, and in some sense holy, has to be experienced through the senses in order for it to work on the mind and conscience" (Tönnies 2001, 50).

Among contemporary scholars, Amy Gutmann has attempted to fill the conceptual "space" between "community" and "group" with an intermediate term – namely, "identity groups." Her criterion for belonging to such a group is the identification of each of its members with one another (Gutmann 2003). Such mutual identification may be based on a shared culture, as well as on the pursuit of a common, selfless cause that inspires the members of the group. Gutmann (2003, 13) distinguishes between identity groups and groups bound by "instrumental interests." The motives for participating in these two types of groups are different: one is for the self-identification with a particular circle of people, while the other is purely for self-interest. However, there is also a significant difference between two kinds of identity groups: groups bound by a common cultural identity and groups whose members identify with one another by their own choice insofar as they have decided, each in their own way, to unite behind a common ideal. In the first case, if we use ethnic groups as an example, the bond between members is a contingent one and self-identification with the group is quite inert and difficult to change by a consciously made decision. In the second case, people unite of their own free will and take on the responsibility of creating, for example, an association for the protection of animals or in support of AIDS victims, and can leave the group at any moment. It goes without saying that this typology refers to modern societies. In an Islamic state, for example, society as a whole is regarded as an identity group, in Gutmann's terms. The same holds true also for totalitarian systems of social order.

Identity: essence or construct?

The "essence-or-construct" dilemma is not just theoretically interesting; it is also directly relevant to the subject of this study. The manner in which minority claims are justified is of decisive importance for the success of the public legitimatization of these claims and, subsequently, for the ability of civil society to exercise its communicative power. It is one thing to try to convince the public that the full realization of a particular identity requires certain conditions if identity is understood as an essence; it is quite another thing if it is understood as a construct.

In the publications on this theme, the conception of identity as an *essence* of its carrier is called "essentialism," while its conception as a *construct* is called "constructionism."[2] As is often the case in social sciences, this debate is asymmetrical because hardly anyone openly defends the essentialist concept of identity, while the number of publications against it is constantly growing.[3] The reason for this apparently puzzling state of affairs is, in my mind, that the methodological tradition in social sciences predisposes scholars to take an essentialist approach to identity. It is somehow natural for them to strive to explore what lies beyond the "surface" – beyond what is visible – and to reveal the essence of the object under investigation (hence the term "essentialism"). It is only natural that a theory which presents its object as unambiguously defined and predictable will be widely appreciated. Having information about the essence of the object allows us to explain, predict and, to a certain extent, manipulate its behavior. A methodological analysis of a random sample of publications on identity will reveal that many of them contain "essentialist" elements, although their authors would not identify themselves as essentialists. Thus, the "fight" against essentialism is not as much a confrontation between two schools in social science as it is a fight of one social scientist or another against herself – that is, against her own inclination to reflect on identity in an essentialist way.

What does it mean to conceive of identity as an essence? Without pretending to be comprehensive, the following list of characteristics may be derived from the various critiques of essentialism. One ascribes to identity – or, rather, *prescribes* to it (by way of a methodologically, yet, not particularly, correct mix of description and prescription) – endurance in time; endurance in the face of external influences (one may also say "sovereignty"); integrity; purity (some authors use the term "discreteness" – see, for example, Modood 1998, 378); internal "hierarchy" of essence and its manifestations.[4]

What do these five characteristics of identity actually mean? In the first place, identity should be able to endure over time; it should not undergo significant change, otherwise its carrier (a group or an individual) would cease to be itself, for it would lose – that is, change – its identity. It follows from this that the essentialist concept of identity presupposes conservatism; what is more, it requires a "conservational" approach to the culture of the community in question. Traditions, folklore, and mores need to be protected from the "erosion" of time. Otherwise, the community will lose its unique way of life and become different even if the sources of the changes are "internal" to it – in other words, if the community is undergoing an "organic" cultural evolution. Without mentioning the term "essentialism" in his essay "Struggles for Recognition in the Democratic Constitutional State," Jürgen Habermas (1994, 130) criticizes the essentialist approach that considers cultural identity to be valuable in itself:

> For in the last analysis, the protection of forms of life and traditions in which identities are formed is supposed to serve the recognition of their members; it does not represent a kind of preservation of species by administrative means. The ecological perspective on species conservation cannot be transferred to cultures.

The essentialist approach to traditional (or, as some call them, premodern) cultures has especially important implications for public policies on minorities. Traditions may be a marker of ethnic, as well as of religious identity. However, it is fully possible that a community's ethnic and religious identity may differ from its traditional mores. In today's world, for example, the question of whether or not, and possibly to what extent, the radical forms of Islam such as Salafism represent the authentic, original spirit of this religion, or are the product of the unwarranted promotion of traditional cultural mores to the status of religious norms, has acquired particular urgency (see, for example, Lacey 2009).

From an essentialist point of view, the answer to the question, "Is the transition from traditional to modern cultural patterns of activity possible without affecting ethnic and religious identity?" is, clearly, "No." Traditional mores are part of the specificity of the respective communities and should also be preserved. Thus, even a moderate change in the existence of identities is declared to be undesirable and preference is given to cultural conservatism.

The same can be said of the notion that identity should not succumb to external influences. Do people who are ready to adapt their way of life to any type of circumstances that may come their way have any identity at all? Could we speak of identity in the case of communities that are uncritically receptive to everything offered on the global "cultural market," such as aesthetic preferences, style of behavior, and all kinds of moral values? One example of an action in support of the "sovereignty" of national identities is the occasional mass protests against the expansion of McDonald's and Coca-Cola in a number of countries around the world (see, for example, Barrett 1999).

Next, in what sense does identity presuppose integrity of the group or of the individual? Let us look at a minority community that comprises different "sub-groups" – groups that have significantly different ways of life and in which the relations of solidarity are organized around more than one "center of gravity." A typical example of this is the Roma minorities in the countries of Central and Eastern Europe. They comprise communities that differ by origin, dialect, religion, degree of integration into society, and so forth (see for example Ringold 2000). Given this state of affairs, what can be said with certainty about Roma identity? If identity is reduced to the abstractly common features of life in all Roma communities, its content will turn out to be quite poor and meaningless. Hence, a scholar may be tempted to ignore the internal differences and to ascribe some characteristics of one of the "sub-groups" to all of the others – that is, to "essentialize" identity in this respect.

This approach to identity is also a source (albeit not the only one) of stereotyping in social sciences. The flaws of such generalizations are pointed out, for example, in a number of methodological analyses of contemporary feminism, such as the following:

> The feminist critique of gender essentialism does not merely charge that essentialist claims about "women" are overgeneralizations, but points out that these generalizations are hegemonic in that they represent the problems of privileged women (most often white, Western, middle-class, heterosexual women) as paradigmatic "women's issues."
>
> (Narayan 1998, 86)

Essentialist cognitive approaches of this kind also account for widespread stereotypes about cultures, such as "It is typical of the Bulgarians that…" or "In such a situation, a German would …"

From an essentialist point of view, cultural homogeneity is also valuable for another reason. It has to do with the attitudes toward cultural syncretism, as well as toward the various forms of cultural "hybridization." These phenomena are often found at the "contact points" of different cultures, where there is an exchange of certain elements from the cultural practices and value systems of the parties involved. In some areas of the Rhodope mountains in southern Bulgaria, for example, Bulgarian Christians, Bulgarian Muslims, and ethnic Turks live closely together. In this situation there is a mix of Christian and Islamic rites, celebrations of the same religious holidays, and performing the other group's religious rituals in the search for a miraculous cure, and so forth:

> Both folk Christianity and folk Islam replicated onto the natural environment their old, pre-monotheistic beliefs, mixing them with notions and rituals which have been imported from elsewhere. This resulted in a plastic module which has preserved known traditions and can accept innovations

with ease. It is understandable and convenient both for Christians and for Muslims. Hence a common cultural pool is formed and starts functioning.

(Georgieva 1995, 165)

From an essentialist point of view, such mutual influences are undesirable: "Conservatives argue that cultures should be preserved in order to keep groups separate, because cultural hybridity generates conflict and instability" (Benhabib 2002, 4). Cases such as the one described above are qualified as "contamination" or even desecration of identity.

From such positions, it is also difficult to come to terms with the so-called "hyphenated identities," which are common in immigrant countries such as the United States and Canada, as well as in Western Europe. For example, what is the identity of a second-generation immigrant Turk who was born and brought up in Germany but is a citizen of the Republic of Turkey? From an essentialist point of view, such persons must decide for themselves whether they are German or Turkish and, having adopted one national identity, do everything possible to distance themselves from the other. Especially interesting arguments against this "hard-line" approach, in the words of Alina Curticapean, can be found in her article "'Are You Hungarian or Romanian?' On the Study of National and Ethnic Identity in Central and Eastern Europe" (Curticapean 2007).

This characteristic of essentialist thinking may be derived from some distinctive features of western civilization; namely, from the Eurocentric tendency to draw distinct dividing lines between all sorts of events, processes, concepts, etc., and to reason by using exclusive disjunctions: logical constructions of the either/or type, as well as dichotomies such as subject/object, mind/body, or culture/nature (Alatas 2002).

Finally, I will look at the "hierarchizing" approach to identity – that is, the tendency to seek an essence "behind" or "under" what is visible, or, as one author puts it, to reveal "a hidden structure underlying the superficial properties by which the kind is recognized" (Haslam 1998, 292). This approach is emblematic of essentialism; in fact, in all likelihood, essentialism "owes" its very name to the hierarchizing approach.

Moreover, if a scholar is intent on drawing the line between essence and expression, this means that she views identity through the lens of essentialism which, then, she will also apply to its other four aspects (endurance in time, endurance in the face of external influences, integrity and purity). No matter what changes are observed in the life of a community, one may claim that it has essentially preserved its identity. In addition, no matter how much a community is susceptible to external influences, there is nothing to stop us from assuming that its essential characteristics remain intact and that its "backbone" is not broken. Furthermore, not even the most dramatic contradictions within a community could convince the essentialist that its identity does not unite the antagonistic parties, even if only at the essential level and without being visible "on the surface." In addition, no matter what contact is made and what mutual influences occur on "the periphery," this cannot affect "the core" of community life.

The distinction between essence and appearance in our context also has other implications. Collective identity turns out to be founded upon a core set of traits that are common (in this particular combination) only to the members of the particular group. A number of authors note that there is a link between essentialism and stereotyping in this respect, as well: "As suggested by Allport's observations, essentialist beliefs about social categories (hereinafter referred to as 'social essentialism') facilitate social stereotyping and prejudice" (Rhodes, Leslie, and Tworek 2012, 13527).

But perhaps the most characteristic expression of essentialist thinking is the association of identity with authenticity. According to this mode of thinking, expressions such as "true" Bulgarian or "unalloyed patriotism" make sense. The manifestations of essence may, or may not, be an adequate expression of the essence itself depending on the "interference" of external factors. It is a moral duty of everyone to withstand such influences. Craig Calhoun (1995, 219) describes as "Romantic naturalism" the "demands for individuals to express and be true to their inner natures" but, as I noted above, I believe the roots of essentialism should be sought also within the very character of scientific research.

The critiques against the essentialist approach to identity will be examined later on. At this point, I will proceed to review the "rival" paradigm in identity studies – namely, that of "constructionism."

Schematically, this paradigm may be represented as the polar opposite of essentialism, according to the five parameters by which I characterized essentialism above. From the constructionist point of view, identity may be developed. Furthermore, there is nothing wrong with adapting identity to the circumstances; in other words, there is nothing wrong with identity being more flexible than sovereign. Nor is there anything to fear about the possibility of internal contradictions or of the fragmentation of identity, as these will not take anything away from identity. By the same logic, the "blurring" of the boundaries of identity and its participation in forms of "hybridization" are fully admissible. Finally, there is no reason – and it is even totally unnecessary – to distinguish essence from manifestation. Any process and interaction within a community may have more or less of a significant impact on its identity, depending on the particular situation. No matter how some people may behave, we have no right to accuse them of "betraying" their identity. Or, as Seyla Benhabib (2002, 8) writes more generally, "We should view human cultures as constant creations, recreations, and negotiations of imaginary boundaries between 'we' and the 'other(s).'"

Development, adaptation to circumstances, internal fragmentation, hybridization, and "shifting" priorities may be "endured" by identity if we conceive of it – and this is the big difference from essentialism – not as a historical fact, but as a construct that is built and continually reproduced by a particular community insofar as it maintains its own self-conscious way of life:

> The constructionist approach, then, sees ethnic and racial identities as highly variable and contingent products of an ongoing interaction between, on the one hand, the circumstances groups encounter – including the conceptions

and actions of outsiders – and, on the other, the actions and conceptions of group members – of insiders.

(Cornell and Hartmann 1998, 85)

Constructionist theories of identity place emphasis on two things: the ability of the community to construct, reproduce, and reform its self-awareness, hence, its way of life, and the dependence of this ability on circumstance. In the constructionist account, identity construction depends both on objective and subjective circumstances – both on real factors and on "externally" assigned characteristics of identity. Cornell and Hartmann (1998, 94) use the special term, "circumstantialism," to characterize constructionism in this respect.

In the constructionist account, identity is viewed, first and foremost, as a process. Stuart Hall, for example, prefers to use the term "identification" instead of "identity." According to Hall (1996b, 4), identities are

> constructed across different, often intersecting and antagonistic, discourses, practices and positions.... [A]ctually identities are about questions of using the resources of history, language and culture in the process of becoming rather than being: not "who we are" or "where we came from," so much as who we might become, how we have been represented and how that bears on how we represent ourselves.

What, more precisely, does identity construction consist of? Publications on the subject point out various "techniques" that are well-known but have been assigned a new meaning. These techniques include: the creation of community-based organizations that are centered on ethnicity, religion, race or gender; the support of research on a community's history and culture; the revival or institutionalization of holidays (for example, for many years now, April 8 has been celebrated as International Roma Day in the countries of Central and Eastern Europe where there are significant Roma minorities); the revision or even rewriting of a community's history; the establishment and promotion of a community's own media (regardless of whether it operates in the minority or in the national language); the popularization of the community's folklore and other cultural traditions; the public promotion of nationally or internationally acclaimed members of the community; the creation and popularization of myths about historical events that have played an important role in the life of the community, and so forth.

The ingenuity of the participants in cultural identity construction and reconstruction is amazing. Not even the lack of empirical "building material," which is evident in some cases, can stop such undertakings. An example of a creative approach in this respect is the attempts (noted by a number of scholars) to positively rethink the objective scarcity of historical achievements, successes and heroic feats of the Romanian people, which can serve as a "mainstay" in the consolidation of Romanian national identity. This is a problem described by Bogdan Ştefănescu (2011, 130) as the Romanians' incapability "of making their own history, either in terms of asserting themselves through a remarkable destiny or in recording their historical exploits." A number of eminent Romanian intellectuals (such as Lucian Blaga, Gheorghe I. Brătianu, Mircea Vulcănescu, Mircea Eliade, Constatin Noica, and Andrei Codrescu) have sought to use the situation to their advantage by interpreting this "void" as a source of constructive energy: "In the process, the regenerative void became one of the most popular compensating strategies for the traumatic self-imaging of a marginal culture" (Ştefănescu 2011, 129). Ştefănescu (2011) characterizes the metaphor "regenerative void" as "an ambiguous image that indicates both the inability to construct a viable collective identity and the compensating mechanism to turn this failure into an unexpected success."

All these different strategies, techniques, and even, inventions, applied in cultural identity re/construction, may be generalized in a formulation proposed by Seyla Benhabib (2002, IX) in the Preface to her book *The Claims of Culture*: "I think of cultures as common human practices of signification and representation, of organization and attribution, which are internally driven by conflicting narratives."

In this connection, I believe a distinction should be made between such actions of a community that are aimed at its mobilization and self-recognition (in other words, actions that serve to bring up to date and consolidate a community's identity without changing it), and those actions that constitute true construction of identity.[5] As a criterion for distinguishing one type of actions from the other I would propose optionality – that is, the possibility of giving alternative answers to the questions that are important for the assertion of a collective self-image. This is the only way a community can have the "leeway" to choose whether to construct its identity in one manner or another.

I will illustrate my thesis by using a classification proposed by Cornell and Hartmann (1998, 81), who distinguish three key issues relevant to identity construction: "the boundary that separates group members from nonmembers, the perceived position of the group within the society, and the meaning attached to identity."

Prima facie, the answer to the question, "What distinguishes our community from all others?" ought to be simple and unambiguous. If we are talking about an ethnic community, then this will be its historical origin; if we are referring to a religious community, then it will be its doctrine and daily rituals of faith, and so forth. But it is possible to provide arguments for alternative views on each of these issues. In the case of Bulgarian ethnicity, for example, there are two main "conflicting" versions (there are also more "exotic" ones that I will not discuss here): the Bulgarian people are either of predominantly Slavic origin, or conversely, of Turkic origin. Bulgaria's contemporary history vividly demonstrates the relationship between the authority of each of the two hypotheses and the political conjuncture. When relations with Russia, or formerly the Soviet Union, were given priority, the first hypothesis was predominant in the Bulgarian teachings of history, as well as in the media; when these relations cooled for one reason or another, then the second was given prominence.

Let us evaluate this case using the criteria of the two approaches to identity. From an essentialist point of view, it is scandalous, for it involves a series of consecutive humiliating distortions of Bulgarian ethnic identity. If we think in constructionist terms, however, there is nothing wrong. It is simply that Bulgarian ethnic identity was constructed based on certain circumstances and those who identify themselves as Bulgarian should not hesitate to reconstruct it as the situation changes.

In the first line of reasoning, identity is associated with an essence that should be founded, if possible, upon factual truths. Hence, the debate on "Slavic or Turkic origins" appears to be a means of establishing the relevant facts. It follows from this that the community has the right, so to speak, to change its identity in relation to its consciousness of its historical origins only if there is indeed new evidence that disproves the currently accepted version. In other words, Bulgarians are arguing about their origin in order to reveal, as correctly as possible, the true *essence* of their cultural being.

From a constructionist point of view, however, historical truth should be regarded as something relative. Either way, history is primarily based on interpretations and myths. There is a lack of evidence to prove either of the two hypotheses as true. What is at stake in the debate between their proponents is not the truth of the matter, but the good of the community. The dispute tends to be a controversy between two "projects" for the further reproduction of the ethnic identity of Bulgarians over the long term, in which the stakeholders are much more interested in the future than in the distant past of the community. On the philosophical level, it would not be an exaggeration to claim that the constructionist paradigm is founded epistemologically on pragmatist presumptions.

Where do things stand with the second dimension in which identity is constructed – in other words, how is the community's self-awareness of its place in society formed? In my opinion, there are two alternatives: the development of such self-awareness either along conformist or along "defensive" lines. If we are talking about the identity of an ethnic, racial, or religious minority, for example, such identity is constructed in the "magnetic field" between two "poles": a tendency toward its integration into and dissociation from the existing socio- and cultural-political configuration. If, for example, we look at the case of the Turkish ethnic minority in Bulgaria, we will see that its identity is influenced by two factors, which have opposite effects. One is loyalty to Bulgarian society at large (manifested, *inter alia*, in the discourse on good-neighborly relations, the so-called "*komshuluk*,"[6] and so forth), and the other – the awareness of its own vulnerability and endangerment on the part of the selfsame Bulgarian society (an awareness expressed in the so-called "ethnic vote" for the DPS[7]). At every historical moment, these two tendencies balance each other out in some way (that is, neither of them ever fully overcomes the other), but the point of equilibrium is constantly shifting depending on the circumstances, with the result being a rather "fluid" picture that represents the reproduction over time of the ethnic identity of Turks.

Last but not least, a few words about the third dimension, the conceptualization of one's self-identity in a more fundamental sense; the awareness of one's (of the community and of the individual) place in the world at large. Here, too, the processes of identity construction and reconstruction develop in two directions: "positive" and "negative." Whatever we think of ourselves, however we discuss our self-concept among us (within our community) or with "Others," it will be along the lines of either the assertion of our worth or of the recognition of our weaknesses. The end result is usually optimistic – although we realize that our mentality and way of life have a number of flaws we need to overcome, we still have a worthy place "under the sun" and reasons to be proud of ourselves; we deserve respect and recognition from the "Others." As Cornell and Hartmann (1998, 81) note, not without irony, the typical formula in this respect is: "we are the people who survived a century of oppression but never lost our courage or our belief in ourselves."

However, identity construction can become "malignant" when under negative external pressure. Sometimes this pressure is so strong that it gets internalized by the community, creating the impression that its members hate themselves. Such cases involve oppressed, "stigmatized" minorities whose social status is so low that it also affects the way they think of their identity. A textbook case of the internalization of the "Others'" negative attitudes and its transformation into a negative self-attitude is the phenomenon of the so-called "Jewish self-hatred," which was the subject of lively debates in the second half of the nineteenth century (see Tajfel 1978, 10).

The thesis that identity has a dialogical character has been well-argued by a number of scholars (especially convincingly by Charles Taylor in his essay "The Politics of Recognition," see Taylor 1994). In constructionist terms, this thesis can be translated as the recognition of the dependence of identity formation and reformation not just on the circumstances but also on the attitudes of the "Others." Identity is constructed and reconstructed through interactions both within the community and with the outside world. A strong critique of the baleful influences of self-denigration on oppressed communities can be found in Frantz Fanon's (1990) book *The Wretched of the Earth*.

In contemporary philosophy, the issue of identity construction "from the outside" is particularly popular among authors who come from poststructuralist (or, more generally, postmodern) backgrounds. Attention is primarily focused on female and sexual-minority (homosexual) identities (see, for example, Calhoun 1995, 218). Their inequality and stigmatization is explained and delegitimized accordingly by "deconstructing" the commonplace notions of what it means to be a woman, a gay man, or a lesbian, while taking into account the fact that those notions are often internalized in the minds of the individuals concerned, who consequently confirm and strengthen, through their behavior, the "Others'" prejudices about them.

Following this line of reasoning, some authors go as far as to reject identity itself as a characteristic of the individual and the group. According to Stuart Hall (1992, 277),

If we feel we have a unified identity from birth to death, it is only because we construct a comforting story or "narrative of the self" about ourselves....

The fully unified, completed, secure, and coherent identity is a fantasy. Instead, as the systems of meaning and cultural representation multiply, we are confronted by a bewildering, fleeting multiplicity of possible identities, any one of which we could identify with – at least temporarily.

This relativization of identity does not make constructionism more convincing. Instead, it tends to be a sort of *reductio ad absurdum*. In all cases, though, we are left with a serious dilemma: should we view identity as a given that is "encoded" in the way of life and mentality of the individual and the community, and which makes them what they are – in other words, should we accept that identity is an essence? Or, conversely, should we regard identity as a construct – a product of the struggle of the individual and the community for survival and self-assertion under particular circumstances?

It is difficult to say why, but many of the authors working in the constructionist paradigm do not attempt to reveal the motives driving the activities of collective identity construction and reconstruction. Some describe an impressive picture of intersecting discourses, practices and positions (see, for example, Hall 1992, 277, quoted above), as well as of the negotiation and renegotiation of boundaries – interactions out of which identities are formed and reformed as if in and of themselves: "Participants in the culture, by contrast, experience their traditions, stories, rituals and symbols, tools and material living conditions through shared, albeit contested and contestable, narrative accounts" (Benhabib 2002, 5).

Others, conversely, view identity construction as a collective act of the respective community, as if it were a conscious being. Here is an example of such an approach: "These works focus much of their attention on the ways that ethnic groups construct their own identities, shaping and reshaping them and the boundaries that enclose them" (Cornell and Hartmann 1998, 78). Further on in the same text, we find a description of how the successes of the civil rights movement in the United States and the federal government's measures for widening the autonomy and self-government of Native Americans encouraged them to take advantage of these transformations and to assert "their own emergent understandings of themselves" (Cornell and Hartmann 1998, 79). In this account, the Native American community seems to have acted as one, as if it were a sort of collective person.

To my mind, both of these notions of identity construction – as an impersonal, decentered process, or as a product of human agency – are at odds with the available empirical information. It is not difficult to find examples pertaining to minorities which show that, insofar as there are activities that may be interpreted as the construction and reconstruction of collective identities, these activities are driven primarily by a struggle of interests within the communities concerned. Whether or not an interpretation of historical or current facts will be accepted as the position of the community, and hence as an element of its identity, does not depend on the way discourses intersect or on the decision of some sort of collective mind; it depends, rather, on the balance of forces between groups and/or leaders in the community. Further on, I will examine a number of examples in this respect. At this point, though, I will consider the case of the identity of Muslims in Bulgaria.

The Muslim community in Bulgaria is not homogeneous. It consists of three categories of believers: ethnic Turks, Muslim Bulgarians (popularly known as "Pomaks"), and Muslim Roma. At the same time, the further development (or maybe "reconstruction"?) of this community's identity can follow one of two alternative paths: that of the so-called "Turkish Islam" (the "successor" to Ottoman Islam), or of Islam in its classical, Arabic form. There are many differences between the two, but the most characteristic ones are that the first form of Islam is greatly "etatized" – that is, it does not question the rule of the state government and it is moderate in its requirements regarding religious practices. The second is the very opposite: the Muslim religion competes with secular institutions and paves the way for various doctrinal tendencies, some of which are radical.

What is it that determines the motivation of Muslims in Bulgaria to take one or the other path, that is, to reproduce their identity in one way or another? It is not difficult to see that the ethnic Turks prefer the first form of Islam listed above, while the Pomaks and Roma prefer the second. In the first case, the motivation is related to some extent to the ethnic identity of the believers, and in the second, to the unwillingness, especially of the Pomaks, to accept a political alignment with a foreign country[8] – that is, in a sense, the preference for the "Arabic" form of Islam is determined by patriotic considerations.

If we examine the situation more closely, though, we cannot but notice that these delicate mechanisms of articulating faith are influenced to a large extent also by the interests of the religious elites who exercise formal and informal leadership over the two categories of Muslims in Bulgaria. Those who belong to the circle of spiritual leaders that gravitates toward the "Turkish" form of Islam may rely on political support from the DPS and on financial support from the Turkish state in advancing their "career." Those who belong to the other circle may have the opportunity to study in an Arabic country, with all expenses paid, and to receive donations from some international Islamic foundations to further their religious activity. On what, and to what extent, then, does the further direction of the "construction" and "reconstruction" of the identity of Bulgarian Muslims depend: on authentic religious motives, on nationalist attitudes, or on pragmatic considerations of the leaders?

Identity construction may be instrumentalized in many, as well as in different, ways. I will give just one more example. In her article, "Engaging or Contesting the Liberal State? 'Muslim' as a Politicised Identity Category in Europe," Fiona Adamson (2011) presents two alternative strategies of Muslim identity construction in the United Kingdom. One is applied by the Muslim Council of Britain, and the other by the organization Hizb ut-Tahrir. In the first case, Muslim identity is deployed as a means of making collective claims on behalf of British Muslims and lobbying vis-à-vis the state, and is presented to the public – both to the Muslim and to the general one – in a way that justifies these claims. In the second, Muslim identity is deployed as a means of asserting a political identity that is in opposition to "the West" in general and, in the name of their religious identity, British Muslims are encouraged "to reject liberalism, disengage from institutionalised participation in British politics, and instead identify themselves *politically* with a broader transnational community of Muslims or the global *ummah*" (Adamson 2011, 900).

The difference between the two approaches to creating a construct that claims to be the true Muslim identity is determined, according to Adamson, by the interests of the leaders of the two organizations; or, as she calls them, by two groups of "political entrepreneurs" who "strategically deploy the *category* of 'Muslim' as a means of constituting and representing an identity community for political purposes, thereby creating a constructed constituency that transcends other ethnic, national or sectarian identities" (Adamson 2011).

These examples clearly show, I hope, that the legitimacy of identity as a factor influencing people's behavior is questionable if it is regarded in a constructionist perspective. If we have to decide what attitude to take, for instance, towards an act of violence performed in the name of some identity – maybe in protest against its oppression, or its desecration, as in the case of the terrorist attacks carried out in Europe as, allegedly, a reaction against the caricaturing of the Prophet Muhammad in print media – we should first answer for ourselves the question of whether the identity concerned is authentic and truly represents somebody's self-awareness of the place of her community and culture "under the sun"; or, conversely, whether it is a set of myths organized in some construct that is configured so as to serve somebody's interests. This question becomes even more difficult if it is asked in a radical sense – not referring to a specific case (that is, whether the identity in question is "true" or only imaginary), but, generally, whether there are authentic identities at all, or are all of them instruments of manipulation – see, for example, Al-Azmeh's (1993, 21) thesis regarding "the fabrication of an Islamic tradition" by Islamists.

In this respect, essentialism is in a more favorable position than constructionism because, from an essentialist standpoint, it is much easier to morally justify a behavior guided by motives founded on identity. If we assume that identity is an essence of the individual or the community – which is to say that identity is what makes them what they are – we may understand (although not necessarily approve of) actions performed in defense of identity. The problem of the legitimacy of identity is more difficult if we consider identity in constructionist terms. Is it at all possible to consciously and deliberately define and redefine identity without engaging in self-interested manipulation?

Identity: an end, or a means?

To answer this question, we must consider another debate, that between the proponents of "primordialism" and of "instrumentalism." This discussion is conducted mostly within the narrower field of national identity theories. Nationalist doctrines are often based on the primordialist concept of the nation as a quasi-natural reality formed in and of itself,[9] while the opponents of nationalism point out that the nation is "artificial" – in other words, they view it precisely as a construct. When this dispute snowballs to encompass the issue of cultural identity in general, it ultimately comes down to answering the question of what the end is and what the means are. From a primordialist perspective, identity is valuable in itself and everything people do in connection with identity is a means of its preservation and assertion – even at the cost of privation and sacrifice on their part. As Pierre L. van den Berghe writes in his book *The Ethnic Phenomenon* (van den Berghe 1981, 27), "blood runs thicker than money." Conversely, from an instrumentalist standpoint it is claimed that individuals act solely to serve their self-interests and their behavior, vis-à-vis identity, is no exception. For individuals, identity is only a means of ensuring their own well-being and all sorts of manipulations of identity are admissible.

Obviously, this is an important question. The solution to the problem of the end and the means will determine, *inter alia*, the degree of freedom in "dealing with" cultural identities – whether we will treat them as sacred, or allow ourselves to use them for our own good and for the good of our communities. In order to avoid an unproductive clash of such extreme views, however, we need greater conceptual clarity that would enable us to seek some kind of synthesis of the two opposite concepts. What is meant, for instance, by the "self-interests" of individuals: selfish pursuit of personal success to the detriment of all others, self-fulfillment through the common good, or perhaps something completely different? In my opinion, we would achieve greater clarity of these concepts if we used some well-elaborated classifications of the types of social action.

One of the best-known typologies of social action is the one proposed by Max Weber (1978) in *Economy and Society*. He distinguishes between four types of action: instrumentally rational (*zweckrational*), value-rational (*wertrational*), affectual, and traditional. In the context of the problems discussed in this chapter, the first two types are most of interest to us. Regarding instrumentally rational action, Weber writes that it is determined by expectations as to the behavior of objects and human beings, where these are viewed as a means for the attainment of rationally pursued ends. Conversely, value-rational action is "determined by a conscious belief in the value for its own sake of some ethical, aesthetic, religious or other form of behavior, independently of its prospect of success" (Weber 1978, 24–25). Persons act in this way when they are driven by, in Weber's words, "'commands' or 'demands'" which they believe are imposed on them; these may involve norms such as "duty, honor, the pursuit of beauty, a religious call, personal loyalty, or the importance of some cause, no matter in what it consists" (Weber 1978, 25).

As one can see, instrumentally rational and value-rational actions are related to their results in exactly opposite ways. In the first case, the expected result motivates the action and the end justifies the means, while the value-rational action is guided by the maxim "Do what is right, come what may."[10] How can this typology help us clarify the relationship between the essentialist and the constructionist approach to identity? Can we apply it in order to make a convincing distinction between morally justifiable and morally condemnable behavior in the context of identity?

At first sight, the case is clear. From an essentialist perspective on identity, only value-rational actions are admissible, while from a constructionist standpoint there are no grounds for such a restriction. There is nothing wrong with acting in an instrumentally rational way in this sphere, either – namely, in modifying one's or another's identity in a way that facilitates the attainment of particular ends.

Weber's typology, however, cannot draw a sufficiently distinct boundary between behavior in the spirit of essentialism and behavior in the spirit of constructionism. What about the status, for example, of an action performed in the name of the community's interest? If it aims to attain some particular result that is in the interest of the whole community, will this action be instrumentally rational or value-rational? In a sense, it will meet the criteria necessary to be classified as belonging to either of the two types. On the one hand, it will be determined by the relationship between ends and means, and on the other, by values such as duty (to the community) and honor.

Recently, an analogous typology, which answers the question asked above was developed by Jürgen Habermas in his theory of communicative action. In his typology, the alternatives to instrumentally rational and value-rational action are, respectively, action oriented to success and communicative action, where the former has two subtypes – instrumental (that is, nonsocial) action and strategic (social) action (see Habermas 1984, 285). What does the eminent German philosopher mean by these terms?

Generally speaking, he distinguishes action oriented to success from communicative action by the way their goals are determined. In the first case, the actors choose the goal of their action themselves, while in the second they coordinate their behavior with the people who are affected by their action – that is, they determine their goal in agreement with the latter. In this sense, communicative action, in the words of Habermas (1984, 286), is "oriented to reaching understanding."[11] In other words, actors do not decide "off their own bat," so to speak, what should follow from their action; rather, they take into account the positions of the other participants in the situation.

The typology of social action proposed by Habermas offers a good frame of reference for distinguishing different types of constructionist activity concerned with identity. If this activity is performed with the participation, or at least with the approval (including tacit approval or, simply, abstention from objection), of all of the parties concerned – which, typically, is all people belonging to the community – then the result should not be morally problematic. In other words, if the construction and reconstruction of collective identity is carried out as a communicative – in the Habermasian sense – action, it should not negatively affect the legitimacy of the collective identity so produced – in other words, it should not compromise its legitimacy as a factor determining the behavior of the group's members. If we ask ourselves whether this identity is really the self-awareness of the community to which it is ascribed, we should answer in the affirmative, considering that although they may be conducted in a purposeful or even calculated manner, the changes in it are made with the understanding and agreement of all members concerned. In this case, the "authorship" of the constructed collective identity will belong to the community, even if not in the naive sense mentioned above – that is, not in the sense that the community makes decisions like some sort of collective agent.

In sum, Habermas's typology of social action enables us to shift the focus of the essentialism/constructionism (or primordialism/instrumentalism) debate from the problem of whether or not, in principle, is it right to manipulate identity, onto a question that is easier to answer: Who is it that manipulates identity, and in whose interest?

Naturally, here we should also consider how one can establish what the case is in real-life situations – whether a given act of identity definition or redefinition is the work of the respective community, or of some of its members who are acting in its name but in their self-interest. If we think, for instance, about the way of nation-building that is characteristic of the relatively younger nations in Central and Eastern Europe, the question will be this: who is behind all the falsifications of history, behind the myth-making, behind the politically-oriented language reforms, and so forth? If all of these things were done with the knowledge and with the more or less tacit approval of the overwhelming majority of the country's citizens, from a constructionist point of view, there should be nothing morally condemnable about them, provided, of course, that this approval can be qualified as "informed consent" (meaning that it was not the result of brainwashing, or of a political passivity instilled for decades through repressive measures). If the majority of these people were convinced that this is better for them and for their descendants, there isn't anything wrong with "inventing" a collective identity for themselves, is there? Isn't the common good more valuable than historical truth?

But the case would be completely different if we were dealing with identity manipulation, which is the exclusive work of members of the respective country's political and cultural elite, and which is done in their self-interest. The product of such undertakings cannot be regarded as an authentic self-consciousness of the respective community. This type of national identity cannot legitimize any actions performed in its defense. Whatever critiques may be leveled against it in essentialist or primordialist terms, they will be justified.

Of course, here I am describing two polar opposite cases: identity construction in a purely communicative and in a purely strategic way. In reality, these processes are more complex and nuanced. Well-intentioned strategic actions, which are performed in the community's "interest" as understood by the actor, are also possible. In that case, people are manipulated "for their own good." A major advantage of the strategic/communicative action typology is that it rejects, in a well-argued way, the possibility that norms that have not been established through communicative agreement may be legitimate. From the perspective of this methodology, good intention in itself cannot serve as grounds for legitimizing identity. History has also shown that such initiatives usually end in failure.

Although the strategic approach to identity construction can be inadvertently presented as communicative, this can also occur not just unintentionally. In nationalist doctrines and policies, as well as in every other ideology, self-interest is usually presented as common interest. In addition, the social technology of nationalism also presupposes legitimizing instrumentalist undertakings by appealing to primordialist ideals. Certainly no one would be inspired by a nationalist political agenda if the true goals of its creators were openly made clear.

On a more general level, some contemporary authors have even made attempts at "synthesizing" essentialist and constructionist values in the same vein as the nationalist doctrines and policies discussed above. Stuart Hall, for instance, presents racial identity as a fiction (that is, he "deconstructs" it completely), but claims, at the same time, that this fiction is necessary in order to make "both politics and identity possible" (see Hall 1996a, 45). Some authors, mostly with a feminist orientation, define "strategic essentialism" as our readiness to act as if essentialism were true even though we are convinced it is not. According to them, such hypocritical behavior is admissible and morally justifiable in certain political situations (see, for example, Spivak 1987; Brah 1992; Veronis 2007). As Marina Falbo (2006, 253) claims, "Strategic essentialism seems a necessary strategy in order to invoke a specific subject, to be recognized as entitled to be a political subject. It helps to establish disadvantaged groups as a recognizable political subject."

Such a tactical move is usually recommended as a means of defending the interests of disadvantaged groups if this is the only way their problems can be included on the agenda of society. But although it is always possible, the instrumentalization of the essentialism/constructionism dichotomy does not, in effect, reduce the contrast between these two approaches towards identity.

Still, we have not yet answered the question of how we can establish in practice whether or not the re/construction of a given collective identity in a particular case is the work of the respective community, or of separate sub-groups in that community which are pursuing their self-interests. Very generally speaking, we can say that we would be able to make this distinction if we know how the collective authorship of identity is possible, what its "mechanisms" are, and hence how we can tell whether there is such authorship in a given situation.

In fact, such collective authorship of a large group of people cannot be achieved to an absolute degree; it can only be an ideal. But it is worthwhile to discuss the ways of getting close to this ideal. This can be done, for example, through various models of coordinating the positions of the community's members on particular issues – both within and beyond the framework of the traditional forms of establishing a "majority." Later, while discussing the legitimacy of minority claims, we will try to answer the question of how, and to what extent, the classic mechanisms of representative democracy can be used for collective decision-making by minority communities. We will see that this is not easy – a serious obstacle is the relative informality of this kind of community. There are alternatives though. I will use as an example the method of *public deliberation*, which will be discussed in detail in Chapter 5, and its capacity as a democratic way of decision-making founded on the force of the better argument, rather than on the right of the majority.

* * *

To recapitulate: what are the relations between the epistemological, moral-normative, and public-political dimensions of the two paradigms in working with cultural identities that we discussed in this chapter? As already noted above, from an essentialist standpoint identity is an essence, which means that it is an objective historical given and the community should act in accordance with it. If not, the community would betray its nature. This is a moral duty and follows from the philosophical presumption of the unconditional value of authenticity in human life. Being yourself is more important than living safely and comfortably, and having all the material goods in the world.

Hence, along these lines, the political behavior of every nation and of every minority community should be driven, first and foremost, by the awareness of the value of its own identity; however, this leads to a number of confrontations in political life. If national identity is equated with that of the ethnic majority in a given country and is understood by the members, or at least by the leaders of this ethnic community, in an essentialist way, its "well-being" will be hardly compatible with the interests of minorities, especially if their identities are also conceived of in essentialist terms by their members. How can a person compromise with her own identity, considering that it is this which makes her what she is? Both nationalist movements and minority chauvinism are rooted in this paradigm of understanding and expressing cultural identity.

All this is not to say that the essentialist methodology does not allow for changes – including radical ones – in policies concerning identity. Admittedly, essence is regarded as self-consistent and enduring in time, but no one can claim to have absolute knowledge of her own or someone else's essence. When social realities expose particular identity policies as obviously inadequate, they can be revised, but not with the apprehension that this is a change of the identity itself. Instead, the revision of the policies can be interpreted as a result of a change in the *understanding* of that essence. The reasoning goes as follows:

> Up until now we have been mistaken about the nature of our essence, but the results of the latest studies show that it is in fact different from what we thought it was; therefore, we must change our policies in order to bring them in line with reality.

The constructionist paradigm was formed as a reaction to the essentialist trends in the social sciences, in ideology, as well as in the respective political practices. In the first case, this paradigm counters an attitude that is typical of scholars because it stems from the very nature of research: the aspiration to discover consistent and predictable characteristics of the subject of study. In the second, it opposes the doctrines and policies that promote segregation, discrimination, and assimilation. All of them are formed, to one extent or another, on an essentialist methodological basis. The philosophy underlying the constructionist way of thinking proceeds from the principles of individualism and rationalism. In effect, it belittles and delegitimizes collective identity. How can we possibly treat collective identity seriously if we consider it as nothing more than a construct fabricated in order to serve the self-interests of one group or another in their struggle for power and material gain?

In real political life this ideology is used in the struggle for the rights of, and a better social status for, mostly those minorities who are not differentiated from the rest of the population on a community basis. I have in mind racial and sexual minorities, as well as women, insofar as from a feminist point of view they, too, are disadvantaged. For groups of this type, the priority is on the struggle against discrimination, as well as for the positive treatment of their differences (for example, the right to same-sex marriage), and not for cultural rights related to the reproduction of their identities over time.

There are no distinct boundaries between the theories and practices developed within the two paradigms discussed above. In some cases, people from one community subscribe to theories that present their own identity as an essence and the "rival" ones as constructs. Such "creative accounting" is used, for example, by most leaders of nationalist or xenophobic political parties who, in their public appearances, readily "deconstruct" minority identities, reducing them to a fabricated instrument for gaining privilege or to a product of the secret services of neighboring countries. The same politicians, however, reason in a radically different way when it comes to their own national and ethnic identities (tacitly and unjustifiably equating the former with the latter).

Another typical variant of the intertwinement of the two methodologies, which was discussed above in connection with nationalism, is the deliberate presentation of a construct as an essence. The theorists of the so-called "Revival Process" in Bulgaria (the forced assimilation campaign against ethnic Turks conducted in 1984–1989 – see endnote 4 in Chapter 2) used a distinctly essentialist and primordialist rhetoric in an effort to motivate the Bulgarian Turks to change their ethnic identity:

> The religious fanaticism, hostility and intolerance, instilled for centuries by the Ottoman authorities and the Islamic Church,[12] impeded the process of the national revival and awakening of the Islamized Bulgarians, and not infrequently also brutally suppressed every open manifestation of that process.
>
> (Yankov 1988, 26)

With hindsight, it is obvious that the category "descendants of Islamized Bulgarians," applied by the theorists of the "Revival Process" to the ethnic Turks who are Bulgarian citizens, was a construct that claimed legitimacy in an essentialist way. According to this ideology, if ethnic Turks in Bulgaria accepted that they were "descendants of Islamized Bulgarians," then they would have returned to their true historical roots – that is, they would have corrected a mistake in their own self-consciousness.

We have also seen that it is possible to define and redefine identity in a constructionist vein – without claiming to discover or rediscover an essence – by acting not in a strategic, but in a communicative (in the Habermasian sense), way. The condition for this is that the community as a whole must positively accept these "manipulations" based on the belief that they correspond to the interests of its members. Of course, such approval is justified only if it is free and rational, that is, if it is not based on coercion and/or deception. In that case, identity may be regarded as legitimate even though we do not view it as an essence and, hence, do not enter into an "essentialist mode," with all of its resulting consequences. The second part of this book will examine the paths of public legitimization of specifically those minority claims that are related to the conditions for reproduction of group identity over time.

Finally, along these lines I would like to mention an unquestionable fact which, to the best of my knowledge, is not discussed in the relevant publications. For their proponents, both the essentialist and the constructionist interpretations of cultural identity are empirically true. If I recognize my identity as an essence, I thereby construct my self-awareness in an essentialist way and therefore behave as if my identity were indeed my essence. This also holds true for the proponents of the constructionist paradigm. Thus, everyone is right for themselves; therefore, resolving this dispute in a rational way is difficult, if at all possible.

Notes

1 In contemporary terms, we would say that *Gemeinschaft* has its roots in the traditional way of life, and *Gesellschaft* in modernity.
2 The term "constructionism" is used by the majority of the authors writing on this subject, but some also use "constructivism" in the same sense (see, for example, Fischer et al. 1999; Isin and Wood 1999, 16).
3 It is very telling that in the many articles criticizing essentialism it is almost impossible to find a quote by an advocate of this approach (that is, by an author who explicitly argues for the advantages of essentialism). Most of those who are described as advocates of essentialism (again by other authors) are, for example, the proponents of "naturalized epistemology" in the philosophy of language (see Haslam, Rothschild, and Ernst 2000).
4 Another typology of the characteristics of essentialism in cultural identity studies, which complements the one described above, is proposed by Seyla Benhabib (2002, 4). She points out the following assumptions as "faulty epistemic premises":

> (1) that cultures are clearly delineable wholes; (2) that cultures are congruent with population groups and that a non-controversial description of the culture of a human group is possible; and (3) that even if cultures and groups do not stand in one-to-one correspondence, even if there is more than one culture within a human group and more than one group that may possess the same cultural traits, this poses no important problems for politics or policy.

5 To my mind, the "undertakings" reviewed from a constructionist perspective by Cornell and Hartmann (1998, 79) are precisely actions of the first type.
6 The term is derived from *komşu* or "neighbor" in Turkish.
7 The Movement for Rights and Freedoms – de facto an ethnic party of the Bulgarian Turks with a nominally liberal ideology is discussed in more detail in Chapter 4.
8 Turkey, Bulgaria's largest and only Muslim neighboring country, is believed by some to exert considerable influence over the Muslim communities in the countries of Southeast Europe.

9　According to some authors, one of the distinctive features of primordialism is the presumption that nations have existed since time immemorial, while others use a special term in this context – "perennialism," where the opposite concept is no longer "instrumentalism" but "modernism" (see Özkirimli and Grosby 2007).

10　Just as in the case of the "community–society" dichotomy, introduced by Tönnies, we have no grounds to apply the "instrumentally rational action vs value-rational action" opposition outside of the modern cultural context. In a totalitarian social environment every action is related, positively or negatively, directly or indirectly to the fulfillment of a mission.

11　"*Verständigung*," rendered as "understanding" in the English translation of *Theorie des kommunikativen Handelns*, does not fully convey the exact meaning of the original term that Habermas uses, not in a cognitive but, rather, in a moral sense, having in mind mutual agreement between two or more persons concerning the coordination of their actions.

12　The use of a term such as "Islamic Church" attests to that author's incompetence in matters of Sunni Islam.

References

Adamson, Fiona B. "Engaging or Contesting the Liberal State? 'Muslim' as a Politicised Identity Category in Europe." *Journal of Ethnic and Migration Studies* 37, no. 6 (2011): 899–915.

Alatas, Syed Farid. "Eurocentrism and the Role of the Human Sciences in the Dialogue among Civilizations." *The European Legacy* 7, no. 6 (2002): 759–770.

Al-Azmeh, Aziz. *Islams and Modernities*, London: Verso, 1993.

Barrett, Amy. "McDonald's Ads in France Try to Head Off Protests." *The Wall Street Journal*, December 9, 1999.

Benhabib, Seyla. *The Claims of Culture.* Princeton: Princeton University Press, 2002.

Brah, Avtar. "Difference, Diversity and Differentiation." In *Race, Culture and Difference*, edited by James Donald and Ali Rattansi, 126–148. Thousand Oaks and London: SAGE, 1992.

Calhoun, Craig. *Critical Social Theory. Culture, History, and the Challenge of the Difference.* Oxford: Blackwell, 1995.

Cornell, Stephen and Douglas Hartmann. *Ethnicity and Race. Making Identities in a Changing World*. Thousand Oaks: Pine Forge Press, 1998.

Curticapean, Alina. "'Are you Hungarian or Romanian?' On the Study of National and Ethnic Identity in Central and Eastern Europe." *Nationalities Papers* 35, no. 3 (2007): 411–427.

Falbo, Marina. "Reinventing Inclusion: From a Politics of Presence to Inessential Coalitions." *Contemporary Politics* 12, no. 3–4 (2006): 247–260

Fanon, Frantz. *The Wretched of the Earth*. London: Penguin Books, 1990.

Fischer, Edward, Quetzil Castaneda, Johannes Fabian, Jonathan Friedman, et al. "Rethinking Constructivism and Essentialism." *Current Anthropology* 40, no. 4 (1999): 473–499.

Georgieva, Tsvetana. "Coexistence as a System in the Everyday Life of Christians and Muslims in Bulgaria." In *Relations of Compatibility and Incompatibility between Christians and Muslims in Bulgaria*, 147–172. Sofia: International Centre for Minority Studies and Intercultural Relations, 1995.

Gutmann, Amy. *Identity in Democracy*. Princeton, NJ: Princeton University Press, 2003.

Habermas, Jürgen. *Theory of Communicative Action*. Boston, MA: Beacon Press, 1984.

Habermas, Jürgen, "Struggles for Recognition in the Democratic Constitutional State." In *Multiculturalism. Examining the Politics of Recognition*, edited by Amy Gutmann, 107–148. Princeton, NJ: Princeton University Press, 1994.

Hall, Stuart. "The Question of Cultural Identity." In *Modernity and its Futures*, edited by Tony McGrew, Stuart Hall, and David Held, 273–326. Oxford: Polity Press, 1992.

Hall, Stuart. "Minimal Selves." In *Black British Cultural Studies: A Reader*, edited by Houston A. Baker, Jr., Manthia Diawara, and Ruth H. Lindeborg, 114–119. Chicago/London: University of Chicago Press, 1996a.

Hall, Stuart. "Who Needs Identity? In *Questions of Cultural Identity*, edited by Stewart Hall and Paul du Gay, 1–17. Thousand Oaks and London: SAGE, 1996b.

Haslam, Nick. "Natural Kinds, Human Kinds and Essentialism." *Social Research* 65, no. 2 (1998): 291–314.

Haslam, Nick, Louis Rothschild, and Donald Ernst. "Essentialist Beliefs about Social Categories." *The British Journal of Social Psychology* 39, no. 1 (2000) 113–121.

Hofstede, Geert. *Cultures and Organizations: Software of the Mind*. New York: McGraw-Hill, 1991.

Isin, Engin and Patricia Wood. *Citizenship and Identity*. SAGE: London, 1999.

Kidd, Warren. *Culture and Identity*. New York: Palgrave, 2002.

Lacey, Robert. *Inside the Kingdom, Kings, Clerics, Modernists, Terrorists, and the Struggle for Saudi Arabia*. New York: Viking, 2009.

Modood, Tariq. "Anti-Essentialism, Multiculturalism and the Recognition of Religious Groups." *Journal of Political Philosophy* 6 (1998): 378–399.

Narayan, Uma. "Essence of Culture and a Sense of History: A Feminist Critique of Cultural Essentialism." *Hypatia* 13, no. 2 (1998): 86–106.

Office of the United Nations High Commissioner for Human Right. *Minority Rights: International Standards and Guidance for Implementation*. New York: United Nations, 2010.

Özkirimli, Umut and Steven Grosby. "Nationalism Theory Debate: The Antiquity of Nations?" *Nations and Nationalism* 13, no. 3 (2007): 523–537.

Parekh, Bhikhu. *Rethinking Multiculturalism. Cultural Diversity and Political Theory*. London: Macmillan Press, 2000.

Rhodes, Marjorie, Sarah-Jane Leslie, and Christina M. Tworek, "Cultural Transmission of Social Essentialism." *Proceedings of the National Academy of Sciences of the United States of America* 109, no. 34 (2012): 13526–13531.

Ringold, Dena. *Roma & the Transition in Central & Eastern Europe: Trends & Challenges*. Washington, DC: World Bank, 2000.

Spivak, Gayatri. *In Other Worlds: Essays in Cultural Politics*, London: Methuen, 1987.

Ştefănescu, Bogdan. "The Regenerative Void: Avatars of a Foundational Metaphor in Romanian Identity Construction." *Philologica Jassyensia* 13, no. 1 (2011): 127–139.

Tajfel, Henri. *The Social Psychology of Minorities*. London: Minority Rights Group, 1978.

Taylor, Charles. "The Politics of Recognition." In *Multiculturalism. Examining the Politics of Recognition*, edited by Amy Gutmann, 25–74. Princeton, NJ: Princeton University Press, 1994.

Tönnies, Ferdinand. *Community and Civil Society*. Cambridge: Cambridge University Press, 2001.

Turner, Terence. "Anthropology and Multiculturalism: What is Anthropology that Multiculturalists Should Be Mindful of It?" *Cultural Anthropology* 8, no. 4 (1993): 411–429.

Van den Berghe, Pierre L. *The Ethnic Phenomenon*. New York: Elsevier, 1981.

Veronis, Luisa. "Strategic Spatial Essentialism: Latin Americans' Real and Imagined Geographies of Belonging in Toronto." *Social & Cultural Geography* 8, no. 3 (2007): 455–473.

Weber, Max. *Economy and Society. An Outline of Interpretive Sociology.* Berkeley: University of California Press, 1978.

Yankov, Georgy. "Formiraneto i razvitieto na bulgarskata natzia I vuzroditelniat protzes." [The formation and development of the Bulgarian nation and the Revival process]. In *Problemi na razvitieto na bulgarskata narodnost I natzia,* edited by Georgy Yankov, Strashimir Dimitrov, and Orlin Zagorov, 7–32. Sofia: BAS Publishing House, 1988.

2 The complexity of minority issues

One of the aims of this study is to demonstrate the complexity of minority issues, in regards to which simple solutions seem unlikely to be effective, especially if they are based on a priori considerations and "a one-size-fits-all approach," as put in an article devoted to the research paradigm known as *intersectionality* (Hankivsky and Cormier 2011, 218). Here I start from the obvious fact that real-life cases of tension and conflict involving minorities are rarely due to a single factor, such as the failure to take into account the cultural identity of members of a given minority group in designing public policies. The practice shows that conflicts of this type are usually the effect of a combination of various influences. Although they may appear to be the work of one factor whose effects are visible, a closer examination will reveal a dissonance in these effects, which can be due only to interference from other factors.

For example, the tragic events during the breakup of Yugoslavia, about which we already have sufficient empirical information, were determined by cultural as well as by social and political circumstances. On the one hand, they were driven by existing ethnic, religious, and linguistic differences, as well as by historical score-settling, and on the other, by the aspirations of the local political elites to emancipate themselves from the central government in Belgrade and to head sovereign states. And, if we are to believe some of the claims of conspiracy theories, it is possible that foreign powers with a stake in the breakup of the federation could also have been involved in one way or another.

The causal determination of such conflicts by a certain type of factor may often appear as being the effect of different ones. Frequently, the relative weights of the various influences may not only change over the course of the conflict, but may also vary from one point of the conflict's location to another. Lastly, the different participants in the conflict may not necessarily share the same motives. Thus, if we ignore the possibility that an ethnic or religious conflict may be due to a combination of factors, some of which have nothing to do with ethnicity or religion, we risk developing an understanding about it that will be misleading in the design of minority public policies.

That is why I will examine issues related to minority policy within a three-dimensional coordinate system. In my opinion, every conflict situation of this kind is exposed to at least three types of influences whose effects may vary in strength. I have in mind cultural differences, group solidarity, and factors of social and political nature. Or, if we use the metaphor of the coordinate system, such a conflict situation can be represented as a point in the three-dimensional "space" defined by the three axes in question. Furthermore, its position in this space can change over time depending on the possible changes in the relative weight of the different types of influences.

Examining a given minority issue within such a coordinate system means making a special effort to establish the degree of "contribution" of each of the three types of factors. Public policies designed to resolve the issue in question must take into account the correlations of these qualitatively different "contributions" which require different public-policy approaches, but generate a common effect and are often involved in relationships of the positive-feedback type, meaning that they "catalyze" each other. So, if we do not adequately "diagnose" the issue, the policies that address it can be at odds with reality and turn out to be counterproductive.

I will illustrate the imperative need for such analytical differentiation of the different "components"[1] of minority issues (with the caveat that these components inevitably interface through the relations of mutual constitution and mutual reinforcement that exist between them) with an elegant formulation by Mari Matsuda (1990, 1189) – namely, the method she calls "ask the other question":

> When I see something that looks racist, I ask, "Where is the patriarchy in this?" When I see something that looks sexist, I ask, "Where is the hetero-sexism in this?" When I see something that looks homophobic, I ask, "Where are the class interests in this?"

The complexity of minority issues is recognized nowadays, above all, in gender studies. It was first addressed by the already-mentioned research approach called "intersectional" by Kimberlé Crenshaw (see Nash 2008, 2). Other similar approaches were developed later, ascribing to minority identities, (especially of African-American women) characteristics such as "multiple jeopardy," "discrimination-within-discrimination," "multiple consciousness," "translocational positionality," "multi-dimensionality," "inter-connectivity" (Dhamoon 2011, 232).

Most of these research methodologies aim to present the disadvantaged position of the respective target group. They use formulations such as "multiply marginalized," "multiply-burdened" subjects (Nash 2008, 4). The exposure of the "multiplicative effect" of the overlapping and mutual reinforcement of more than one form of discrimination (based on race, gender, sexuality, class) legitimizes, in a particularly spectacular manner, the claims for developing public policies that will alleviate the situation of the marginalized group in question.

However, studies devoted to the complexity of minority issues often point out the difficulty of making the move from the identification of this phenomenon in principle, to the elaboration of methods for the investigation of the relative weight of the relevant factors in determining a given minority issue, and further, to the elaboration of adequate policy responses to specific cases (Hankivsky and

Cormier 2011). They mention certain attempts to, for instance, introduce "space as an analytical dimension in intersectionality policy analysis" (ibid., 220), or to develop a method for "mapping" information about separate "strands" within the field of social care, such as gender, race, ethnicity, ability, religion, age, and sexual orientation (ibid., 223), but they are not particularly optimistic about the quality of these attempts and methods.

In this study, I will take into account the region-specific (to Central/Eastern Europe) nature of the minority issues under review, and will focus on the above-mentioned three dimensions of its complexity: the manifestations of cultural differences, of group solidarity, and of the effect of social and political factors. On the methodological level, I am most interested in the opportunities offered by the "deconstruction" of specific minority issues along those three axes, especially in the opportunities for countering some manipulation that is characteristic of the public legitimization of minority claims. What I have in mind is the justification of some claims for particular public policies over others through selectively emphasizing one dimension of the given minority issue while ignoring or belittling the other ones. Situating public communication, which aims to legitimize minority claims, within the said three-dimensional coordinate system obligates the participants involved in the communication to thoroughly examine all three types of influences as they pertain to each individual case.

Cultural differences

Considering the subject of my study, I will examine the three types of influences on minority issues that public policies should take into account in the context of a liberal-democratic social system, or if we use J. Rawls's famous formula, of a "well ordered society" (Rawls 1997, 765). In this context, how should the question of cultural differences be viewed? How should minority identities be treated, ideally, and how are they actually treated in different societies depending on the specific cultural and social circumstances there?

One obvious possibility is the exertion of assimilation pressure on national, ethnic, and religious minorities. This may be done openly, through public legitimization of such policies. However, it may also be pursued discreetly, where minority members are subjected to informal pressure aimed at motivating them to seek to improve their quality of life and prospects for professional and social advancement by disowning their identity.

Two quite different models of assimilation are possible in theory and found in practice. One is characteristic of the so-called "civic" nations. In these nations assimilation[2] is conducted not by replacing the minority identity with another, but by its systematic belittling and encouragement of its subjects to identify with the nation as a civic, rather than cultural, community. Individuals are expected to be guided, above all, by universal values instead of cultural traditions and group solidarity, Emblematic in this respect is the French ("republican") model of dealing with minority issues – at least in its traditional form (see for example Laurence 2003, 1; Iskandar and Rustom 2006, 2).

Nominally, this kind of pressure on cultural identities is not qualified as assimilationist because it does not aim at changing them, but rather at relativizing their importance. In fact, however, what we have here is the clandestine assimilation of the minorities by the majority on the pretext of securing national civic unity.[3] Majority is equated with normalcy (see Várady 2001, 139), national identity is equated with the cultural identity of the dominant group because national identity cannot be entirely culturally neutral (see, for example, Taylor 1994, 43; also Iskandar and Rustom 2006). Even with the best intentions in the world, it is impossible to teach history, literature, and the national language at school in a culturally neutral way (in the rare cases of official bilingualism, the two languages are taught in a culturally balanced rather than neutral way). The very idea of a culturally neutral national culture is an oxymoron, therefore, it is impossible to realize in practice.

More generally, the relationship between cultural identity and civic consciousness is usually viewed in the relevant publications as problematic:

> Citizenship, conceived as a matrix of rights and obligations governing the members of a political community, exists in tension with the heterogeneity of social life and the multiple identities that arise therefrom. This tension expresses itself in the clash between the "universal" citizen and numerous dispersed identities of which citizenship is but one.
>
> (Purvis and Hunt 1999, 457)

The other mechanism of assimilation is applied in the so-called "ethnic" nations where members of minority groups are pressured to identify with the majority. A glaring example of this type of assimilation was the so-called "Revival Process" in Bulgaria.[4] To motivate the ethnic Turks to change their identity, the concept was developed that all members of this group were distant descendants of ethnic Bulgarians who, during Turkish rule,[5] had been Islamized and eventually assimilated ethnically. It was claimed, therefore, that a process of "re-Bulgarianization" would not constitute assimilation but a return to the authentic, true identity of these people – hence the official name of the campaign, "Revival Process":

> The main argument was historical. It included the thesis that all Bulgarian Turks were descendants of Bulgarians converted to Islam during Turkish rule rather than of Turkic colonizers; that they were now reawakening from a centuries-long slumber; that they were now happy to restore their "true names" along with their true national self-identity.
>
> (Kanev 1998, 77)

This study is not concerned with the complex relationships between universalist and particularist trends in multicultural societies that have been addressed by the politics of recognition and identity politics in recent decades and which are reflected in, at first glance, paradoxical categories such as cultural or even religious citizenship (Hemming 2011). Here, I will content myself with the conclusion that certain problems in the relations between a minority and the mainstream society could be traced back to possible assimilation pressures. This is a particularly sensitive issue for national minorities, especially for those of them which – justifiably or not – have a certain sense of cultural superiority over the majority of their country's population. In such cases, even the requirement to have command of the official language could turn out to be a *casus belli* – as, for example, in the case of Russian minorities in the countries of the former Soviet Union (see, for example, European Agency for Fundamental Rights 2010).

But the relations between different cultural identities in a given society may also cause tension and conflict "in the opposite direction." The tendencies toward minority self-segregation can be just as problematic; their main, and largely legitimate, source is the value of group identity to those who share it. Scholars who have written on the matter tend to agree – to my mind, with good reason – that the opposite, that is, self-hatred of one's identity, is a pathological condition that causes unnecessary suffering for the carriers of this identity, and that inciting self-hatred is morally condemnable (Fanon 1990; Taylor 1994).

To what extent is the defense of the cultural identity of minority groups – and hence, resistance against assimilation – justified? This question is addressed mainly in studies devoted to multiculturalism. Here, I will briefly comment on two of the best-known arguments, which fit nicely into the context of liberal values. Arguably, the most popular one of these is formulated by Charles Taylor in his seminal essay on "The Politics of Recognition" (1994). According to this argument, it is our moral duty to accept all cultures (or at least those that have proven their significance historically, having formed the mentality of entire societies for long periods of time – see Taylor 1994, 66) as valuable in an absolute sense – that is, regardless of the point of view. At the beginning of his essay, Taylor (1994, 33) refers to a more or less obvious characteristic of identity – that it is dialogical in nature, and that we define our identity and answer the question, "Who am I?," based on not only what we see in ourselves, but also on what the persons who are important in our lives see in us. It follows from this that the demonstration of a negative, or even just contemptuous, attitude toward the Other cannot be taken as an innocuous expression of personal opinion, for "a person or group of people can suffer real damage, real distortion, if the people or society around them mirror back to them a confining or demeaning or contemptible picture of themselves" (ibid., 25). Hence, recognition is not just "a courtesy we owe people. It is a vital human need" (ibid., 26).

With this argument, Taylor presents recognition as something that is owed to every individual to the extent where refusal to grant recognition would be unjust. In his view, what should be recognized is not one's identity in a general, abstract sense, but precisely the cultural identity of the individual. I fully agree with this view. Could I grant recognition to somebody while demonstrating a negative attitude toward the culture he or she identifies with?

It turns out that recognizing the worth of another's culture is a matter of fairness. That is why the recognition paradigm, as interpreted by Taylor, fits – at least nominally – into the context of liberal values. It is one of the sources used to justify, theoretically and morally, multicultural public policies from a liberal point of view. Following the logic outlined in Taylor's essay, the conclusion that the self-respect of an individual depends not only on the way she views herself, but also in the way she "sees" herself, through the eyes of others, leads to slogans of the "let's celebrate diversity" type, which were very popular in the 1990s. The solution to the dilemma of whether we will like or dislike a particular achievement of another culture is not a matter of our personal taste. Appreciation of other cultures is required, not as a show of courtesy or of political correctness, but as nothing less than the fulfillment of a moral duty.[6]

The next argument I will look at belongs to another authoritative exponent of multiculturalism, Will Kymlicka. This argument is based on the ideal of the liberal neutrality of the state. Kymlicka insists that this ideal should be complemented by the recognition of the importance of what he calls "societal culture." The Canadian philosopher questions the liberal ideal of the neutrality of public institutions with regard to conceptions of the good life, including culture, and of limiting the powers of these institutions only to the fair regulation of social interactions. According to Kymlicka, the state de facto actively participates in the functioning of a "societal culture," which is (at least partly) institutionalized, as well as laden with cultural content. He proposes the following definition of societal culture:

> a culture which provides its members with meaningful ways of life across the full range of human activities, including social, educational, religious, recreational and economic life, encompassing both public and private spheres.
>
> (Kymlicka 1995, 76)

Kymlicka argues that societal culture is a necessary prerequisite for individuals to live a full life, and that the realization of societal culture mandates the participation of public institutions. In other words, individuals should expect public institutions to not only safeguard their interests against unjust infringement, but to also support their culturally determined way of life.

What does all this entail for public policies on minorities? Schematically, Kymlicka develops his arguments on two levels. First, he substantiates the proposition that the liberal ideal of the individual's autonomy entails the need for the individual's participation in a "societal culture." On the second level, Kymlicka (1995, 84) asks whether it matters which "societal culture" will provide a given individual, who belongs to a minority group, with the context that shapes that individual's choice of a certain way of life. In other words, does it matter whether minority members will model their way of life after their own national or ethnic culture, or whether they will resort to the "services" of the "mainstream" one?

Kymlicka answers this question on two levels, too. First, he offers several arguments in support of the thesis that the individual's self-identity is important and valuable to her; therefore, the possible decision to assimilate into the societal culture of another ethnic group (that is, of the majority) by adopting it as her own culture, is not of the same order of importance as the decision to change her home or job.[7] Then he formulates the thesis that justice requires allowing the individual to freely decide whether to do one thing or another – that is, whether to assimilate or to seek ways to satisfy her need of a societal culture, starting from her existing self-identity. Or, in other words, to fight for group-specific rights for herself, as well as for the other members of her group, so that they could use those rights to collectively develop their own minority societal culture:

> I believe that, in developing a theory of justice, we should treat access to one's culture as something people can be expected to want, whatever their more particular conception of the good. Leaving one's culture, while possible, is best seen as renouncing something to which one is reasonably entitled.
>
> (Kymlicka 1995, 86)

As we can see, it is by no means impossible to formulate arguments in favor of the value of minority identities, which are in accordance with the principles of liberal democracy. But what about the question of how such a philosophy can be applied as a methodology in designing minority policies? If the value of minority identity is understood in essentialist terms, even without "paying tribute" to communitarian leanings, this is very likely to lead to the encouragement of self-segregation among the members of minority groups. As the development of multicultural practices in some Western-type democratic societies has shown, policies that support minority identities can lead to self-segregation of minority communities (see Guzzetta 1997, 63). Efforts to preserve a specific way of life, as well as, and resistance to, the temptations of assimilation, can result in the distancing of the members of a minority group from mainstream life in the country they live in, prompting them to give priority to their own culture-specific values and norms over the civic values and norms governing public life in their country. Such efforts could also lead to limiting the freedoms of the individual members in the name of keeping archaic cultural traditions alive (see Devore 1997, 41; Guzzetta 1997, 66).

As for the countries of Central and Eastern Europe, the factors determining the tendencies of self-segregation in the life of minorities are compounded by the burden of historical legacies of interethnic and interreligious relations. It is a fact that all large autochthonous minorities in this region – with the exception of the Roma – emerged as such as the result of the redistribution of territories among states, including the disintegration of empires or federations. These processes were usually accompanied by bloody armed conflicts which left their mark in the collective memory of the respective minorities. Another source of intergroup tension can be found in the mechanisms of national identity formation and reproduction; among which a particularly important role plays the mechanism of distinguishing one's identity from other identities, and juxtaposing it to them – the "us versus them" syndrome (see Golubović 1999, 34; Gergova 2002, 151). For example, in the Balkan countries that were constituted as a result of the disintegration of the Ottoman Empire, there are tendencies to demonize the Turks and Islam, especially in the way history and literature are taught at school (Zhelyazkova 1997; Stoyanov 1998; Bosakov 2010). These tendencies inevitably affect the attitudes toward the respective minorities.

Thus, the cultural identity of a given minority group is a potential source of tension and conflict – even in a democratic society – insofar as it can be the subject of assimilation pressure, or be the driving factor behind the self-segregation of the group. But cultural differences can be the cause of minority problems in and of themselves, too. A number of typologies of cultural differences have been produced within the framework of the academic discipline of Intercultural Communication, drawing on comparisons of empirical data (with methodologies borrowed primarily from cultural anthropology and social psychology) about manifestations of cultural attitudes and values by members of different cultural communities. The most-discussed cultural differences are those in terms of contextuality (high-context and low-context, see Hall 1976), power distance, and uncertainty avoidance (see Hofstede 1991), as well as dichotomies such as individualism/collectivism, masculinity/femininity (see Hofstede 1991), universalism/particularism, achievement/ascription, and specific/diffuse cultures (see Trompenaars and Hampden-Turner 1997).

Problems arise when persons with different cultural attitudes have to interact – for example, when people from different ethnic backgrounds live in close proximity to each other in a small town or village, or in the same neighborhood. In everyday life, as in economic and public life, certain contrasts between the mores of people who depend – not of their own will – on one another can result in the unpredictability of the Others' behavior, in lack of mutual trust, and in irritation at the behavior of the Other, which can deviate from our standards of what is acceptable and what is not. One of the indications that such "co-residence" is problematic is the mass departure of members of the majority from neighborhoods that have become predominantly inhabited by minority groups, which leads to the spatial and, hence, cultural segregation of the respective minority community.

The social implications of cultural differences are especially important in primary and secondary education. When there are discrepancies between the school regulations, teaching methods, content taught, and teaching style, on the one hand, and the cultural attitudes of children from ethnic or religious minorities, on the other, the result is alienation of children from school life as they perceive the time spent in school as useless and depressing, as well as loss of motivation to participate in the learning process, there will be conflicts with schoolmates, and so forth (Sotirova 2008; Totseva 2008; Tilkidjiev et al. 2009).

Another important aspect of the role of cultural differences as a factor in minority problems is the contrast between the traditional mores that are prevalent among some minority groups in Central and Eastern Europe and the modern[8] social order. The Roma minorities are a case in point in this respect. A number of differences between the way of life of some Roma groups and "mainstream" society – such as much higher birth rates, as well as early marriage and early motherhood, which prematurely burden young people with family duties and prevent them from attaining proper education and vocational training, thereby diminishing their chances of fully and successfully participating in society (Tomova 1995) – can be explained precisely as a "clash" between manifestations of traditional and modern cultural identities. The problems of some Muslim minorities, particularly of those living in rural areas far from major urban centers, are of the same type. They are characterized by significant self-isolation from mainstream public life, an insufficient capacity for orientation in the changing political climate, an inclination to form clientelistic political dependencies, and a susceptibility to radical Islamist influences (see Georgieva 1998; Zhelyazkova 1998).

The theoretical and public-policy challenges posed by these types of minority issues primarily stem from the dilemma of whether the attitude toward them should be based on a culturally-relativistic tolerance of differences, or on a culturally-evolutionistic intolerance toward the backward mores that are believed to hinder the integration of large groups of citizens into contemporary society. In the first case, there is a danger that minority policies may do a disservice to their target groups by deterring their cultural development (in a sense, this is what Habermas has in mind in his critique of the "ecological" approach to cultural identities, mentioned in the previous chapter, see Chapter 1). In the second, the risk is that such policies may actually lead to assimilation pressure on minority groups.

Group solidarity

When dealing with categories of people, groups, and communities, we should not ignore the question of intergroup relations. It is especially important because the interactions of subjects of different identities are often problematic. After all, every ethnic or religious conflict inevitably involves, in some way, the identities of the participants.

Cultural identity has been presented so far in this study as relatively innocuous. Why, then, does it often prove in reality to be the "apple of discord"? Why can the mores of a particular cultural community provoke aggression on the part of the members of another one who happen to live in the same neighborhood? Some authors (I will examine this question later) disagree that identities may be a source of hostility between their subjects, and attribute ethnic and religious conflicts to purely instrumental – economic and political – motives (see, for example, Cornell and Hartmann 1998, 149). Regarding the infamous civil wars in the territory of the former Yugoslavia, one will still hear people asking in bewilderment, "But how did they manage to live together peacefully for so many years before the conflict?" Moreover, considering that there was no change in the identities themselves, how come they suddenly became incompatible?

One of the challenges facing social sciences today is the connection between cultural difference and discrimination (Jetten 1997). Differences in mentality and way of life, which in themselves should not significantly affect relations between people, may cause the unequal treatment of the Others that often deteriorates into systematic oppression of minorities. What could be the reason for this? Let us discuss the hypothesis that intergroup relations produce conditions in which cultural differences can give rise to tension and even open conflict between their subjects.

Intergroup relations have been the subject of social psychology research for decades. Here, I will look at one of the most influential theories, that of social identity. It attempts to explain relations between groups from the vantage point of their members' personal motivation for action. This explanation can be represented schematically as follows.

The basic assumption of social identity theory is that in their social lives all individuals conceive of themselves as members of groups (it is this self-concept that constitutes their social identity – see Abrams and Hogg 1990). Furthermore, it is a well-known fact that, typically, people prefer to have a positive rather than a negative self-image – that is, they strive for high self-esteem. Group membership undoubtedly is of importance for an individual's self-esteem. Since individuals tend to identify with a group to which they belong, if the latter has a high status in society this has a positive effect on the self-image of its members, and vice versa. Hence, social identity theory concludes that individuals regard the relations between their "in-group" – the group (or category) they belong to by virtue of some shared trait,[9] and the "out-groups" – the groups that differ in that aspect, as competitive. This is because the superiority of one's in-group over the Others' groups is perceived by individuals as evidence of their group's merits, and hence, as grounds for maintaining or improving their self-esteem. It follows that groups may find themselves in relationships of competition even if there are no objective reasons for it.

The founder of social identity theory, Henri Tajfel, substantiates this hypothesis by providing evidence from the so-called "minimal group experiments." In these experiments, groups formed on the basis of trivial criteria are made to compete against each other in some way. It turns out that regardless of how trivial the goal of the competition was, group members eagerly join in. Writing about one of these experiments, which were conducted on schoolboys, Tajfel (1978, 14) notes that

> The establishment of a difference between two groups in favour of their own was often more important to the schoolboys with whom we worked than the absolute amounts of monetary rewards that they could get.

This conceptual frame of reference provides an answer to the question we asked above – namely, why are the interactions among persons of different cultural identities so problematic. There does not have to be an objective reason for the existence of competitive relations between such groups. The very fact that they differ in some respect – in this case, culturally – is enough to give rise to a struggle for superiority which, depending on the circumstances, can be overt or covert, peaceful or violent, moderate or extremist.

Actually, according to some authors, the smaller the cultural contrast between identities, the more intense the competition between them. If we assume that it is important to members that their in-group stands out as superior to other groups, then maintaining this superiority when comparing their in-group to an out-group that is barely any different is an even greater challenge: "the more similar the out-group is to the in-group, the greater the efforts needed to differentiate between the two groups and, hence, the stronger will be the intergroup discrimination and in-group bias" (Johnston and Hewstone 1990, 188). In addition, when there are small differences between groups, their relations are aggravated by their members' fears about the preservation of group identity:

> But the more similar the out-group is to the in-group, the more likely it will define itself and its social identity using similar dimensions to the in-group. Such an out-group would then be a threat to the in-group's unique identity. The in-group is more likely to discriminate against a group posing a threat to their identity than against one posing no such threat.
>
> (Johnston and Hewstone 1990, 188)

That is how social identity theory explains the seemingly paradoxical fact that peoples which live in close proximity to each other and share a number of common cultural traits are often at odds with each other. Sigmund Freud offers another explanation for this paradox. According to him, the reason ultimately lies in the inherent human inclination toward aggression, which groups try to direct outward, at other groups, in order to maintain good relations among their members. Freud (1989) calls this search for an "outlet" of intragroup aggression "the narcissism of minor differences" (he uses as an example the tensions between the Spaniards and the Portuguese, the North and South Germans, and the English and the Scots). In recent times this phrase became popular after Michael Ignatieff (see Ignatieff 1998, 50) used it to describe the conflicts in the territory of the former Yugoslavia. Social identity theory, however, looks for a less pretentious explanation for the paradox, proceeding from the commonplace fact that people prefer to have a positive rather than a negative self-image, and tend to identify with groups to which they belong in some way or another. This can explain many displays of antagonism in intergroup interactions, such as negative stereotyping, prejudice, and discrimination, as well as in-group solidarity.

What social identity theory cannot explain convincingly, though, is positive intergroup relations – which are also a fact, even if not as common as intergroup conflict. If we assume that in-group/out-group competition is unavoidable, we commit ourselves to the view that intergroup hostilities have no alternative – a view that is morally problematic, as well as empirically untrue.

Another challenge to social identity theory is posed by, for example, the instances of overlapping of in- and out-groups. What happens when an individual belongs to one group by virtue of a certain trait, but also belongs to a second group by virtue of another trait, and the latter is an out-group vis-à-vis the former? With whom will this individual identify? With the members of which of the two groups will she feel a bond of solidarity? The literature on this topic in political psychology recognizes the problematic nature of so-called *multiple identities:* "In a large, pluralistic society, then, multiple criss-crossing social identities can become a source of increasing fractionation or enhanced stability, depending on how competing identities are managed" (Brewer 2001, 123; see also Stryker 2000).

In Bulgaria, for example, the Muslim Bulgarians (or the so-called "Pomaks") would be expected to solidarize themselves with the ethnic majority based on ethnic origin and with the Turkish (and part of the Roma) minorities based on religion. This means that the attitudes of the people from the Muslim Bulgarian community toward the Turkish community would be contradictory. For them, the latter would be an out-group in terms of ethnic origin and an in-group in terms of religion. Hence, depending on the way the given multiple social identity is "managed," it could fall into a state of quasi-schizophrenic split or, conversely, develop into a link between the two communities.

In the case of Muslim Bulgarians, the multiplicity of their identity has in fact led to the significant disintegration of this community. Some of these Bulgarian citizens tend to identify with the ethnic Bulgarian majority and to distance themselves from Islam (some even convert to Christianity while others, who are more moderate, simply secularize themselves to one extent or another), but others identify themselves as Turks (see Georgieva 1998, 234). Still others turn to history in an effort to "rediscover" (in essentialist terms) their ethnicity as non-Bulgarian and non-Turkish, but as a separate "Pomak" one, thus radically reconstructing their identity (Mitrev 2008).

This example shows how important is the way individuals perceive themselves as belonging to a particular social group or category. The social-psychological theory of self-categorization (Haslam et al. 1996) focuses precisely on this aspect of self-awareness. Viewed philosophically, here we have a mixture of description and prescription, of judgments about facts and judgments about values, which is as theoretically interesting as it is practically problematic. Depending on which of the overlapping aspects of a given multiple identity is regarded as more important by the subject of that identity, the latter can play objectively very different roles. And insofar as these roles can produce socially constructive or destructive effects, the management of multiple identities can also have quite significant moral implications, which makes the very term "management" somewhat inadequate. In cases of this kind, an individual's self-identification (or self-categorization) in a particular way also entails taking on significant moral responsibility.

A case in point considers the tendencies to *instrumentalize* self-identification. If the leaders of a given social group stand to gain from its confrontation with another (in terms of in-group versus out-group), and if the two group identities objectively overlap (as in the case of Muslim Bulgarians, on the one hand, and the other Muslim communities in Bulgaria, on the other), these leaders will seek to influence the complex processes of self-identification of the ordinary members of their group so as to belittle everything that connects them to the out-group in question and to emphasize the importance of everything that separates them from this other group. But if the confrontation between the two groups is objectively harmful to their ordinary members, such behavior on the part of their leaders will be morally condemnable. Conversely, mutual identification of the ordinary members with one another will create possibilities for intergroup cooperation – that is, for developing relations of the "win-win" type.

I will end this section on the role of group solidarity as a factor determining minority issues with a brief discussion of the feedback relationship between the manifestations of group solidarity, on the one hand, and the effects of the other two types of factors influencing minority issues, on the other. At the beginning of this chapter, I pointed out that cultural differences, group solidarity and social and political relations exist in a mutually reinforcing relationship with each other. What can we say in this respect about the relationship between discrimination (as a typical form of in-group – out-group rivalry) and cultural differences?

I think that for everyone who has dealt with this topic the answer is self-evident. Depending on the circumstances, discrimination can trigger hyper-trophied, defiant, and inexplicable – if viewed in isolation – displays of cultural differences (for example, radicalization of the forms in which a given group or an individual professes Islam). But it can also prompt a "downplay" of the cultural differences: a suppression of culturally-distinctive traits and behavior on the part of the group or the individual in an effort to avoid giving "the discriminators" reasons for unequal treatment. In the first case, discrimination and cultural differences are in a positive-feedback relationship. Discrimination provokes displays of cultural differences which, in turn, reinforce the discriminatory attitudes and reactions of the other side, thereby creating conditions for even more extreme exhibits of such differences, and so forth. In the second case, it would be reasonable to expect that the feedback relationship would be negative, but practice shows that the result is usually a further exacerbation of the relations. For the "discriminators," the very fact that the culturally different Others are "keeping a low profile" is cause for suspicion (as this demeanor can be interpreted as ostentatious or insincere); for the victims of discrimination the suppression of their cultural identity causes inner psychological and moral struggle on both the individual and group levels, which may instigate future minority-related tension.

As for the relationship between group solidarity and social and political interaction, this is a well-known and widely researched subject. Tension between religious, ethnic, and national groups is a favorable environment for the pursuit of social and political interests. Furthermore, the struggles between representatives of opposite interests of this kind unavoidably fuel religious, ethnic, and national conflicts which, in turn, aggravate social and political rivalries.

Social and political factors

To begin with, I would like to discuss the most commonly-held notions of the difference between the social and cultural aspects of public life by using a description offered by Nancy Fraser in Chapter One of the book *Redistribution or Recognition? A Political-Philosophical Exchange* (Fraser 2003).

Fraser (ibid., 13) gives three examples each of social and cultural injustice. Those of social injustice are:

> exploitation (having the fruits of one's labor appropriated for the benefit of others); economic marginalization (being confined to undesirable or poorly-paid work or being denied access to income-generating labor altogether), and deprivation (being denied an adequate material standard of living).

The examples Fraser (ibid.) gives of cultural injustice are:

> cultural domination (being subjected to patterns of interpretation and communication that are associated with another culture and are alien and/or hostile to one's own); nonrecognition (being rendered invisible via the authoritative representational, communicative, and interpretative practices of one's own culture); and disrespect (being routinely maligned or disparaged in stereotypic public cultural representations and/or in everyday life interactions).

There are also significant differences in the possible remedies for these two types of injustice. Social injustices can be remedied by restructuring economic relations – for example, by "redistributing income and/or wealth, reorganizing the division of labor, ... democratizing the procedures by which investment decisions are made," (ibid.) and so forth. Cultural injustices, according to Fraser (ibid.), can be remedied by:

> upwardly revaluing disrespected identities and the cultural products of maligned groups; recognizing and positively valorizing cultural diversity; or transforming wholesale societal patterns of representation, interpretation, and communication (in ways that would change everyone's social identity).

To my mind, the non-distinction of social and cultural relations leads to conceptual problems on two levels. On the fundamental level, there is the question of whether the one type of relationship can be reduced to the other – that is, whether the former can be represented as an *epiphenomenon* of the latter. For example, identities and group solidarity can be regarded as constructs created by economically and politically dominant groups in society in order to maintain and strengthen their domination (see, for example, Cornell and Hartmann 1998, 57; Fischer et al. 1999, 478). And, conversely, social relations can be interpreted as an expression of basic cultural characteristics of the population concerned. For example, the capitalist organization of the economy can be construed as a product of Protestantism, or socialism (as it existed in the Soviet Union and some other East European countries) can be seen as having been made possible by the collectivist mentality of non-modern cultures (Landes 2000; Porter 2000).

If that is so – if it is true that only the one type of issues really exist – then all efforts to resolve those of the other type are a waste of the resources of society. It is in this sense that what we have here is not just a theoretical but also a public-policy dilemma. Perhaps the most urgent questions in this respect are the following: isn't the significance of cultural conflict (ethnic, religious, racial, and so forth) being deliberately exaggerated in order to divert the attention from the unjust distribution of material wealth? Aren't the struggles for recognition a per-version of the struggle for social justice?

A more moderate approach to the ambiguous relationship between social and cultural issues would recognize the existence of both types of relationships, but then the question arises – and this is the second level of the conceptual problem that we are dealing with – what is the relative importance of the social and cultural factors in each particular case of conflict. Let us take, for example, a situation where some ethnic minority is fighting for independence – that is, for secession from the state it lives in. Are the proclaimed values and ideals in the name of which this fight is conducted truly related to the desire of these people to preserve and assert their cultural identity (a desire that usually motivates such undertakings – at least visibly); or are they merely a smokescreen hiding the material interests of the community's intellectual and political elite? If identity and solidarity still have leading roles in the given situation, this does not neces-sarily exclude the possibility that instrumentally rational (*zweckrational* in the sense of Weber 1978) considerations may prevail elsewhere, and vice versa. Each situation should be examined on a case-by-case basis in order to determine how people should treat individual claims, and what types of public policies addressing these claims are advisable and morally legitimate to pursue. Unless we have clear criteria for distinguishing social from cultural relationships, we will not be able to make a correct "diagnosis."

Moreover, we should keep in mind that the effects of social and cultural factors are often intertwined and even mixed up at times – as a result either of well-calculated manipulation or of *bona fide* misunderstandings. Motivations for political action, which claim to be cultural (as in the above example of the hypo-thetical separatist ethnic minority), are usually "deconstructed" and exposed as social ones by political opponents in an attempt to delegitimize that action in the public eye. It is assumed that a political struggle for the protection of identity can claim public legitimacy much more than the struggle for satisfying some-body's power ambitions or economic interests.

The choice of the particular public-policy measures that need to be taken in order to resolve intergroup tension and conflict is another and, no less important, issue. To find an adequate "remedy," we need to make an accurate diagnosis. If the spatial self-segregation of an ethnic or religious minority community in a large town is due primarily to social reasons (for example, if these families can afford only cheap housing in run-down neighborhoods), the solution to the problem should include measures such as improving the neighborhood infra-structure and reducing unemployment among the minority population. If, however, the reasons are cultural (the desire to live among people of your own who do not look down on you and treat you with contempt, as well as to live in an environment that is arranged according to your customs and where you feel secure and at home), the above-mentioned measures are desirable in a more general sense but will certainly not solve the problem. The solution should be of quite a different nature.

Of course, in real life these two types of factors usually work hand in hand – and they do so in a positive-feedback relationship. As Seyla Benhabib (2002, 69–70) notes, successful acts of the recognition of members of culturally discriminated groups can have positive effects in the other "dimension," too:

> Such changes have distributive consequences, in that the transformation of the cultural status of misrecognized groups can result in the improvement of their lot socioeconomically, in the extension to them of unemployment, retirement, medical, and schooling benefits, and in their inclusion in the democratic public sphere.

However, the consequences are truly disastrous when the positive-feedback relationship between the effects of cultural and social factors works in a negative direction – for example, when discrimination engenders poverty and poverty becomes "culturalized," in turn "justifying" and fueling discrimination and, thereby, adding further impetus to the downward spiral to the bottom, that is, to a state of anomie from which there is no escape. Obviously, in such cases it is necessary to implement both cultural and social measures, but they should have different targets. That is why distinguishing social from cultural issues is a necessary condition for the design of adequate minority policies.

Without pretending to be comprehensive, I will propose two criteria for distinguishing between social and cultural issues in public life in a modern social and cultural setting (see my comments above on the "community vs society" and "instrumentally rational vs value rational action" oppositions – Chapter 1). One of them is based upon the difference between rational and contingent reasons for our behavior. In my view, social actions (those that are not undertaken from the positions of and with a view to identities, but are rather determined by interests) can be entirely rational, while cultural ones (or, perhaps more precisely, ones related to identity) are ultimately determined by contingent circumstances.

What do I mean here by "rational" and "contingent"? Most dictionary definitions of "contingent" associate this word with uncertainty of being. Contingent is something that may or may not happen, because it is "… likely but not certain to happen; not logically necessary; happening by chance or unforeseen causes; not necessitated; subject to chance or unseen effects; intended for use in circumstances not completely foreseen" (*Merriam-Webster's Collegiate Dictionary*). I am using the term "contingent" here not in the sense of randomness but, rather, of a reality that is not necessary in itself – or, as Spinoza writes in *The Ethics* (Part IV, Definition 3), "Particular things I call contingent in so far as, while regarding their essence only, we find nothing therein, which necessarily asserts their existence or excludes it" (Spinoza 2009).

In this sense, cultural identity can be regarded as contingent because it does not necessarily stem from something and is not an element of some rationally organized whole; it is the product of a historical concurrence of circumstances. The question of why it is what it is has no answer. Admittedly, from a constructionist perspective, its origin can be traced to some instrumentally rational considerations of its hypothetical creators, but from such a viewpoint there is in fact no identity. It is an epiphenomenon. If we admit that identity exists at all – that is, that it is not merely a semblance – we must accept it as a given. The behavior that is determined by a particular identity may be otherwise rational, but its fundamental motives are not. People may be able to explain why they behave in one way rather than another regarding every aspect of their actions except for the most important one – why is it important for them to hold on to a particular identity in the first place?

A main element of ethnic identity, for example, is the consciousness of common descent of a group of people (see, for example, Krasteva 1998, 19). The boundaries dividing "us" and "them" are not drawn by this consciousness on a rational basis. They are determined by some set of concurrent historical circumstances, real or imagined, but they are quite significant to us. As we can see from recent ethnic conflicts, solidarity that is uncritically accepted as a given may prove to have significant implications for the life and death of many people.

In what sense can social behavior – unlike identity-based behavior – be entirely rational? As we have seen, the difference between these two kinds of conduct becomes clear when one asks the question about the fundamental motives underlying human acts. What is it that ultimately guides one to act in a particular way? Is it at all possible to base behavior on entirely rational foundations?

One of the possible affirmative answers to this question is given by Immanuel Kant in his ethical theory (*The Critique of Practical Reason*, 2014). True to his critical philosophical position, Kant does not dogmatically postulate any foundations of morality; he does not expect us to take anything for granted. The German philosopher starts from the self-evidence of our reasonability, from which logically follows that it is our "duty" to be true to ourselves, abiding by *rationality* – that is, by the *self-consistency* of our behavior. In his view, acting rationally means acting according to principles that must never contradict themselves. In *The Critique of Practical Reason*, Kant defends the thesis (here it is not necessary to trace each step in his argumentation) that the rationality of our behavior can be guaranteed by the observance of what he calls the "Fundamental Law of the Pure Practical Reason," alias the "categorical imperative," namely: "Act so that the maxim of thy will can always at the same time hold good as a principle of universal legislation" (Kant 2014, First Part, Book I, Chapter I, Par. VII).

This brings us to my first proposal of a criterion for distinguishing cultural from social behavior. Acts motivated – in a more or less mediated way – by identity can never be wholly rational. In the final analysis, their motivation is founded on premises that the actors take for granted as binding upon them. I believe this is more or less what Alasdair MacIntyre (1988, 350) has in mind in his account of the role of cultural identities in constituting different rationalities:

> The conclusion to which the argument so far has led is not only that it is out of the debates, conflicts, and enquiry of socially embodied, historically contingent traditions that contentions regarding practical rationality and justice are advanced, modified, abandoned, or replaced, but that there is no other way to engage in the formulation, elaboration, rational justification, and criticism of accounts of practical rationality and justice except from within some one particular tradition in conversation, cooperation, and conflict with those who inhabit the same tradition.

Conversely, a behavior that is not related to identity can be wholly rational, therefore communication among people in the social dimension of their activity can take place smoothly and in a universally accessible form. The Others, whatever their origin, are predictable and their motivation can be "transparent" to us, and vice versa. In my opinion, this is also the crux of the thesis regarding the universal accessibility of arguments as a necessary condition for the public legitimization of norms and policies, a thesis that is supported by authors such as John Rawls (1997) and Jürgen Habermas (2005), and which will be discussed in Part II of this book. Besides, civic values and attitudes – the ones that are supposed to unite all the members of a modern nation – unlike cultural ones, can be rationally made sense of and substantiated.

Another indicator by which cultural issues differ from social ones is, in my opinion, the character of associations among people. Put in traditional terms, this ought to be a difference between relationships of community (*Gemeinschaft*, on the cultural level) and of society (*Gesellschaft*, on the social one).[10] However, since these terms have been the target of multiple critiques and attempts at reformulation, I will try to use a more general and neutral criterion for distinguishing these two types of factors – namely, the mutual identification of the participants in the life of society with one another. We can establish whether certain activities are of a cultural or social nature by seeing whether the participants in them identify with one another or not. I will explain what I generally mean by "identifying with one another" by quoting a very eloquent formulation from Ferdinand Tönnies' book *Gemeinschaft und Gesellschaft* (2001, 33): "the direct interest of one being in the life of another and willingness to share in his or her joys and sorrows." In the terms of social psychology (and social identity theory in particular):

> Identification with a social group occurs when individuals see themselves in terms of a group they belong to and accept the group membership as a part of their self-concept and self-definition. Through identification with groups, individuals derive a sense of meaning and guidelines for understanding the world and interacting with others.
>
> (Settles and Buchanan 2014, 161)

To make this determination I will also use the results of Amy Gutmann's (2003) study on what she terms "identity groups," which was mentioned briefly in the previous chapter. In my opinion, she introduced this term in order to blur the boundary between the two types of social relations whose extreme, polar opposite forms are "community" and "society" (in Tönnies' sense). The community/society dichotomy has been criticized for failing to account for many types of real relations that cannot be classified in either of these two categories. Gutmann (2003, 2) proposes the category of "identity group" instead of "community," pointing out that identity groups are "politically significant associations that attract people because of their mutual identification." According to her (ibid.), "People identify with others by ethnicity, race, nationality, culture, religion, gender, sexual orientation, class, disability, age, ideology, and other social markers."

Groups that are not based on identity are defined by Gutmann as "interest groups," a term that largely overlaps with Tönnies' "society" (*Gesellschaft*). Gutmann's idea, though, is to find a place in her typology for cases that cannot be classified either as communities or as society – for example, groupings of individuals by traits such as race, disability, or age. These are categories of people that are not bound by a sense of community by virtue of their belonging to the respective category, but who can engage in relationships of mutual identification. Within one and the same category of individuals, such relationships may exist in some cases and be absent in others. They can vary in intensity – ranging from strong and binding, to weak mutual identification.

In brief, by replacing the community/society dichotomy with a less contrasting classification – namely, on the one side, a wide spectrum of "identity groups" varying by type and intensity of relationships, and on the other, "interest groups" – Gutmann breaks with the all-or-nothing logic characteristic of Tönnies' paradigm.

I believe that the "identity groups/interest groups" typology also has another advantage over that of "community/society." Although an identity group can be similar to a "community," described by Tönnies as some quasi-organized, close-knit group of people, it can also be very different, very amorphous – with its members (here the term "member" can be used only provisionally) not even knowing one another. To identify with someone on the basis of a common ethnicity, religion, race, and so forth, one does not necessarily have to have personal contacts with her. It is enough to share a sense of common belonging to some cause, or of a common historical background. In this respect, the typology proposed by Gutmann is, indeed, less contrasting, and therefore closer to reality and more convincing.

So, what criterion for distinguishing the effects of cultural factors from those of social factors can we formulate on the basis of the "identity groups/interest groups" typology? The simplest, but not sufficiently precise solution, would be to distinguish between a behavior that is motivated by its subject's identification with other people (it would be even more clear, but also more imprecise, to call this "collectivist behavior"), and a behavior that is motivated solely by the individual's self-interests, which may be defined as individualistic. However, it would be inaccurate to assume that every act performed from the position of identification with some group of people is culturally determined. This is because (at least in the popular view) culture is an overall way of life, whereas, as Gutmann (2003, 2) convincingly shows, identification with others is also possible on the basis of other aspects of human existence outside of culture alone. That is why it seems that we should limit the scope of culturally motivated behavior only to acts performed by individuals from the position of their self-identification with people who share the same overall way of life.

Is all this to say that the cultural and social dimensions of public life are not interconnected, and that we are dealing with some sort of dualism of two types of factors that are at work independently of each other? As already noted above, real-life events offer enough proof to the contrary – there are significant relationships between people's acts in these two dimensions. Conflicts of a cultural nature can be catalyzed or toned down by social factors. In conditions of material deprivation the relationships between coexisting racial, ethnic, or religious minorities, for example, usually become aggravated. And conversely, immigrants in countries with a high standard of living are usually treated tolerantly by society at large. On the other hand, the cultural gaps arising from racial, ethnic, or religious differences invariably "push" minority communities toward poverty. There are exceptions, of course, but cultural alienation – in the form of discrimination against the Others, the "ones different from us," and the lack of motivation on their part to seek self-realization in "mainstream" economic activities – leads to economic self-/segregation and orientation of the social energy of young minority members mainly toward activities within their community, including criminal ones.

Thus, not only cultural differences and group solidarity, but also social factors may engender minority problems – usually all of them "working" together and in various configurations. The last of these three categories also includes purely political undertakings that belong to the instrumentally rational (in the sense of Weber, 1978) or strategic (in the sense of Habermas, see Chapter 1) type of action. The fact that they are instrumentally rational or strategic is usually concealed by value-rational rhetoric designed to legitimize them in the eyes of the public at both the national and international levels. For example, one country's irredentist claims on another – which may be motivated by the government's desire to seize natural and demographic resources and/or to strengthen its positions in domestic politics – are usually represented as the defense of legitimate interests and rights of a national or ethnic minority in the other country. If this is done in a sufficiently competent and active manner, it can inspire genuine separatist sentiment among the minority group in question, even if there are no objective grounds for such attitudes (such as acts of discrimination against its members, for example). In such cases the effects of cultural and social factors become intertwined in a complex way, making the question of who is in the right incredibly difficult to answer. For, as history shows, the opposite is also possible: an oppressed minority's entirely legitimate claims to rights and freedoms can be represented by the authorities as the product of manipulation by foreign powers. But I will discuss the political approaches to minority issues in more detail in the next chapter.

Notes

1 Some authors call them "mutually constituted differences" (Dhamoon 2011, 230).
2 One may argue whether this kind of minimization of the significance of the cultural identity of members of minorities can be qualified as "assimilation." Later, I will explain why I have chosen to use this term in the present context.
3 At the cost of minimizing the significance of – allegedly – *all* cultural identities in public life.
4 A large-scale campaign for the assimilation of ethnic Turks in Bulgaria was launched in the winter of 1984/1985, and included, in the first place, motivating – through various forms of pressure – these Bulgarian citizens to apply to the authorities with a request that their names be changed (from Muslim to Christian or Slavic ones). However, since the ideological justification of this campaign was based on the thesis that Bulgarian Turks were, in essence, descendants of long-since assimilated ethnic Bulgarians, the campaign also included a ban on speaking Turkish in public, and even *ex-officio* renaming of deceased persons in the civil status records, as well as a number of restrictions on the practice of Islam.
5 From the end of the 14th century to 1878 the Bulgarian lands were part of the Ottoman Empire.
6 In another respect, the question arises here as to whether, and to what extent, what Taylor calls recognition on demand (Taylor 1994, 68; see also Blum 1998) is possible, but this question is not directly relevant to the subject of this study.
7 As an example, here are two of these arguments, which Kymlicka has borrowed from eminent exponents of liberal thought. Cultural identity gives individuals a sense of security because it connects them to a group of other people through relationships of solidarity based on belonging, not accomplishment (see Margalit and Raz 1990, 447). Cultural membership adds additional meaning and value to our actions, which become not only acts of individual accomplishment, but also part of a collective, historically significant, continuous creative effort whereby culture is made and remade (see Tamir 1993, 72).
8 The question as to which is the most adequate qualification for the prevalent moral and legal norms in contemporary European societies – "modern," "postmodern," "late-modern," or other – is addressed in Part II of this book.
9 Such as male or female, high- or low-educated, urban or rural resident, resident of a particular town, fan of a particular football team, member of a particular ethnic or religious community, and so forth.
10 The community/society (*Gemeinschaft/Gesellschaft*) typology was introduced in 1887 by Ferdinand Tönnies (2001) in his eponymous book.

References

Abrams, Dominic and Michael Hogg. "An Introduction to the Social Identity Approach." In *Social Identity Theory. Constructive and Critical Advances*, edited by Dominic Abrams and Michael Hogg, 1–9. London: Harvester Wheatsheaf, 1990.
Benhabib, Seyla. *The Claims of Culture*. Princeton: Princeton University Press, 2002.
Bosakov, Veselin. *Integratziata na mjusjulmanite v Bulgaria* [The Integration of the Muslims in Bulgaria]. Sofia: IVRAI, 2010.

Blum, Lawrence. "Recognition, Value and Equality." In *Theorizing Multiculturalism. A Guide to the Current Debate*, edited by Cynthia Willet, 73–99. Oxford: Blackwell, 1998.

Brewer, Marilynn B. "The Many Faces of Social Identity: Implications for Political Psychology." *Political Psychology* 22, no. 1 (2001): 115–125.

Cornell, Stephen and Douglas Hartmann. *Ethnicity and Race. Making Identities in a Changing World*. Thousand Oaks: Pine Forge Press, 1998.

Devore, Wynetta. "Has the Focus on Multiculturalism Resulted in Inadequate Attention to Factors such as Gender, Social Class and Sexual Orientation? Yes." In *Controversial Issues in Multiculturalism*, edited by Diane de Anda, 39–61. Boston: Allyn and Bacon, 1997.

Dhamoon, Rita Kaur. "Considerations on Mainstreaming Intersectionality." *Political Research Quarterly* 64, no. 1 (2011): 230–243.

European Union Agency for Fundamental Rights. *European Union Minorities and Discrimination Survey. Main Results Report*. Luxembourg: Publication Office of the European Union, 2010.

Fanon, Frantz. *The Wretched of the Earth*, London: Penguin Books, 1990.

Fischer, Edward, Quetzil Castaneda, Johannes Fabian, Jonathan Friedman, et al. "Rethinking Constructivism and Essentialism." *Current Anthropology* 40, no. 4 (1999): 473–499.

Fraser, Nancy. "Social Justice in the Age of Identity Politics: Redistribution, Recognition, and Participation." In *Redistribution or Recognition? A Political-Philosophical Exchange*, by Nancy Fraser and Axel Honneth, 7–109. London and New York: Verso, 2003.

Freud, Sigmund. *Civilization and Its Discontents*. New York: W.W. Norton & Company, 1989.

Georgieva, Tsvetana. "Pomaks: Muslim Bulgarians." In *Communities and Identities in Bulgaria*, edited by Anna Krasteva, 221–238. Ravenna: Longo Editore, 1998.

Gergova, Petya. "The Image of the Neighbour in Commentaries." In *Bulgaria – Yugoslavia. Journalism in Intercultural Dialogue*, edited by Valery Roussanov, 148–153. Sofia: ACCESS Foundation, 2002.

Golubović, Zagorka. "Models of Identity in Postcommunist Societies." In *Models of Identity in Postcommunist Societies*, edited by Zagorka Golubović and George F. McLean, 25–40. Washington, DC: The Council for Research in Values and Philosophy, 1999.

Gutmann, Amy. *Identity in Democracy*. Princeton, NJ: Princeton University Press, 2003.

Guzzetta, Charles, "Should Pograms and Service Delivery Systems Be Culture-Specific in Their Design? No." In *Controversial Issues in Multiculturalism*, edited by Diane de Anda, 62–78. Boston: Allyn and Bacon, 1997.

Habermas, Jürgen. *Religion in the Public Sphere*, lecture presented at the Holberg Prize Seminar. 2005. www.holbergprisen.no/images/materiell/2005_symposium_habermas.pdf#nameddest=habermas, accessed October 5, 2015.

Hall, Edward. T. *Beyond Culture*. New York: Anchor Books, 1976.

Hankivsky, Olena and Renee Cormier. "Intersectionality and Public Policy: Some Lessons from Existing Models." *Political Research Quarterly* 64, no. 1 (2011): 217–229.

Haslam, Alex, Penny Oakes, John Turner, Craig McGarty, Richard Sorrentino, and Edward Higgins. "Social Identity, Self-categorization, and the Perceived Homogeneity of Ingroups and Outgroups: The Interaction between Social Motivation and Cognition." *Handbook of Motivation and Cognition 3*. New York: Guilford Press, (1996), 182–222.

Hofstede, Geert. *Cultures and Organizations*: *Software of the Mind*. New York: McGraw-Hill, 1991.

Honneth, Axel and Nancy Fraser. *Umverteilung oder Anerkennung? Eine politisch-philosophische Kontroverse*. Frankfurt am Main: Suhrkamp, 2003.

Hemming, Peter J. "Educating for Religious Citizenship: Multiculturalism and National Identity in an English Multi-faith Primary School." *Transactions of the Institute of British Geographers* 36 (2011): 441–454.

Ignatieff, Michael. *The Warrior's Honor*. New York: Henry Holt and Co, 1998.

Iskandar, Adel and Hakem Rustom. "From Paris to Cairo. Resistance of the Unacculturated." *The Ambassadors* 9, no. 1 (2006), www.ambassadors.net, accessed December 2, 2015.

Jetten, Jolanda. *Dimensions of Distinctiveness: Intergroup Discrimination and Social Identity*, Amsterdam: Thesis Publishers, 1997.

Johnston, Lucy and Miles Hewstone. "*Intergroup Contact: Social Identity and Social Cognition.*" In *Social Identity Theory. Constructive and Critical Advances*, edited by Dominic Abrams and Michael Hogg, 185–210. London: Harvester Wheatsheaf, 1990.

Kanev, Krassimir. "Law and Politics on Ethnic and Religious Minorities." In *Communities and Identities in Bulgaria*, edited by Anna Krasteva, 55–95. Ravenna: Longo Editore, 1998.

Kant, Immanuel. *The Critique of Practical Reason*, eBooks@Adelaide, 2014.

Krasteva, Anna. "Ethnicity." In *Communities and Identities in Bulgaria*, edited by Anna Krasteva, 11–40. Ravenna: Longo Editore, 1998.

Kymlicka, Will. *Multicultural Citizenship. A Liberal Theory of Minority Rights*. Oxford: Clarendon Press, 1995.

Landes, David. "Culture Makes Almost All the Difference." In *Culture Matters. How Values Shape Human Progress*, edited by Lawrence Harrison and Samuel Huntington, 2–13. New York: Basic Books, 2000.

Laurence, Jonathan. "The New French Minority Politics." The Brookings Institution (March 2003). www.brookings.edu/fp/cusf/analysis/laurence.pdf, accessed April 28, 2015.

MacIntyre, Alasdair. *Whose Justice? Which Rationality?* Notre Dame: University of Notre Dame Press, 1988.

Margalit, Avishai and Joseph Raz. "National Self-Determination." *Journal of Philosophy* 87, no 9 (1990): 439–461.

Matsuda, Mary. "Beside My Sister, Facing the Enemy: Legal Theory Out of Coalition." *Stanford Law Review* 43 (1990): 1183–1192.

Mitrev, Anguel. "The Imagined Ethnos of Political Nepotism." *Le Monde Diplomatique* (Bulgarian Edition) No 10 (2008)

Nash, Jennifer C. "Re-thinking Intersectionality. *Feminist Review* 89 (2008): 1–15.

Porter, Michael. "Attitudes, Values, Beliefs, and the Microeconomics of Prosperity." In *Culture Matters. How Values Shape Human Progress*, edited by Lawrence Harrison and Samuel Huntington, 14–28. New York: Basic Books, 2000.

Purvis, Trevor and Alan Hunt. "Identity versus Citizenship: Transformations in the Discourses and Practices of Citizenship." *Social Legal Studies* 8 (1999): 457–482.

Rawls, John. "The Idea of Public Reason Revisited." *University of Chicago Law Review* 64, no. 3 (1997): 780–807.

Settles, Isis H. and Nicole T. Buchanan. "Multiple Groups, Multiple Identities and Intersectionality." In *The Oxford Handbook of Multicultural Identity*, edited by Verónica Benet-Martínez and Ying-yi Hong, 160–180. Oxford: Oxford University Press, 2014.

Sotirova, Maya. "Interkulturniat konflikt v uchilishte – priroda, tipologia, kompetentnost za upravlenie na konfliktite na uchitelja." [Intercultural Conflicts at School – Nature, Typology, Conflict-Management Competence of the Teacher]. In *Educational and Cultural Integration of Roma Children*, edited by Kiril Kostov, Raya Madgerova, Angelina Manova, Yosif Nounev, and Maya Sotirova, 44–69. Doupnitza: NCTTEIRC, 2008.

Spinoza, Benedict. *The Ethics*. A Project Gutenberg EBook, 2009.

Stoyanov, Valery. "*Turskoto naselenie v Bulgaria mezhdu poljusite na etnicheskata politika*." [The Turkish Population in Bulgaria between the Poles of Ethnic Politics]. Sofia: LIK, 1998.

Stryker, Sheldon. "Identity Competition: Key to Differential Social Movement Participation?" In *Self, Identity, and Social Movements*, edited by Sheldon Stryker, Timothy Owens, and Robert White, 21–40. Minneapolis: University of Minnesota Press, 2000.

Tajfel, Henri. *The Social Psychology of Minorities*. London: Minority Rights Group, 1978.

Tamir, Yael. *Liberal Nationalism*. Princeton, NJ: Princeton University Press, 1993.

Taylor, Charles. "The Politics of Recognition. In *Multiculturalism. Examining the Politics of Recognition*, edited by Amy Gutmann, 25–74. Princeton, NJ: Princeton University Press, 1994.

Tilkidjiev, Nikolay, Valentina Milenkova, Kamelia Petkova, and Natasha Mileva. *Otpadashtite romi*. [Roma Dropouts]. Sofia: Open Society Institute, 2009.

Totseva, Yanka, "Nachalnite uchiteli i obrazovanieto na detzata s razlichna etnichnost." [Primary-School Teachers and the Education of Children of Different Ethnicity]. In *Diversity without Borders*, edited by Plamen Makariev, Yanka Totseva, and Ivan Ivanov, 28–40. V. Tarnovo: Faber, 2008.

Tomova, Ilona. *The Gypsies in the Transition Period*. Sofia: IMIR, 1995.

Tönnies, Ferdinand. *Community and Civil Society*. Cambridge: Cambridge University Press, 2001.

Trompenaars, Fons and Charles Hampden-Turner. *Riding the Waves of Culture: Understanding Diversity in Global Business*. London: Nicholas Brealey Publishing, 1997.

Várady, Tibor. "On the Chances of Ethnocultural Justice in East Central Europe." In *Can Liberal Pluralism Be Exported? Western Political Theory and Ethnic Relations in Eastern Europe*, edited by Will Kymlicka and Magda Opalski, 135–149. Oxford: Oxford University Press, 2001.

Weber, Max. *Economy and Society. An Outline of Interpretive Sociology*. Berkeley: University of California Press, 1978.

Zhelyazkova, Antonina. "Formiraneto na mjusjulmanskite obshtnosti I kompleksite na balkanskite istoriografii." [The Formation of Muslim Communities and the Complexes of Balkan Historiographies]. In *The Muslim Communities in the Balkans and in Bulgaria*, edited by Antonina Zhelyazkova, Bozhidar Alexiev, and Zhorzheta Nazarska, 71–98. Sofia: IMIR, 1997.

Zhelyazkova, Antonina. "Turks." In *Communities and Identities in Bulgaria*, edited by Anna Krasteva, 287–306. Ravenna: Longo Editore, 1998.

3 Political power and minority policies

As I noted in the Introduction, I see serious problems in the empowerment of minorities by ensuring the participation of their representatives in the exercise of political power. At first glance, this looks like a promising way to align minority policies with the interests of minority groups. However, power relations have a logic of their own and when that logic governs the protection of the interests of minority groups as well, this leads not to an improvement of a minorities' plight, but to results of a completely different nature.

As we know, political power can be attractive in its own right; that is, for many people who are involved in it in some way it can be not just a means but also an end in itself. The struggle for gaining and retaining political power imposes certain patterns of behavior on those who exercise it, patterns that have little to do with promoting the interests of the citizens represented. This is a systemic problem for every democratic society, but because of the specific issues of minority groups it is especially acute in cases when – as I will try to show in this chapter – minorities manage to get their representatives into the institutions of political power. The prospects for these representatives to benefit from participation in power play a role in this respect, along with the tendencies toward minorities' self-segregation, which are fueled by the "amalgamation" of power and community relations.

In this chapter I will illustrate the above considerations by examining three of the most widely applied models of minority empowerment through their deliberate involvement in the exercise of political power. I will consider the so-called "socialist internationalism" that is familiar from the recent past, consociational democracy, and the policy of setting quotas for minority representatives in institutions of political power as it is conceptualized and theoretically justified by Anne Phillips in her theory of "the politics of presence." I will also comment on whether or not the creation and operation of ethnic or religious political parties is justified. As a whole, I will argue for the view that the communicative empowerment of minorities is preferable to the deliberate inclusion of minority representatives in the exercise of political power.

Socialist internationalism

The term "socialist internationalism" refers to, among other things, the minority policies that were carried out in former socialist countries such as the Soviet Union and Yugoslavia – two countries whose populations were ethnically and linguistically diverse and which were structured as federations with a complex hierarchy of union republics, autonomous republics or provinces, nationalities, and so forth (see Roberts 1978).

Unlike the *millet* system in the Ottoman Empire, the different ethnic groups in the multinational socialist states not only had significant cultural autonomy but also political rights, including the right to participate in government. A union republic or an autonomous province had their own legislative and executive bodies. Their representatives took part in legislative decision-making at the federal level (within bodies such as the Chamber of Nationalities of the Federal Assembly of Yugoslavia, according to Yugoslavia's 1946 Constitution – see Radan 1998, 189). In the classic model[1] of socialist internationalism, however, this "empowerment" was only nominal as the institutions in question did not actually make political decisions. The countries were de facto ruled by the communist party (also called the "United Socialist Party" in the German Democratic Republic, or the "United Workers' Party" in Poland, and so on). In turn, the communist party was ruled by a political elite concerned exclusively with keeping and consolidating its dominant positions:

> As the Soviet and earlier Yugoslav experiences indicated, a strong and disciplined party can dominate and impose its will despite the presence of a federalist constitution. With Tito at the helm, the LCY[2] was able to assert its dominance and keep the republic elites loyal to Tito and Yugoslavia.
>
> (Radan 1998, 198)

Thus, the participation of representatives of different ethnic (or national) communities in government was only ostensible: "Federalism under party control was meant to satisfy aspirations for national autonomy and expressions of national identity" (Hodson, Seculić, and Massey 1994, 1540).

This state of affairs, however, was not "invented" by the people in power in the Soviet Union or Yugoslavia. It has theoretical roots in Marxist-Leninist ideology itself. The category "socialist internationalism" evolved from a classic Marxist category, that of "proletarian internationalism." In its capacity as a strongly modernist project, Marxist ideology treats community solidarity and identity as remnants of the traditional forms of social organization: "modern industry labour, modern subjection to capital, the same in England as in France, in America as in Germany, has stripped him [the proletarian] of every trace of national character" (Marx and Engels 1969, 20[3]). For its part, national identity is a "superstructural" phenomenon. It is determined by the mode of production. That is why class solidarity ought to take precedence over ethnic and national ones:

We are opposed to national enmity and discord, to national exclusiveness. We are internationalists. We stand for the close union and the complete amalgamation of the workers and peasants of all nations in a single world Soviet republic.

(Lenin 1974, 43)

Minority problems are regarded as a temporary phenomenon. They will "vanish" on their own after the universal and ultimate triumph of the socialist revolution:

National differences and antagonism between peoples are daily more and more vanishing, owing to the development of the bourgeoisie, to freedom of commerce, to the world market, to uniformity in the mode of production and in the conditions of life corresponding thereto.

The supremacy of the proletariat will cause them to vanish still faster.

(Marx and Engels 1969, 25)

From this point of view, the fictitious nature of the "empowerment" of ethnic and national communities is not morally condemnable; it is not an instance of political hypocrisy. The participation of their representatives in political decision-making at the federal level is just a transitional form of the defense of their community interests, which are bound to become increasingly irrelevant anyway (see Hodson, Seculić, and Massey 1994, 1539).

In reality, however, this led to a paradoxical situation. Each of the factors I mentioned so far worked more or less against the affirmation of minority identities. But probably because of the complex configuration in which these processes occurred, the ultimate result was – in a way and, at least, on the superficial level – positive for minorities. Precisely because their cultural life was set within dimensions that were irrelevant to the mechanisms of real power, it was given enough room for expression. Insofar as cultural activities related to the reproduction of the cultural identity of minority groups over time were innocuous with regard to power – despite the nominal presence of minority representatives in institutions of political power – they were granted relative freedom and material support by the authorities.

In Bulgaria, for example, after the so-called "socialist revolution" of 1944, minority education developed extensively and many opportunities were provided for the expression of minority identities in the field of the media and the arts:

Along with the elementary "Turkish schools" (more than 1000 in number), there were seven Turkish high schools. A high school for girls opened in Rousse, while in Sofia, Kurdzhali and Razgrad there were institutes training teachers for the Turkish schools. More than ten Turkish-language or bilingual newspapers and one magazine were published in this period, including the local papers in Shoumen, Haskovo, Razgrad, Silistra and other cities ... Bulgarian radio had regular Turkish-language broadcasts. The state theaters in Haskovo, Shoumen and Razgrad staged Turkish-language productions.

(Kanev 1998, 73)

Intercultural relations were also largely free from antagonism. Minority communities had no particular reason to compete with one other as they all were in the same situation – that is, nothing depended on any of them. The fate of each minority group was decided elsewhere, not in the interactions between the communities themselves.

This picture shows that it is possible to draw certain analogies between socialist internationalism and the *millet* system in the Ottoman Empire. In both cases minorities enjoyed significant cultural autonomy and peaceful intercultural relations, but in a way that minimized their actual say in the political decisions affecting them. Hence, their cultural autonomy was, to a large extent, fictitious. It wholly depended on factors that were beyond the control of the communities concerned and, therefore, there were no guarantees for its further existence. In addition, the cultural autonomy of minorities was not only vulnerable to external influence; it also had no sources of stability within itself. As history has shown, it could have been very easily replaced by conflict situations where the very same people who viewed their identity as a basis for a dignified and meaningful life could have suddenly turned it into a justification for aggression against their neighbors. This type of cultural autonomy is not conducive to the formation of a responsible attitude toward one's identity. The breakup of Yugoslavia is a sad example of a shocking switch in the positions of the local political and cultural elites in the former Yugoslav republics – from praise of the fraternity and unity of the peoples of the federation to militant nationalism – in the course of a single decade. Such an abrupt about-face in attitudes and policies attests, in my view, to the fictitious, fabricated, hypocritical character of the "legitimacy" of the order in interethnic relations that had been established in this multinational country.[4]

However, there were also similar, albeit smaller-scale, volte-faces in minority policies in other countries from the erstwhile "socialist camp." For example, in Bulgaria socialist internationalism was an official policy of the regime until 1956, but then, just two years later, in 1958, the Central Committee of the Bulgarian Communist Party held its so-called October Plenum at which it adopted the "Theses on Work among the Turkish Population":

> Those strongly worded "theses" condemned "the manifestations of nationalism and religious fanaticism" among Bulgarian Turks. From that point on, "the struggle against nationalism," often seen as any attempt at expressing Turkish self-identity, became the battle cry of all attempts at forced assimilation, during and after the 1984–1985 forced name change included.
>
> (Kanev 1998, 75)

In addition to the multinational Yugoslavia and Soviet Union, socialist internationalism was also applied at various times in other countries of Central and Eastern Europe – in the form of the inclusion of certain individuals from ethnic or national minorities in the bodies of the legislative and executive branches of government (especially at the local level of administration), and even in ruling structures of the communist (regardless of its nominal name) party itself. This was done without a public normative regulation. The "cadres" from the respective community were "elevated to leading positions" (to use the political parlance of the day) because of their individual organizational skills and political loyalty that had been assessed as useful for the advancement of the party line by the respective party leadership which did not owe the public any explanation for its decisions. The promotion of minority "cadres" was meant not only to demonstrate the absence of discrimination against ethnic minorities, but also to display an even higher appreciation for their cultural identity (something like granting recognition in the sense in which this term was introduced later by Charles Taylor 1994).

Consociational democracy

Another model of cultural community empowerment, the *consociational democracy* model, involves the inclusion of minority representatives in institutions of political power. The term was introduced by Dutch political scientist Arend Lijphart, but the model itself had been applied for many years before that. It involves a "technique" of fair (at least, by design) *power sharing* among communities that may be ethnic, as well as religious or racial.

Consociational democracy is a consensual form of government in which all major groups of a multicultural society are represented. In this model, cultural pluralism is extended to the institutional level. Lijphart (1977, 25) defines consociational democracy in terms of four major characteristics: government by a grand coalition of the political leaders of all significant segments of the plural society; mutual veto or "concurrent majority" rule; proportionality as the principal standard of political representation, civil service appointments, and allocation of public funds; a high degree of autonomy to run its own internal affairs.

According to Lijphart (1977, 1), cooperation of community elites "is the primary distinguishing feature of consociational democracy." He contrasts this style of leadership with the British one, which prevails in the political world. The former is *coalescent*, while the latter is *competitive*, or, as other authors call it, "*adversarial*" (ibid., 25). Another specific feature of consociational democracy is that it makes, at least initially, plural societies more thoroughly plural: "Its approach is not to abolish or weaken segmental cleavages but to recognize them explicitly and to turn the segments into constructive elements of stable democracy" (ibid., 42).

In Europe, Lijphart finds elements of consociational democracy in the constitutional system of the Netherlands, Belgium, Switzerland and Austria. In the rest of the world, this model is applied to a large extent in Malaysia (see, for example, Giordano 2005), Uruguay, and Suriname; in the 1960s and 1970s it was also reasonably successful in Lebanon. Of special interest to this study is the case of Bosnia and Herzegovina. Its population is comprised of three major communities: Bosniaks, Croats, and Serbs. In terms of political system, Bosnia and Herzegovina is "a sort of 'asymmetrical confederation,'" as Mirjana Kasapović (2005, 4) puts it. It consists of two entities: the unitary Republika Srpska and the multiethnic Federation of Bosnia and Herzegovina. The latter consists of ten cantons. The two entities, as well as the ten cantons of the Federation, have broad autonomy, albeit at different levels. As Kasapović (ibid.) points out:

> The powers of the central state institutions are limited to foreign policy and trade, customs, monetary and migration policies, air-traffic control, the implementation of international obligations and regulations, the regulation of transport between the entities.

The three communities are proportionally represented at all levels of government. One-third of the members of the House of Representatives, the first chamber of the Parliamentary Assembly, are elected in the Republika Srpska, while the remaining two-thirds are elected in the Federation. In the House of Peoples, the second chamber, one-third of the seats (five) are for members elected by the National Assembly of the Republika Srpska, and two-thirds are for members – five Bosniaks and five Croats – elected by the House of Peoples of the Federal Parliament. The State Presidency is made up of three members, one from each community. No more than two-thirds of the members of the Council of Ministers (the national government) can be from the Federation. The Chair of the Council (the prime minister) and her deputies, as well as the ministers and their deputies, must come from different communities. The same principle of national proportionality is applied in the cantonal legislative, executive, and judicial governments. All important decisions in both Houses of the National Assembly are made by consensus or by qualified majorities. The Constitution prescribes that when making decisions by simple majority vote, the representatives must "put in maximum effort for that majority to include at least one-third of the votes of the delegates or members from each entity's territory" (Kasapović 2005, 6). The decisions of the Presidency are made by consensus or, if that proves impossible, by a majority of two votes, where the outvoted member may then declare a decision to be detrimental to the vital interests of the entity he or she comes from. If this claim is confirmed by a two-thirds vote in the parliament of the entity in question, the challenged Presidency decision does not take effect (see Kasapović 2005, 6).

As we can see, the constitutional system of Bosnia and Herzegovina is an example of the detailed implementation of the model of consociational democracy. However, opinions differ as to how successful it actually is. Lijphart himself does not claim that consociational democracy can serve as a *universal* model for the institutional regulation of relations between different cultural communities in a given country. He identifies a number of "favorable conditions" under which consociationalism is likely to be successful. These are: a certain balance among the groups competing for power; a multiparty political system; a relatively small size of the country; the cross-cutting of the cleavages that constitute the plurality of this society; the overarching of loyalties; traditions of elite accommodation (see Lijphart 1977, 54). Other authors add more conditions of this kind, referencing the situations in particular countries. Michael Kerr (2006, 27), for example, proposes (based on the power-sharing arrangements in

Northern Ireland and Lebanon) the following condition: "existence of positive external regulating pressures, from state to non-state actors, which provide the internal elites with sufficient incentives and motives for their acceptance of, and support for, consociation."

Can we assume that if these conditions are in place, the model of consociational democracy will solve the problem I described above – that is, is it possible for representatives of minorities to participate, on an equal footing, in the design and implementation of minority policies in a way that is acceptable for all? In my mind, one must first note that, judging from historical experience, consociational democracy is more or less successful in societies where there is a significant presence of traditional forms of solidarity and legitimacy.[5] Most of the variants in which consociationalism is applied do not provide formally regulated mechanisms for legitimizing the leadership in communities which should represent[6] the "segments," as Lijphart puts it, of the democratic structure of society. In other words, we have to assume that in many cases this leadership is of a traditional type – it is exercised by families that have "always" held authoritative positions in the respective community and, consequently, there has not been the need to legitimize their status. However, in such cases the processes of modernization, whatever their specific form may be, will inevitably have a negative effect on consociational democracy; therefore it can, at best, be accepted as a possible provisional solution to minority problems in countries such as those in Central and Eastern Europe.

Along this same line of reasoning, we should note that the condition stipulating the existence of a tradition of cooperation between community elites, which is rightly identified by Lijphart as a necessary prerequisite for the success of the consociational model, is also hardly compatible with modernization. This also holds true for cooperation as a paradigm of political life in general. In the rare cases of real and successful consociational democracy, what we have is rather a cooperation of traditional type, and not dialogue of the type referred to by, for example, Jürgen Habermas in his theory of communicative action (Habermas 1984).

Lijphart himself anticipates a number of critical arguments against his model and tries to answer them. One of the shortcomings of grand coalition governments, for example, is that such a configuration of political power minimizes the role of the opposition, thereby leaving little or no room for a critical assessment of the government's policies (see Lijphart 1977, 47). Another one is that the segmental organization of the exercise of political power brings about the excessive domination of the political elites in their groups. A lot of responsibility is concentrated in the hands of the segmental leaders in order to defend the interests of their groups before the leaders of the other segments and, at the same time, to justify before their group members the concessions that they often have to make to the Others. "It is therefore helpful if they possess considerable independent power and a secure position of leadership" (Lijphart 1977, 50).

Furthermore, we should bear in mind that the collective rights of minorities (in consociational democracy the relationship between the individual member of a community and society at large is mediated by the community's leaders, which is characteristic of collective minority rights) are, generally, in a problematic relationship with the principles of democracy. If anything, they entail a curtailment of the autonomy of the individual: "Although consociational systems arguably do not have the purpose of 'nullifying or impairing' individual rights, they inevitably have the effect of favouring members of one group over another on the basis of their ethnicity" (Wippman 1996, 209). More generally, as Lijphart admits, "... consociational democracy results in the division of a plural society into more homogeneous and self-contained elements" (Lijphart 1977, 48).

Besides, the segmental organization of power is basically inert and inefficient. It is difficult to reach agreement in a grand coalition with a number of partners who may have radically divergent interests and visions and who have the power to veto certain types of decisions. And if proportionality is applied as a standard of recruitment, civil service is likely to be inefficient because segment membership would be regarded as more important than individual capacities and performance. Furthermore, segmental autonomy presupposes a multiplication of the number of governmental and administrative services, which makes government excessively costly (see Lijphart 1977, 51).

We should also factor in the possibility (which is often the case in reality) that community leaders may have their own agendas, which do not always coincide with the interests of their communities. In the case of Bosnia and Herzegovina, for instance, the elites of the three communities turned out to have very divergent views regarding the institutional regulation of the relations between Muslims, Croats, and Serbs within a single state:

• the Bosniak political elite advocates a unitary civil state;
• the Serbian political elite advocates the exclusive status of Republika Srpska as a nation-state of the Bosnian Serbs and its union with the rest of the state;
• the Croatian political elite advocates the state as a union of three national entities (Kasapović 2005, 20).

As a result, society in Bosnia and Herzegovina remains divided on many important issues of political, economic, and cultural life to this very day. According to the prevailing opinion, the realization of the model of consociational democracy in this country is far from the ideal.

Finally, again judging from historical experience, the "segmentation" (to use Lijphart's term) of society through power sharing ultimately has a negative effect on its stability. It contributes to "the reification of ethnic divisions," as Donald Horowitz (1985, 575) puts it. The communities that are elements of such a political system are sufficiently ready for a relatively autonomous way of life (as, for example, in Bosnia and Herzegovina where the consociational arrangement of society has reinforced the existence of "self-sufficient ethnically homogenous societies" – Balić and Izmirlija 2013, 132) and may respond to any crisis in their relations (which may be caused also by external factors, as was the case in Lebanon) by switching from partnership to rivalry, or even to separatist actions.

The politics of presence

As was the case with consociational democracy, the concept of the "politics of presence," first developed by Anne Phillips (1995), defined and morally justified a trend that had existed in minority policies for decades. It concerns a set of political rights granted by law to some minorities in a number of countries: setting quotas for minority representatives in the legislative and executive branches of government; drawing election-district boundaries so as to give minorities a local majority and improve their representatives' chances of winning seats in elective bodies (see Pildes 2000, 119); and the right of minority representatives to veto decisions affecting their communities.

An example of such legislation is Act LXXVII, passed in 1993, on the Rights of National and Ethnic Minorities in Hungary.[7] It empowers minority communities to act against institutions that violate their rights, including vetoing appointments and municipal government decrees (Articles 26–29). Similar rights have since been granted to the minorities in the Republic of Macedonia under the Ohrid Agreement of 2001. For example, Article 69 (2) stipulates that for laws directly affecting culture, use of language, education, personal identification documents, and use of symbols, the Assembly makes decisions by a majority vote of the attending Representatives, provided that this vote also includes a majority vote of the attending representatives of minority communities (formulated in the official text of the Ohrid Agreement as "Representatives attending who claim to belong to the communities not in the majority in the population of Macedonia").

What are the most common arguments in favor of "the politics of presence"? As I noted above, there are legitimate grounds for dissatisfaction with the conditions for a dignified life which the standard democratic system offers to people who care about their cultural identity (provided it is different from that of the majority). Decision-making by majority vote jeopardizes the rights of people who belong – in the above sense – to cultural minorities.

One of the solutions to this problem is, as Anne Phillips calls it, the "politics of ideas." It is based on a presumption that is characteristic of the liberal worldview – namely, that the significant differences among people are mainly related to "beliefs, opinions, preferences, and goals, all of which may stem from the variety of experience, but are considered in principle as detachable from this" (Phillips 1996, 140). If this is true, then there is no particular reason why the interests of people who have certain beliefs, opinions, preferences, etc., cannot be represented in and before institutions of political power by other people who do not share these beliefs, opinions, and so forth, but, rather, profess ideas that motivate them to stand up for their fellow citizens:

> The interests of pensioners or the long-term unemployed can then be championed by those who are neither retired nor out of work; the interests of geographical localities can be represented by people who no longer live in the area; the interests of mothers with young children can be represented by childless men.
>
> (Phillips 1996, 140)

In this model of democratic relations, "what is to be represented then takes priority over who does the representation" (ibid., 140–141).

It is clear that such an approach to relations between minorities and society at large will eliminate the problem of their numerical inequality in voting strength. If decision-making is motivated by the clash of ideas, it does not matter which group is a majority. There is no reason why the interests of people from a minority cannot be taken to heart and even defended by their fellow citizens who do not belong to their community.

According to Phillips (1996, 141) and the other proponents of the politics of presence,[8] however, the politics of ideas does not adequately deal with the experiences of "those social groups who by virtue of their race or ethnicity or religion or gender have felt themselves excluded from the democratic process." What is at issue here is experience and identities that cannot be exchanged between people. For example, a man may represent programs or ideals that are supported by women, but could he represent women as women per se (see Phillips 1995, 6)? According to Pablo de Greiff (2000, 397), people from different minorities have specific experiences and points of view that are difficult to understand for someone who has not had the same experiences. Hence, even with the best intentions, people from the majority can be mistaken about the fairness of the norms regulating the status of minorities. This necessitates the participation of minority representatives in government at all levels. If they are allowed to have a say, to evaluate decisions affecting minority communities from the specific point of view of members of those communities, this would help avoid many injustices. In addition, the participation of minority representatives in institutions of political power has a positive effect on the legitimacy of these institutions in the eyes of the respective groups: "When people can look and see people like themselves, they are much more likely to identify with an institution and have a sense of ownership" (Sawer 2001, 58).

The findings of studies on the adequacy of women's representation in government are especially convincing. For example, a number of surveys of the priorities of parliament members have been conducted in various countries (see Wängnerud 2000). On the whole, they confirm Phillips' thesis that "the gender of politicians is an important factor in representative democracy" (Wängnerud 2000, 68). More specifically, the results of the survey conducted by Lena Wängnerud (ibid.) in the Swedish Riksdag:

> show for example that issues of social welfare policy are weighted more heavily on the agendas of female politicians than on those of male politicians. We see as well that it is almost exclusively female politicians who pursue issues of equality between the sexes.

However, Anne Phillips herself is well aware that the politics of presence is not flawless either. In her book, *The Politics of Presence*, she lists several standard critiques against this methodology. One of them is that if public policies focus exclusively on the interests and aspirations of culturally diverse groups, this could pose a threat to national unity and may lead to the "balkanization" of society (see Phillips 1995, 22). A significant advantage of the politics of ideas is that identical beliefs can be professed by people belonging to different communities, the result being a sort of "cross-fertilization" of differences that mitigates their disintegrating effect on society. If, however, the politics of presence is applied, it exaggerates, rather than tones down traditional cultural differences, thus creating prerequisites for further, as well as intensified ethnic, racial, religious, and other conflict.

Another objection discussed by Phillips is that the politics of presence, unlike the politics of ideas, makes it more difficult for voters to hold their representatives in power accountable for the *quality* of their representation (she refers to "the anxieties of establishing accountability" – see Phillips 1995, 23). In the case of the politics of ideas, it is more or less clear what voters may demand from their representatives: the defense of a particular, more or less articulated, specific cause. But what does it mean to hold our representative in power accountable for whether or not she represents us properly as a person with a particular ethnic or racial or religious identity? Let us assume that in a given case our representative has acted in a way we think was right. But other people, with the same identity as ours, might not approve of these actions because they think of themselves in a different way and their self-awareness is not the same as ours even though we nominally belong to the same community. In many cases, minorities are not "a homogenous group whose interests can be simply 'represented,' but rather a group with multiple identities and interests that form a complex political culture" (Maddison 2010, 667).

In general, the politics of presence presupposes an essentialist understanding of identity – insofar as it justifies minority communities' claims to group-political – that is, collective – rights. It is based on the assumption that a minority community is a homogeneous group of individuals who think and feel in the same way, and who are organized around a clear understanding of their common interests and the respective agenda (see Falbo 2006, 253). The relationship between each one of them and the "outside world" is mediated by the leaders of the community who are unquestionably assumed to personify its aspirations and ideals. Such stereotypes are not merely naive and misleading; they can lead to inadequate public policies. Furthermore, they can also encourage a real essentialization of minority identities, with all the negative consequences that this entails for political life in the given country. As I noted in Chapter 1, which focused on cultural identity, essentialism and constructionism are not just descriptive but also normative theories, therefore their predictions can be self-fulfilling prophecies. If we conceive of our identity as an essence or as a construct, we will be inclined to behave accordingly, thus indeed ending up with an identity that is precisely what we think it should be.

As for the question of the accountability of minority community representatives in power, practice shows that their relations with the people whose interests they are meant to protect are not typical of representative democracy. In general, politicians compete for votes under conditions of relative political pluralism.

This motivates them to keep their commitments to their constituents because otherwise they, or at least their party, will suffer the consequences of voter discontent in the next elections. In other words, more than one relatively equal candidate competes for the votes of the same electorate. Their electoral success depends on the credibility of their promises, on their abilities as politicians, on their past record, and so forth – all of which are indicators directly relevant to the quality of their possible activities as representatives of the interests of the people who will vote for them.

What is the situation with minority representatives in political power under the conditions of the "politics of presence"? If we assume, while doing everything to avoid the temptations of essentialism, that we are talking about representatives of communities (in the sense of Tönnies 2001), or of individuals united by mechanical solidarity (in the sense of Durkheim 1997), or of identity groups (in the sense of Gutmann 2003), then we have to admit that in such conditions there is not much room for political pluralism. The relations of solidarity, of mutual identification of individuals who belong to the same ethnic or racial or religious minority,[9] are hardly compatible with competition. Insofar as there is pluralism in such communities, it is – at least, judging from the examples around us – on a clan or clientelistic basis. Or, as one Canadian author concludes, "Most ethnocultural communities are not well equipped to deal with dissent" (Jedwab 2001, 14).

What is more, against the background of the priority given to collectivist values such as unity, solidarity, and loyalty, any show of dissent, which outsiders would regard as a sign of healthy pluralism, can be viewed by the community as betrayal (leading to the phenomenon of "ethnic outbidding," to be discussed below). This is why the criteria used by voters, in general, as well as by voters from minority communities (under the conditions of the "politics of presence") to evaluate a candidate for government office are quite different, which determines the differences in the way an already elected representative views her accountability to the electorate. So it is no surprise that the policy of setting quotas for representatives of ethnic and/or religious groups in government often leads to the formation of complacent and corrupt minority political elites, while the situation regarding the rights and interests of the people they are supposed to represent does not change for the better.

Identity relations and political power

So far we have examined three models of institutional regulation of relations between minorities and society at large. Under *socialist internationalism*, minority groups are de facto excluded from the process of making political decisions that affect them. Under the other two models, *consociational democracy* and *the politics of presence*, minority representatives do participate in the process of making such decisions, but this poses a number of problems related both to the integrity of society at large and to the interests of the minorities themselves. Here, I will consider the question of whether it is at all possible to combine power relations and identity relations without producing effects that are detrimental to social life. To do this, I will use as my starting point a well-known debate on ethnic parties.

As forms of direct empowerment of minorities, both consociational democracy and the politics of presence presuppose the existence of parties organized along ethnic or religious lines. Here, I will not discuss the criteria by which a political party can be identified as ethnic or religious, which is a question that is certainly interesting and important in itself. Historical practice shows that there are no hard-and-fast rules in this respect. A party such as, for example, the Movement for Rights and Freedoms (DPS) in Bulgaria, may officially identify itself as a nationwide movement yet still be widely regarded as an *ethnic* party (in the case of the DPS, as a party of Bulgarian Turks). This question, however, is not relevant to the present study. By "ethnic party" I mean a party that de facto represents the interests of an ethnic community.

The debate on ethnic parties is well-represented in contemporary academic literature (see Rabushka and Shepsle 1972; Horowitz 1985; Breen 2000; Chandra 2005; Roeder 2005; Mitchell, Evans, and O'Leary 2006; Rosenblum 2007; Zuber 2013). Several "classic" arguments against the operation of such parties (in some countries in Central and Eastern Europe, such as Bulgaria, there is even a constitutional ban on ethnic or religious political parties; in others, they are banned by the courts on an ad hoc basis) are listed by Nancy Rosenblum in her paper examining the justifications for banning ethnic, religious, and racial parties. According to Rosenblum (2007, 29), it is widely assumed in democratic theory that such parties often take intransigent, uncompromising, militant, and extremist positions in politics; they aim to impose the interests of a single cultural identity on public life; they are authoritarian in their organization and goals; they impose loyalty on members on the basis of ascriptive rather than voluntary identity politics; their leaders are of dubious legitimacy. Rosenblum (2007, 25) identifies four categories of justification for banning such parties: "violence, incitement to hate, altering the character of the nation, and an additional category that I think deserves scrutiny – outside support or control."

A very popular conception that reveals a systemic problem within ethnic parties is that of "ethnic outbidding." It was developed by Alvin Rabushka and Kenneth Shepsle (1972), and Donald Horowitz (1985). According to the proponents of this conception, the main problem of an ethnic party is that it competes for votes only within the respective ethnic group. When two or more such parties compete for support from the same ethnic community, each one of them naturally strives to persuade the members of the community that it can represent their interests better than the other (or others), and this drives these parties to "bid" for votes by making ever more radical and extremist claims with regard to society at large. Such competition inevitably leads to centrifugal dynamics in the party system (see Rabushka and Shepsle 1972: 82–86).

The "defenders" of ethnic parties offer both empirical and theoretical counterarguments against these critiques. Authors of surveys conducted in recent years have published their results, which point to a much more complicated picture than that of the ethnic outbidding and extremist claims that we would expect from ethnic parties if we were guided by the above-mentioned theoretical considerations (see, for example, Szöcsik 2012; Gleason 2015): "Integrating recent findings, ethnic party strategies are defined by the criteria of appeal and policy position as 'static bidding,' 'ethnic underbidding,' 'ethnic outbidding,' 'lateral bidding,' 'lateral underbidding' and 'lateral outbidding' " (Zuber 2013, 758).

If we consider the complexity of minority issues discussed in the previous chapter of this book, we should be very cautious in drawing conclusions from such surveys. The fact that the findings of a particular survey do not confirm the theoretical prediction that ethnic parties are "naturally predisposed" to provoke political tension and conflict may be due to the falsity of this prediction; but it may also be due to entirely different factors that prevent the emergence of such tension and conflict in the long or short term. Regarding the DPS in Bulgaria, for example, its dominant political influence among the Turkish ethnic community cannot be seriously jeopardized by rival political parties, which also claim to exclusively represent the interests of the ethnic Turks in Bulgaria (such as the People's Party "Freedom and Dignity," NPSD), not because the DPS successfully outbids them with extremist claims, but because it has established such strong clientelistic networks[10] in the areas with numerous ethnic Turkish populations that any attempt to conduct rival political activity in these areas is "nipped in the bud" by influential local activists of the DPS. The ways such parties defend and pursue their political interests may vary greatly depending on the specific conditions, i.e. on the specific "constellation" of relevant factors. But these constellations are prone to change, and there are no guarantees that if they do change, the DPS – if we return to our example – would not resort to ethnic outbidding or other forms of extremist political behavior, should there arise the need for it to defend its political interests.

There are also some noteworthy theoretical arguments in favor of ethnic parties. As an example, I will cite a statement by the eminent Bulgarian political scientist Petar-Emil Mitev regarding the so-called "Bulgarian ethnic model."[11] According to Mitev (2005, 9–10), the Bulgarian ethnic model represents

> the transformation of ethnic contradictions and conflicts into a political process that neutralized them and enabled restoring the good neighborly relations in the everyday life of Christians and Muslims that had existed prior to the conflict situation. The opposite process took place in Bosnia, where political contradictions were transformed into an ethnic conflict.

Indeed, from a moral point of view, it is more acceptable, as well as more prudent, to seek to resolve ethnic problems by political means instead of satisfying political interests by provoking ethnic conflict. But can the resolution of ethnic issues through the use of politics be achieved only by means of politicizing the ethnic relations themselves? Wouldn't it be more reasonable to use politics to this end without conflating identity relations and power relations; for example, by using as a "mediator" what Jürgen Habermas calls "communicative power," that is, by exerting pressure on institutions of political power by way of the public sphere? The *communicative empowerment* of ethnic and, for that matter, of other minorities would achieve similar effects without binding the struggle for minority protection to political power games, which makes this struggle prone to abuse in the pursuit of selfish individual and group interests.

I would like to conclude this chapter by proposing one more argument against the direct empowerment of minorities through the inclusion of their parties in politics. Generally speaking, I am referring to the dangers that come from mixing power relations with community relations. As noted above, minorities are characterized by various degrees of group solidarity depending on the nature of their identity and on specific historical, cultural, and social circumstances. A racial minority, for example, represents a certain category of people, that is, people who are not necessarily bound by solidarity. National, ethnic, and religious minorities are all identity groups (in the sense used by Amy Gutmann, i.e. their members identify with one another), but these mutual identifications can vary in their degree of intensity. In many cases the said groups exist as communities, which are close-knit cultural entities.

My apprehension is related specifically to political parties representing national ethnic or religious *communities*. What do I have in mind? First, what follows if the relations among people who share a common ethnic, religious, or national identity are communal in character? To answer this question, let us consider the two classic theories of community noted above – those of Ferdinand Tönnies and of Emile Durkheim.

Chapter 1 offered a summary of Tönnies' concept of this type of social relations as expounded in his book *Gemeinschaft und Gesellschaft* (see Chapter 1). According to Tönnies, the main thing that distinguishes relations of community from relations of society is the mutual identification of the community's members with one another. The solidarity and trust among them do not come from a more or less self-reflected sharing of common values, but are perceived by members as unconditional mutual commitment, as their destiny.

When one considers Tönnies' praise for relations of community, the fact that Durkheim calls them relations of "*mechanical* solidarity" becomes puzzling. In his book *The Division of Labor in Society*, the French scholar, in ways similar to his German colleague, discusses two kinds of "positive solidarity." The first one presupposes "a more or less organized society composed of beliefs and sentiments common to all the members of the group," and the second, "a system of different and special functions united by definite relationships" (Durkheim 1997, 83). The solidarity that is derived from "similarities" makes the individual consciousness dependent on the collective one. Where there is such solidarity the individual "does not belong to himself," as Durkheim (ibid., 85) puts it. This kind of solidarity can be called mechanical by analogy with the ways in which inorganic bodies are linked, in contrast to the mutual dependencies characteristic of life. Here "mechanical" signifies the passive dependency of the part on the whole and of the individual on the collective.

The other kind of solidarity (which is related to the division of labor) is based, not on the similarities, but on the differences between people. It stems from the need for mutual complementarity, and that is why Durkheim (ibid.) reflects on it by using the analogy of the structure of the living organism and calls it "organic." Emblematic cases of mechanical solidarity are kinship relations and religious communities, while organic solidarity is manifested primarily in the development of the professional organization of society.

It is remarkable that the two classical sociologists offer contrasting evaluations of the same facts. They describe the life of communities in more or less the same way. However, what is regarded with approval and even admiration by one, is considered by the other as something oppressing and humiliating for people. The bonds of mutual identification of the community's members, of intimacy, of mutual trust, of solidarity, are, at the same time, also a means of suppressing individuality, that is, of "absorbing" the individual into the collective.

What follows if we decide to view minority communities the way that Tönnies and Durkheim suggest? More specifically, can we use their viewpoint to draw any conclusions about the desirability of the political "empowerment" of minorities? To discuss this question, I would like to first comment on a particularly characteristic argument for banning parties organized along ethnic or religious lines – namely, that such a ban is necessary in order to avoid "ethnic or religious antagonism" (see, for example, the Bulgarian Constitutional Court's Decision No. 4 of 21 April 1992 – *Durzhaven Vestnik* [*State Gazette*], no. 35 of 1992).

This argument begs the question: why is it that only ethnic or religious political parties are viewed as a potential source of ethnic or religious tension among the population of a country, while the nongovernmental organizations of ethnic or religious communities, for example, are not viewed this way? In my opinion, the pro-ban position is convincing in this respect. Special importance is given to political parties because their activity concerns political power, which allows for the legitimate use of violence. This is why political organizations have a great destructive potential regarding life in the country and it is advisable to avoid politicizing difficult, potentially conflictual, relationships.

However, this brings us to another question regarding the reasoning of the constitutional ban: why is special priority given to ethnic and religious antagonism and not, for example, to social or class antagonism? Why are political antagonisms of the first kind regarded as inadmissible, while those between employers and employees, or between rural and urban populations, are assumed to be "normal" (otherwise socialist, as well as agrarian parties, would also have to be banned)? The relevant statutory documents do not provide an answer to this question. It is obviously left to intuition. But considering that there is no constitutional ban on ethnic or religious parties in many countries, I think that a more detailed argument is necessary in this case.

I believe that such an argument can be found if we assume that ethnic and religious relations are community relations, in contrast to, for example, class relations. People acquire individual identity within a particular culture, which is characterized by some ethnic and religious specificity. They do not choose the community in which they are born and grow up; and once their personalities are formed, it is difficult for them to change their attitudes of loyalty and solidarity that have played a constitutive role in their formation. Conversely, one of the significant determinants of an individual's rational acts outside the community is her aspiration to improve, that is, to change her social status and move from one social category to another.

There is also another difference between relations of community and relations of society (in the sense of Tönnies) which is directly relevant to the problem of the special significance of ethnic, racial, and religious antagonism as compared with the other social antagonisms. As a rule, relationships in communities are organized within a closed, self-sufficient system. Conversely, relations of society – or, in Durkheim's words, of "organic solidarity" – are relations of complementarity. A community does not essentially need other communities in order to function and to reproduce its internal bonds in time. All it needs is some – any, as a matter of fact – outside social world in order to maintain the us versus them juxtaposition as a condition for in-group solidarity. In contrast, relations of society are based on the division of labor. A social class cannot make do without what Hegel calls "the other of itself" (*das Andere seiner selbst*).

Hence, the principled difference in treating the Other differently is based on whether or not her "Other-ness" comes from her belonging to another community or to another social category altogether. The conflicts that develop within society are played against the "background" of some awareness, or at least the intuition, that the "adversary" is necessary for us – that there is some, albeit distant, unity of interests. Conversely, unlike the antagonistic relationships that exist within a society, the antagonisms between communities are unbridled and leave no room to spare the Others. In my opinion, this is also the reason why civil wars involving a religious or ethnic factor are much more brutal than the most intense social conflicts.

If we approach the specific nature of ethnic and religious relations with these considerations in mind, we will have to conclude that a constitutional ban on ethnic and religious political parties is justified. The existence of such parties politicizes relations between communities – that is, it drags them into the struggle for power, which could have dangerous consequences for political peace in the country. Such politicization can only be afforded by countries with national, ethnic and religious minorities that are insignificant in terms of number and influence, as well as by countries with an established (usually as the result of centuries-long struggles) tradition of the peaceful resolution of conflicts between communities.

I would like to conclude this chapter, which was devoted to political models of minority empowerment, by pointing out that, in my view, all power-based approaches to these issues have yielded controversial results to date. Classical representative democracy places minorities in an unequal position when it comes to voting. For its part, the politics of ideas fails to take into account the specificity of culturally-different lifeworlds. The various forms of participation of minority representatives in power have, in turn, an essentializing effect on the respective collective identities, thereby weakening the integrity of society. The only winner from the "politics of presence" is the minority political elite that is formed for the purpose of taking part in the exercise of political power. All this leads to the conclusion that the possibilities for finding ways to harmonize relations between minorities and society at large in the "vertical" dimension are quite limited. It is also necessary to look for ways to empower minorities in the non-power "horizontal" dimension of public life.

Notes

1 These forms of representation of the different ethnic groups in power structures changed over time, in some cases also at the constitutional level, through a shift toward more centralized or decentralized governance depending on the balance of centripetal or centrifugal interests and sentiments among politically influential circles in the respective country. The case of Yugoslavia is an especially clear example of this process – see Radan (1998).
2 The League of Communists of Yugoslavia – that is, in fact, the Yugoslav Communist Party.
3 The page numbers refer to the Internet version of the publication.
4 This remarkable transition from a persistently demonstrated national and ethnic tolerance to indiscriminate nationalism has been the subject of multiple studies and explanations from the positions of different theoretical models (see Hodson, Seculić, and Massey 1994). Here it is of interest only as evidence of the fictitious nature of one form of empowerment of ethnic and national communities within a multinational country.
5 I will venture to question Lijphart's thesis that in West European countries such as the Netherlands, Belgium, Switzerland, and Austria there is (even if partly) consociational democracy – at least in the variant described by him.
6 The case of Bosnia and Herzegovina is an exception – detailed mechanisms for electing the representatives of the different communities to government bodies do, indeed, function there. However, the end result is far from encouraging.
7 The Hungarian legislation on minority issues has since been significantly amended.
8 Similar ideas have been expressed in different terms by other authors – for example, as "descriptive representation" (see Chaney and Fevre 2002).
9 In this respect the politics of presence yields quite different results in the representation of women in power, on the one hand, and of national, ethnic, and religious minorities, on the other.
10 Made up of local businesspersons and officials in the local administration, which in these areas is usually under the control of the DPS – the invariable winner in local government elections in the regions where ethnic Turks predominate in number.
11 This term refers to a set of public policies and public discourses universally regarded as having helped Bulgaria to avoid violent ethnic and/or religious conflicts in the transition to democracy – conflicts similar to those that broke out in the former Yugoslavia (see Zhelyazkova 2001). There definitely were objective preconditions for the outbreak of such conflicts in Bulgaria at the beginning of the 1990s. Bulgaria is home to large autochthonous Turkish and Roma minorities (according to the latest census of 2011, approximately 9 percent and 5 percent respectively), as well as to a large Muslim minority (almost all ethnic Turks, a significant part of the Roma, and some 130,000 Muslim Bulgarians). On the eve of the transition, the communist regime conducted a forced assimilation campaign against the Bulgarian Turks (the so-called "Revival Process"), which strongly damaged ethnic and religious relations.

Generally, the "Bulgarian ethnic model" is considered to have three dimensions:

the first relates to the country's peaceful transition in the years after 1989, which sets it apart from developments in the former Yugoslavia; the second refers to the successful political participation of the Turkish minority which has played a stabilizing role in postcommunist Bulgaria; and the third is its association with traditions of ethnic and religious tolerance.

(Rechel 2007, 1201)

From a political point of view, the most important role in this model is that of the DPS, an ethnic party of Bulgarian Turks which, however, nominally has as its mission the protection of the rights and freedoms of all Bulgarian citizens; that is why the constitutional ban regarding parties organized along ethnic or religious lines was not enforced against it (a petition to declare the DPS unconstitutional was rejected by Bulgaria's Constitutional Court). The most characteristic thing about this role is the moderate way in which the DPS protects the interests of the Turkish ethnic community and which, according to many observers of political processes in Bulgaria, legitimizes the elevation of this party, and more particularly, of its leaders, to key positions in the governance of political processes (even when it is in opposition), and hence, to levers of influence over economic interactions, including over the allocation of financial resources from various EU funds. As a result, the party's leaders have unlimited opportunities for securing personal and group gains and for joining oligarchic political and economic circles (see Rechel 2007, 1212). The "Bulgarian ethnic model" is a fine example of the complexity of minority issues (as noted in the previous chapter) as it exemplifies how specific events can be shaped by changeable configurations of intertwining influences of cultural differences, group solidarity, and social and political relationships.

References

Balić, Lejlap and Midhat Izmirlija. "Consociation in Bosnia and Herzegovina: Practical Implementation of the Theoretical Principles." *South-East European Journal of Political Science* I, no. 3 (2013): 121–135.

Breen, Richard. "Why is Support for Extreme Parties Underestimated by Surveys? A Latent Class Analysis." *British Journal of Political Science* 30, no. 2 (2000): 375–382.

Chandra, Kanchan. "Ethnic Parties and Democratic Stability." *Perspectives on Politics* 3, no. 2 (2005): 235–252.

Chaney, Paul and Ralph Fevre. "Is There a Demand for Descriptive Representation? Evidence from the UK's Devolution Programme." *Political Studies* 50, no. 5 (2002): 897–915.

De Greiff, Pablo. "Deliberative Democracy and Group Representation." *Social Theory & Practice* 26, no 3 (2000) 397–415.

Durkheim, Emile. *The Division of Labor in Society.* New York: Free Press, 1997.

Durzhaven Vestnik [State Gazette], no. 35 of 1992.

Falbo, Marina. "Reinventing Inclusion: From a Politics of Presence to Inessential Coalitions." *Contemporary Politics* 12, no. 3–4 (2006): 247–260

Giordano, Christian. "Governing Ethnic Diversity in Postcolonial Societies. The Politics of Citizenship and Multiculturalism in Southeast Asia." In *Interethnic Relations and Politics of Multiculturalism: Between Southeast Europe and Southeast Asia*, edited by Christian Giordano, 58–83. Sofia: Marin Drinov Academic Publishing House, 2005.

Gleason, Kelly A. *Ethnic Parties, Bans, and Civil Unrest* (electronic publication), https://pantherfile.uwm.edu/kgleason/www/PBans.pdf, accessed November 17, 2015.

Gutmann, Amy. *Identity in Democracy*. Princeton, NJ: Princeton University Press, 2003.

Habermas, Jürgen. *Theory of Communicative Action*. Boston MA: Beacon Press, 1984.

Hodson, Randy, Dusko Sekulić, and Garth Massey. "National Tolerance in the Former Yugoslavia." *The American Journal of Sociology* 99, no 6 (1994): 1534–1558.

Horowitz, Donald. *Ethnic Groups in Conflict*. Berkeley, CA: University of California Press, 1985.

Jedwab, Jack. "Leadership, Governance, and the Politics of Identity in Canada." *Canadian Ethnic Studies* 33, no 3 (2001): 4–22.

Kanev, Krassimir. "Law and Politics on Ethnic and Religious Minorities." In *Communities and Identities in Bulgaria*, edited by Anna Krasteva, 55–95. Ravenna: Longo Editore, 1998.

Kasapović, Mirjana. "Bosnia and Herzegovina: Consociational or Liberal Democracy?" *Politička misao* XLII, no. 5 (2005): 3–30.

Kerr, Michael. *Imposing Power-Sharing: Conflict and Coexistence in Northern Ireland and Lebanon*. Dublin: Irish Academic Press, 2006.

Lenin, Vladimir I. *Pismo k rabochim I krestjanam Ukraini po povodu pobed nad Denikinim. Polnoe sobranie sochinenij*, vol. 40. [A letter to the workers and peasants of the Ukraine on the occasion of the victories over Denikin]. Moscow: The Political Writings Publishing House, 1974.

Lijphart, Arend. *Democracy in Plural Societies*. New Haven: Yale University Press, 1977.

Maddison, Sarah. *Black Politics: Inside the Complexity of Aboriginal Political Culture*. Sydney: Allen & Unwin, 2009.

Maddison, Sarah. "White Parliament, Black Politics: The Dilemmas of Indigenous Parliamentary Representation." *Australian Journal of Political Science* 45, no. 4 (2010): 663–680.

Marx, Karl and Friedrich Engels. *The Communist Manifesto*, Selected Works, Vol. One, Moscow: Progress Publishers, 1969.

Mitchell, Paul, Geoffrey Evans, and Brendan O'Leary, "Extremist Outbidding in Ethnic Party Systems is not Inevitable: Tribune Parties in Northern Ireland." *Political Science and Political Economy Working Paper*, Department of Government, London School of Economics and Political Science 6 (2006): 1–41.

Mitev, Petar-Emil. "Bulgarskiat etnicheski model – problematizirano postizhenie v obedinjavashta se Evropa." [The Bulgarian Ethnic Model – A Problematic Achievement in United Europe]. In *Etnichesko mnogoobrazie i obedinjavashta se Evropa*, 5–28. Sofia: Solidarno Obshtestvo Foundation, 2005.

Phillips, Anne. *The Politics of Presence*. Oxford: Clarendon Press, 1995.

Phillips, Anne, "Dealing with Difference: A Politics of Ideas or a Politics of Presence?" In *Democracy and Difference: Contesting the Boundaries of the Political*, edited by Seyla Benhabib, 139–154. Princeton, NJ: Princeton University Press, 1996

Pildes, Richard H. "Diffusion of Political Power and the Voting Rights Act." *Harvard Journal of Law & Public Policy* 24, no. 1 (2000): 119–140.

Rabushka, Alvin and Kenneth Shepsle. *Politics in Plural Societies: A Theory of Democratic Instability*. Columbus, OH: Charles Merrill, 1972.

Radan, Peter. "Constitutional Law and the Multinational State: the Failure of Yugoslav Federalism." *UNSW Law Journal* 21, no. 1 (1998): 185–203.

Rechel, Bernd. "The 'Bulgarian Ethnic Model'-Reality or Ideology?" *Europe-Asia Studies* 59, no. 7 (2007): 1201–1215.

Roberts, Adam. "Yugoslavia: the Constitution and the Succession." *The World Today* 34, no. 4 (1978): 136–149.

Roeder, Philip. "Power Dividing as an Alternative to Power Sharing." In *Sustainable Peace: Power and Democracy after Civil Wars*, edited by Philip Roeder and Donald Rothchild, 51–82. Ithaca and London: Cornell University Press, 2005.

Rosenblum, Nancy L. "Banning Parties: Religious and Ethnic Partisanship in Multicultural Democracies." *Law & Ethics of Human Rights* 1, no. 1 (2007): 1–59.

Sawer, Marian. "Representing Trees, Acres, Voters and Non-voters: Concept of Parliamentary Representation in Australia." In *Speaking for the People. Representation in Australian Politics*, edited by Marian Sawer and Gianni Zappala, 36–57. Melbourne: Melbourne University Press, 2001.

Szöcsik, Edina. *Ethnic Minority Parties in Political Competition*, Dissertation, 2012. www.e-collection.library.ethz.ch/eserv/eth:6949/eth-6949-02.pdf, accessed November 25, 2015.

Taylor, Charles. "The Politics of Recognition. In *Multiculturalism. Examining the Politics of Recognition*, edited by Amy Gutmann, 25–74. Princeton, NJ: Princeton University Press, 1994.

Tönnies, Ferdinand. *Community and Civil Society*. Cambridge: Cambridge University Press, 2001.

Wängnerud, Lena. "Testing the Politics of Presence: Women's Representation in the Swedish Riksdag." *Skandinavian Political Studies* 23, no. 1 (2000): 67–91.

Wippman, David, "Powersharing as a Response to Cultural Dominance." *Proceedings of the Annual Meeting of the American Society of International Law* 90 (1996): 206–211.

Zhelyazkova, Antonina. "The Bulgarian Ethnic Model." *East European Constitutional Review* 10, no. 4 (2001): retrieved from www3.law.nyu.edu/eecr/vol. 10num4/focus/zhelyazkova.html, accessed November 10, 2015

Zuber, Christina Isabel. "Beyond Outbidding? Ethnic Party Strategies in Serbia." *Party Politics* 19, no. 5 (2013): 758–777

Part II

Identities and communicative power

Introduction II

The main objective of this study – as I noted in the Introduction – is to find new ways through which minority groups can publicly legitimize their claims on policies that affect them. In my understanding, the available mechanisms for exerting such influences on institutions of political power do not work well. That is why it seems necessary to seek new possibilities for motivating the authorities to align their actions with the interests of minorities.

In the first part of the book I outlined some problems which, in my opinion, are of critical importance for minority policies in the countries of Central and Eastern Europe. Their solution can be facilitated by legitimizing minority claims in a manner that is convincing enough to win the support of public opinion for making the necessary changes in public policies. These problems concern collective identities, especially with regard to education, language, the media, the arts, and religion. For example, should pupils from minority communities be taught in their mother tongue at school, or, at least, should they be offered some form of education in their mother tongue? Should the study of minority culture and history be introduced in school curricula, and if yes, in what form? Should official status be granted to alternative names of towns, villages, localities, rivers, and so forth, in areas where a large part of the population belongs to an ethnic or national minority? Should the minority language in such areas have the status of a second official language? Should the law allow the creation and operation of mass media that deal exclusively with the problems of a particular minority, which are managed mostly by members of this minority and, possibly, use the minority language? Should the public expression of religious identity – such as the wearing of headscarves by Muslim women in public institutions – be tolerated?

Indeed, those questions are directly relevant only to the collective identities of minority groups; on a more general level, however, they are also important from a social and political point of view. As noted in Chapter 2 of this book, we have sufficient grounds to assume that cultural differences, group solidarity, and social and political relationships are closely interlinked in the area of minority issues. If a given country is enacting public policies that negatively affect the collective identities of minority communities, the resulting tensions – as reflected in group solidarity and intergroup rivalries – are bound to also affect the social status of the members of those communities, as well as the overall political situation. Contemporary history abounds in examples, especially in Central and Eastern Europe, of the use of controversies that are not particularly significant in and of themselves – for example, disputes about the possibility of the official use of alternative place names, or of the daily broadcast on national television of a ten-minute news program in a minority language (currently a "hot" issue in Bulgaria: see, for example, *Sega* from October 2, 2000; *Praven Svjat* from December 16, 2009) – as a pretext for launching political campaigns on minority issues, which are designed more to "gain points" in the struggle for political power than to resolve conflicts.

How could the policies in the above-mentioned areas be "fine-tuned" so as to secure a balance between the interests of society at large and those of minority groups? One of the most widely used ways of doing that currently is through struggles for recognition and the observance of human rights that go beyond the universal ones: specifically, collective, or – according to other interpretations – group, or group-specific rights. I have already mentioned that this approach has been subjected to serious criticism. It refers mostly to the dangers of the disintegration of public life (including the use of various situations related to collective rights as a *casus belli* by political forces), as well as to the restriction of freedoms of some individuals within their communities.

In the context of this study, though, other arguments against this way of protecting the interests of minorities can also be presented. If we accept the constructionist interpretation of cultural identity and, at the same time, assume that public policies should take into account the complexity of minority issues (specifically, the above-mentioned interrelationships of cultural differences, group solidarity, and social and political factors), what we will see behind the overt disagreements, tensions, and conflicts between minority groups and society at large, is a complex picture of intertwined cultural and social interactions that give rise to the problems in this area. Undoubtedly, public policies should be directed more at the causes of the issues that the minority groups are facing rather than at their consequences. But, if at the causal level we find a whole host of interrelated, diverse, dynamic, and "fluid" social processes, how could they be reorganized and diverted in a socially desirable direction by applying such universalizing and equalizing instruments as collective rights? For, if in a certain context – in a certain country, in a certain area, regarding a certain aspect of minority issues, with regard to a certain ethnic (or religious, or national) community, and at a certain historical moment – the recognition and observance of collective rights indeed helps to balance the interests of a particular minority group and of society at large, then, in a different context, the need to regulate a given set of intertwined social processes through public input and political decision-making may be completely different. What will happen if someone tries to apply a "remedy" that was effective in a particular case to a case of a different sort, not knowing in advance what the effect would be? Moreover, it is precisely the discrepancies in actual cases between real needs and *a priori* recognized collective rights that provide pretexts for nationalist political leaders, as well as for minority ones, to instigate ethnic or religious conflicts.

Another widely used mechanism for aligning public policies with the interests of minority groups is direct empowerment of the latter by including their representatives in the struggle for and, possibly, the exercise of political power. In Chapter 3, I presented critiques that question the capacity of this instrument to balance the interests of minority groups and society at large. We can distinguish between two types of arguments in this respect. The first type stems from the claim that the "logic" of the struggle for political power, as well as the efforts to retain it, is very different from the "logic" that befits the struggle for the defense of the interests of minority groups. When the former substitutes the latter and begins to inform actions that are supposed to enable members of minority groups to participate in public life as full-fledged citizens whose opportunities to preserve, enjoy, and develop their cultural identity are equal to those of everyone else, the result is minority-related policies similar to Frankenstein's monster. As for the other type of critique, it focuses on the dangers of conflating political power (including the power to use coercion or even violence) and community-based, exclusivist solidarities.

Hence, and this is one of the theses of this study, it is reasonable to look for possibilities for the communicative empowerment of minorities, that is, for the public legitimization of their claims in such a way that the relevant policies of institutions of political power would prove to be predetermined – with the help of public opinion – by those claims.

Of course, attempts at such legitimization of minority claims are being, and have been, made for decades, but they have mostly had a limited effect. The capacity of representatives of minorities to influence public opinion is incomparable to that of the mainstream political parties, social movements, and large economic "players." Effective use of the various instruments for influencing public opinion – such as mass media, the arts (e.g., film and literature), public events, and academic discussions – requires investing significant material and intellectual resources, which members of minority groups rarely have at their disposal. When it comes to winning the narrative in the battle for public opinion they are in an inherently disadvantaged position.

That is why in my study I focus on an instrument for influencing public opinion whose efficacy – at least by design – does not depend on power, material, and other such resources, to which minorities have limited access. I am referring to the collective decision-making method called "public deliberation" and, more generally, to the model of deliberative democracy. The principal advantage of this paradigm in our case is that the main criterion for the legitimacy of a binding decision, or of a social norm, or of a public policy, is "the unforced force of the better argument" (Habermas 1996, 306).

From the perspective of this paradigm the attitude of a given public toward a purportedly legitimate claim should not be determined by the number of people who declare their support, by the charisma of some public figure, by someone's authority, or by the popular appeal of some public message (all of which require investing significant material and intellectual resources), but by the rational awareness of the bulk of the public of their own best interests. If arguments that no one can convincingly refute show that satisfying the said claim is in the equal interest of all, then there would be no means for influencing people's psyche that could hinder the recognition of the claim's legitimacy.

In my view, it is this aspect of the method of public deliberation and of the model of deliberative democracy that opens promising opportunities for the communicative empowerment of minority groups. But there are also a series of obstacles to the use of such a means for the public legitimization of minority claims. Some of them are related to problematic elements of the deliberative paradigm itself. For example, what makes one argument more convincing than another? Could this depend on the value-system, intellectual experience, and other such characteristics of the addressees of those arguments? Could it be possible that a given argument may be convincing for one group or category of people, but not for another?

Other difficulties in this respect stem from the particular cultural traits of specific minority groups. Could the validity of arguments which refer to particular characteristics of a minority group's lifeworld be judged by people who do not belong to it? For example, if representatives of an ethnic community claim that, as a result of certain events in its historical background, its members are particularly sensitive about the place names in this area that are associated with its historical past, can this claim be judged to be true or false by people outside of this community who come from a completely different historical background?

Hence, in the next chapters of this book, I will examine some general problems of public legitimization and then, in brief, the theory of public deliberation (including its latest form, which is public deliberation through internet communication), as well as the specific challenges of conveying public legitimization across the "barrier" of cultural differences. In the final chapter, I will present my proposal for overcoming these obstacles to the communicative empowerment of minorities.

Reference

Habermas, Jürgen. *Between Facts and Norms.* Cambridge, MA: The MIT Press, 1996.

4 Communicative power

Public legitimization within the framework of the Habermasian model of the public sphere

The numerous publications on the subject propose different concepts and definitions of "public sphere." Here, I use this term in the most general sense, as an open network of communication streams in which citizens' opinions and wills regarding issues of public importance are formed.

Viewed in this way, communicative interactions in the public sphere differ from those in the private sphere – in people's private lives as well as in various cultural or professional circles; or, if we use a term of Jürgen Habermas's (borrowed from phenomenology), in various "lifeworlds" (Habermas 1996). Public communication deals with issues that actually or potentially concern all citizens, rather than just those who belong to a particular group or category that they can leave if they want to (see Rawls 1997, 769). This is precisely why the will-formation of the participants in public debates is a particularly responsible job. A religious community, or a fan club, for example, may discuss issues that are of exclusive interest to its members; moreover, it may discuss them in a way that is specific to the group in question. The participants in such discussions have no responsibilities to people outside their circle. As the outcomes of such debates do not concern anyone other than the members of the group, the participants do not have to take into account anyone else's rights and interests, or the capacities of non-members to understand their arguments and to judge how convincing they are. In a nutshell, such communicative interactions may be "confined" to narrower or wider circles of participants, and in this sense, they are not public.

Furthermore, relations in the public sphere differ from relations of power. Convincing people to act or behave in a certain manner and coercing them to do so are two alternative ways of producing motivation. In fact, public communication is often used as an instrument of political or economic domination, but such instances are considered to be foreign to the public sphere. The authorities may exercise censorship of the media, or even obligate them to publish materials that serve the government's interests without allowing for criticism. They may organize public debates on issues where anyone who voices a point of view that deviates from the official "party line" is liable to be punished. However, these forms of public communication do not qualify as belonging to the public sphere, which functions as such only if communicative interactions within it are not conducted under political or economic pressure.

This, however, is not to say that within the institutions of political power themselves, there cannot be debates of a public nature, which take place within what John Rawls calls the "public political forum" (Rawls 1997, 767). It comprises, according to Rawls,

> the discourse of judges in their decisions, and especially of the judges of a supreme court; the discourse of government officials, especially chief executives and legislators; and finally, the discourse of candidates for public office and their campaign managers, especially in their public oratory, party platforms, and political statements.
>
> (Rawls 1997, 767)

Debates of this sort are public, however, only if they are conducted from positions of equal power, or outside of any power relations whatsoever – that is, if the decision is determined by the "power" of the presented arguments, not by the will of the power-holder(s).

By the same logic, institutions of political power may participate in the public sphere through news conferences, press releases, interviews of government ministers, PR campaigns designed to win public support for government policies, and so forth. To qualify as genuinely belonging to the public sphere, however, such actions must employ only communicative means, not instruments of power such as favoring some media over others, or pressuring their management. Institutions of political power may correctly play a role in the public sphere only if they are on equal footing with all other participants.

Considering the subject and tasks of my study, here I will use a specific model of the public sphere which is associated mainly with the names of Immanuel Kant and Jürgen Habermas. In several of his publications, and especially in *Perpetual Peace: A Philosophical Sketch*, Kant formulated the idea that the relation between politics and morality is mediated by the *"Publizität."* In an appendix titled *Of the Harmony Which the Transcendental Concept of Public Right Established between Morality and Politics*, he proposes a "transcendental formula of public law" which says: "All actions relating to the right of other men are unjust if their maxim is not consistent with publicity" (Kant 1983, 62). Later in the same text he offers another, affirmative version, of the same principle: "All maxims which *stand in need* of publicity in order not to fail their end, agree with politics and right combined" (Kant 1983, 62; emphasis in original).

Kant's argument in favor of this principle looks simple. If I cannot make public the maxim of certain political actions of mine "without inevitably exciting universal opposition to my project, … [this] is due only to the injustice with which this maxim threatens everyone" (ibid.); it necessarily follows from this that the maxim, or project in question, is contrary to morality. And vice versa – if a political project is in accord with the public's universal goal, happiness, it can be made public (and this will remove the public's distrust in the maxims of politics), thus contributing to "the union of the goals of all possible" (ibid.). In other words, Kant's message here is that publicity is the touchstone for whether or not a given policy conforms to the norms of morality.

Jürgen Habermas outlined in his book *The Structural Transformation of the Public Sphere* (first published in German in 1962; first English edition in 1989), a picture of certain patterns of communication in bourgeois social circles in the late seventeenth to early nineteenth centuries, which he qualified as *Öffentlichkeit* (translated into English as "*public sphere*" – see Habermas 1991). This was, in his account, free and open communication on issues of common concern. As such, it had a powerful legitimizing (or delegitimizing) effect on the norms of social life (especially on the legal ones), and on public policies. Furthermore, Habermas claimed, in the critical spirit of the Frankfurt School, that in modern mass society, characterized by a welfare state and consumerist culture, the public sphere is in decline due to the pressure of commercialized mass media, ideological propaganda and public relations campaigns. Its legitimizing function is being manipulated from behind the scenes and cannot be trusted any more.

This very influential work of Habermas's was criticized by quite a few authors (for example in some of the papers in the collection *Habermas and the Public Sphere*, which was dedicated to the first English-language edition of *The Structural Transformation of the Public Sphere* – see Calhoun 1992) for being historically incorrect, especially as far as the free and open nature of the legitimizing communication among representatives of the bourgeoisie is concerned (what about the chances of the proletariat or women to participate in it, for example). However, it is undoubtedly an impressive presentation of a modernist ideal of legitimizing communication. Much later, in the early 1990s, Habermas developed a more articulate version of this ideal, without relating it to a specific historical period (especially in his *Faktizität und Geltung*, published in 1992 and translated into English as *Between Facts and Norms* – see Habermas 1996).

The main function of the public sphere, according to Habermas's model, is to exert influence via public legitimization on the formulation and adoption of the norms of social life, and also on the design of public policies and their enforcement by the institutions of political power. In his description of the mechanisms of policy legitimization Habermas presents civil society as the necessary social environment for the functioning of the public sphere. This qualification applies to debates that take place within and among informal associations, social movements, professional organizations, intellectual circles, mass media, and other social entities not involved in the exercise of political power, which deal with issues of common concern.

It is the public sphere which, "as a network for communicating information and points of view (that is, opinions expressing affirmative or negative attitudes)," filters and synthesizes the streams of communication in such a way that they "coalesce into bundles of topically specified public opinions" (Habermas 1996, 360). Habermas regards the public sphere as a self-regulating network of communication streams that forms the opinions and the will of citizens. This enables him to discern within it the capacity to transform the diverse messages, contributions, and claims, which originated in the lifeworld, into unified forms that regulate social processes. It is through the public sphere that culture-specific arguments are transformed into arguments that are generally accessible to everyone.

Public opinion on various issues is formed as a result of the functioning of the public sphere. It may be described both as a recapitulation of the debates that occur informally and as the instrument that exerts direct influence on debates on the formal level (those that are within the framework of institutions of political power), as well as on the decisions made by those institutions. Public opinion shows the power-holding elite – and, in a wider sense, political elite in general – "what the public of citizens would accept as legitimate decisions in a given case" (Habermas 2006, 418). In this way, the "weak" public, i.e., the informal public sphere that functions at the civil society level, influences the "strong" (in Habermas's terms) one, i.e., the institutions of political power (the distinction between these two types of public led Habermas to introduce the term "two-track model of deliberative politics" (see Habermas 1996, 304).

How can the influence of public opinion on the institutions of democratic societies be explained? Why do the latter tend to comply with the former? A key formulation that casts light on this issue is Jon Elster's "the civilizing force of hypocrisy" as presented in his "Introduction" to a collection of articles entitled *Deliberative Democracy* (1998, 12). That is to say that the interest to preserve – or rather the concern not to lose – the legitimacy of one's own political conduct in the eyes of the public, who will eventually comprise the electorate, is the source of what Habermas terms "communicative power." He states that, "Not influence per se, but influence transformed into communicative power, legitimates political decisions" (Habermas 1996, 371).

What does Habermas mean by the term "legitimates" in this sentence? Judging from the context of his statement, I believe that here we should understand "legitimating" in the widest sense – in the sense of presenting a norm or social fact as justified in light of someone's beliefs. To say that someone accepts something as legitimate is to say that the person in question assumes it is what it ought to be and is ready to conform to it, be it a law, requirement, claim, decision, policy, or institutional arrangement. Hereinafter, I will use a very concise phrase to denote what we refer to as "legitimate"– namely, *norm or social fact.*

The plurality of the public sphere

Public communication in Habermas's model of the public sphere is most often characterized as "free and open"; these traits are necessary conditions for its legitimizing function. Any communication that is not free cannot be trusted at all, including its legitimizing messages. And why should it be open – that is, why should all the relevant information be accessible, why should there be no "taboo" topics, and why should nobody be excluded a priori from communication? The reason is that, if this is not the case, the effect of the legitimizing function of public communication would be either fictitious (if it does not provide all the available relevant information), or incomplete (if some people are not allowed to speak because they might reveal certain truths, in the light of which the legitimizing messages might seem less convincing, or not convincing at all).

However, it is exactly the openness of public communication that is the target of most criticism against the Habermasian model. This requirement is so important for the legitimizing capacity of public communication, and yet so unrealistic. Open public communication is possible only in a unitary public sphere. The greatest obstacle to the universal accessibility of a process of public communication is not technical. It comes from the different criteria used by the participants in this process to evaluate the legitimizing force of the various means of communication. Some people may recognize a passionate rhetorical address by a charismatic political leader as having a powerful legitimizing effect; meanwhile, people from a different social and cultural background may completely disregard the legitimizing pretensions of such appeals and prefer dispassionate, argument-based types of communication. Furthermore, within the latter type of public, discord may arise with regard to the discursive resources which they consider to be convincing, and so on.

Regarding the openness of public discourse as a necessary element of the modernist ideal of legitimizing public communication, Nancy Fraser (1989, 164) points out the importance of the "sociocultural means of interpretation and communication." By this she means "the historically and culturally specific ensemble of discursive resources available to members of a given social collectivity in pressing claims against one another" (ibid.). These typically are: officially recognized idioms, vocabularies, paradigms of argumentation, narrative conventions, and modes of subjectification (see ibid.). Configured in a certain way, these patterns of argumentative communication are exclusively recognized in a given sociocultural environment as convincing. If a certain reason is formulated and presented in a substantially different manner, it will not be regarded in this environment as valid – not (or not only) because of *what* is being claimed, but because of *how* it is being claimed.

Fraser insists that the means through which a debate is conducted are not indifferent to its outcome – actually they may pre-decide this outcome. Consequently, if some of the citizens in a given society (e.g., a social class, or an ethnic community) have established as authoritative a means of interpretation and communication that presents their economic and political superiority as legitimate, they have great chances of perpetuating this domination. If among the rest of the citizenry certain opposition against the status quo begins to take shape, these people will have little chance to articulate claims that could convincingly contest the domination of the said class or community. This is simply because the public at large will not accept as cogent arguments that do not conform to the hegemonic standards of communication. As a result of the diversity in the patterns of public communication, a debate on some issue of common concern may turn out to be virtually inaccessible, that is, not open to some citizens who might have important information to share – information that might dramatically change the course of the discussion and influence its legitimizing effect – but who use a means of communication that is not recognized as convincing, or even relevant, by the other participants.

Many scholars working on this topic today share the opinion that no unitary public sphere exists. Elizabeth Butler Breese (2011, 132), for example, states that:

> Twenty years after the translation of *The Structural Transformation*, nearly all scholars of the public sphere agree that our social world is composed of multiple, overlapping, and unequal publics. It is more accurate to talk of (and research) *publics* and *public spheres* than to refer to *the public sphere*.
>
> (Elizabeth Butler Breese 2011, 132; emphasis in original)

Other authors claim that communication barriers exist between citizens who are divided by class differences; it then follows, for example, that a "proletarian" public sphere exists alongside the bourgeois one (see Negt and Kluge 1993, originally published in German in 1972). Many more point to *cultural differences* as grounds for the formation of separate religious, ethnic, racial, and gender publics (Hess and Todd 2009; Swaine 2009). Noteworthy in this respect are the hegemonic, in a Gramscian sense, relations that develop when a discourse that is specific to a particular public is imposed as an allegedly universal one upon other publics through the monopolization of discursive resources by an economically and politically dominant group (see Fraser 1989, 67). When other social entities are led to adopt that discourse as their own, they are deprived of any opportunity to become aware of their true interests and of the injustices carried out against them, whereby they perpetuate their subordinate position.

Apart from views of this kind, which focus on the existence of separate, stable publics that are divided by substantial cultural or social differences, we also find in publications on the subject accounts of the formation and dissipation of contingent publics, which emerge as a result of particular debates:

> Audiences that coalesce into publics who talk about political issues – and begin to enact their civic identities and make use of their civic competencies – move from the private realm into the public one, making use of and further developing their cultures of citizenship.
>
> (Dahlgren 2006, 275)

Many of the publications devoted to the plurality of the public sphere and the issues of the so-called counterpublics discussed further on in this study, are informed by an emancipatory impulse. They focus not merely on the diversity of the means of persuasion in public communication and the consequent fragmentation of the public sphere into separate publics, but also on the inequality of the latter. The plurality of the public sphere is seen as a means of perpetuating the domination of the social groups or classes that have imposed, in one way or another, their discourse as the one that exclusively forms public opinion and, *ipso facto*, have deprived other, excluded or marginalized, groups of the possibility of legitimizing their own positions and interests (see, for example. Elsadda 2010; McCann 2011; Eckert and Chadha 2013; Wexler 2013). The resulting normative conclusions primarily focus on finding ways to overcome this systemic injustice and to give the separate publics equal opportunities in the struggle – or, at least, competition – to exert a stronger influence on public opinion. The question of whether or not there may also be possibilities for coming to some type of understanding, as well as engaging in a joint search for the fairest solution to the problems – despite the undeniably existing dissonance in public communication – is somehow relegated to the background.

This second approach to the plurality of the public sphere (see, for example, Wilson 2010; Mccallum 2011) is much more compatible with the Habermasian model of the public sphere. The key question in this respect is: does the undeniable fact of a parallel existence of different publics indicate that this model is not realistic? Habermas argues that the ultimate result of a properly functioning public sphere is the influence produced by the legitimizing effect of public opinion upon the institutions of political power. But can a unified public opinion on an issue of common concern be formed out of a "cacophony" of voices coming from a variety of publics? Seyla Benhabib (2008, 5) observes in this regard that

> ... it is difficult to understand how to connect decentered anonymous networks of flowing and interconnecting conversations to a decisional public sphere; the centered model. I think that one of the most interesting normative questions is how to conceptualize the interaction between these networks of communication, information and opinion building on the one hand, and public articulation in terms of decisional articulation on the other.

As Nicholas Garnham (1992, 371) notes, if the exercise of "communicative power" aims at a general political effect, then

> a series of autonomous public spheres is insufficient. There must be a single public sphere, even if we might want to conceive of this single public sphere as made up of a series of subsidiary public spheres, each organized around its own political structure, media system, and set of norms and interests.

Public opinion clearly does play a prominent role in the societies that can be characterized as liberal democracies. In spite of the multitude of voices coming from the various publics, public opinion *is* a factor that governments and local authorities tend to comply with. Publications on this topic offer a number of explanations for the apparent paradox of, on the one hand, a diversity of publics and patterns of public legitimization and, on the other, a unified public opinion on many important issues of common concern. One aspect of this problem, which will be discussed – in its normative dimension – in the final chapter of this book, is the issue of how claims "generated" within a minority public can be legitimized with respect to a more general public.

Genuine and fictitious legitimacy

Another important element of the Habermasian model of the public sphere pertains to the methods utilized for minimizing the manipulation of public communication. Within this model, public communication is regarded as the main factor for the formation of the opinions and wishes of the citizens related to issues of public importance. In other words, it plays a main role in the legitimization (or delegitimization) of the binding norms that are imposed by the institutions of political power and their policies: "liberal policies are legitimate because they can be presented as being the object of some sort of hypothetical agreement between those subject to their authority, in so far as the public justification of political principles guarantees their acceptability" (Rossi 2014, 10). The manipulation of public communication, however, produces fictitious legitimacy, thereby perverting social life.

This kind of manipulation is one of the major themes in the studies on the modern public sphere, beginning with *The Structural Transformation of the Public Sphere* (Habermas 1991). The publications on this subject provide ample criticism of the quality of our contemporary public spheres, including how they function in democratic, Western-style societies (see, for example, Greider 1992; Sandel 1996; Schiller 1996; Eisenstein 1998; Eliasoph 1998). The *mal*functioning of public legitimization in a given society may be due, not only to such machinations as ideological propaganda, brainwashing, and the like, but also to the prevailing general social conditions. These include, first and foremost, the commercialization of the public sphere in modern mass society, which has been the subject of bitter criticism by Habermas in his *Structural Transformation*.

Therefore, besides genuine public legitimacy, i.e., the reasonable acceptance of certain norms and/or practices as justified by the addressees of the legitimizing messages, there can also be a fictitious legitimacy that relies upon the approval by some citizens of norms and practices for false reasons. For example, if some people are misled by corrupt mass media into believing that a given law is beneficial for their society, even though it in fact serves certain private interests at the expense of the common good, they will consider it to be a legitimate norm. In this type of situation we have nothing more than a false legitimacy.

Legitimizing public communication can be distorted in a myriad of ways. Instead of freedom of the formation and expression of journalists' opinions on matters of common concern, we may have tacit censorship by the management of mass media and, in addition, self-censorship by intellectuals who sometimes prefer to "trim" the truth in their publications if that is necessary in order to not jeopardize their careers. Instead of argument-based communication aimed at convincing the public, there are many instances in which the mass media, quite literally, exert brutal pressure on the senses of their audience. Furthermore, frequently, iconic figures are painstakingly promoted with the goal of influencing the hearts and minds of the people in order to advance a particular cause, with a complete disregard for the possible negative effects on society as a whole. Instead of the debates being open to incoming relevant information, "invisible" barriers are being created as a result of the drastic differences in the patterns of argumentation that prevent people from recognizing the validity of "strange" reasons.

Karl Boggs (2000, 9) writes the following about the detrimental effects that the investment of colossal material resources into public communication by large business corporations have had on the public sphere:

> Without doubt corporate power and wealth shape politics in the United States today more than ever – in corporations' very growing presence in the economy, their extensive lobbies and influence over legislative activity, their ownership and control of the mass media, their preponderant influence over election campaigns, their capacity to secure relief from myriad regulatory controls, their massive public relations apparatus, their general subsidies to the two major parties and the convention process, and so forth.

Boggs (2000, 9) claims that "corporate behemoths," such as Time Warner, Disney/ABC, Bertelsmann, Viacom, or Rupert Murdoch's News Corporation, control mass communications to a large extent, thereby exercising great influence on film production, TV, print journalism, and book publishing, and thus have established an ideological hegemony that allows them to trumpet "those virtues or attributes most consonant with perpetuation of that very system of power and wealth, namely, free markets, consumerism, personal responsibility, competitive individualism, and lessened reliance on the public's input or state governance." Other authors point out, more specifically, certain propensities of the public in mass societies that make it vulnerable to manipulation: the "citizens' 'rational ignorance' (i.e., their deficient willingness to be informed)" (Azmanova 2010, 48); their readiness to "form 'top of the head' impressions under the impact of sound bites and headlines" (ibid.); the publics' vulnerability to "pressure by the more advantaged" (ibid.), and so forth.

However, in reality, the extreme instances of absolutely genuine and absolutely fabricated legitimacy are rare. Typically, the substantive criteria concerning what is good and what is bad with respect to the interests and values of a given public take shape in the process of public communication. And, insofar as this process may be corrupted in one way or another, it can be difficult to judge what is right and what is wrong, what is true and what is false. Conversely, there still must be some way in which to distinguish between valid and manipulative types of public legitimization. If this were not possible, then the entire model of the modern public sphere would be meaningless.

This type of differentiation, which is characteristic of the Habermasian critical approach to public communication, should not be confused with another one that is traditional for social sciences – namely, the differentiation between factual judgments and value judgments, alias between description and prescription. In his article "Legitimacy and Justice" (published in the collection edited by Jörg Kühnelt, *Political Legitimization without Morality?*), Wilfried Hinsch presents the difference between the empirical and the normative understanding of legitimacy as follows: "To call an institutional arrangement legitimate [in the empirical sense] … implies that there are people who sincerely believe that these arrangements should be regulative for their conduct irrespective of external sanctions" (Hinsch 2008, 40). In other words, in this case there is no *judgment* on the part of the author of the description. That a given norm, policy, or institutional arrangement is legitimate to some people is simply ascertained as a matter of fact. Those who perform this cognitive act may have an entirely different attitude towards the object of legitimization:

> One may maintain that a particular arrangement is legitimate in the empirical sense – i.e., that it finds the approval of those who have to abide by it – and still believe that it is highly unjust or unacceptable for other reasons.
>
> (Hinsch 2008, 40)

Conversely,

> To say that an institutional arrangement is legitimate in the normative sense is not simply to say something about the subjective state of mind of particular individuals. It is to say that the arrangement meets certain substantive requirements – say standards of justice and rationality expressed in a normative conception of legitimacy – irrespective of whether people believe that they are met or not.
>
> (Hinsch 2008, 40)

This means that the legitimacy of a given norm, policy, or institutional arrangement is assessed through some substantive criteria. One and the same norm (policy or institutional arrangement) may be assessed from different, alternative points of view by applying alternative substantive criteria that are an expression of particular value positions.

Should we take the above-mentioned critiques against the present-day public sphere to mean that some scholars are critical of the current state of public communication because its legitimizing function does not meet their substantive criteria, which often vary in the different schools of thought? Does exposing the manipulative mechanisms through which the public is persuaded to accept as legitimate some norms or social facts for false reasons simply mean identifying a discrepancy between certain patterns of legitimization, on the one hand, and the legitimacy criteria that the adherents of a particular research paradigm accept as valid, on the other?

In my opinion, the situation is more complex. All legitimizing public communication involves presenting some purportedly legitimate norms or policies as corresponding to its addressees' own beliefs. The legitimizing communication is manipulative if the public is being persuaded that such correspondence exists when, in fact, it does not. Furthermore, in this context, the legitimizing communication is manipulative not because those who are performing the communication are deceiving themselves – in good faith – that the above-mentioned correspondence exists, but because they know it does not and are consciously deceiving the public in question. Or, as James Fishkin (2009, 6) writes,

> A person has been manipulated by a communication when she has been exposed to a message intended to change her views in a way she would not accept if she were to think about it on the basis of good conditions.

Therefore, what we have here is not a contradiction between facts and someone's value position, but an objective, factual contradiction between actual beliefs, on the one hand, and actual characteristics of norms, social facts, or institutional arrangements to which those beliefs are related, on the other – Habermas (1996, 148, 182, 308) refers to this by the term "distorted" communication.

At a more abstract level, identifying manipulation in public communication may take the form of a value judgment, such as when a person who exposes a given manipulation thinks that it is not right and that it is something that should not be done. But this denial of the legitimacy of the manipulatively justified particular norm or policy is not motivated by the discrepancy between the norm and some particular substantive criteria applied by the critic. In such cases, what we have is a value judgment based on the substantive conviction that, as a matter of principle, people should not be persuaded to agree to norms or social facts that conflict with their beliefs or their awareness of their own best interests.

This principle is not a self-evident truth. We may believe that some persons, possibly including ourselves, have the right to mislead others into approving things that they should not be in agreement with. Nevertheless, we must bear in mind that such manipulation also conflicts with the very concept of legitimization. Any legitimizing public communication that consciously misleads its addressees constitutes, to put it in Habermasian terms, a strategic action that claims to be communicative; that is, here we have an objective internal inconsistency of the legitimizing communication itself.

Habermas uses the notion of public deliberation as a means for elaborating his views concerning public legitimization at a later stage of development of his model, as it was presented, for example, in *Between Facts and Norms* (Habermas 1996): "Deliberative politics acquires its legitimating force from the discursive structure of an opinion- and will-formation that can fulfill its socially integrative function only because citizens expect its results to have a reasonable quality" (ibid., 304). Along these lines, he discusses a number of procedural criteria for the legitimacy of collective decisions within the theory of public deliberation that would help distinguish between proper (or, as I will be calling it further, *bona fide*) and fictitious legitimization. The general idea is that if a public debate which leads to consensus of all the parties involved is procedurally correct, then the decision made should be regarded as genuinely legitimate. Quite a few scholars who subscribe to the proceduralist approach to public legitimacy have discussed the meaning of "procedural correctness" in this context (see, for example, Bohman 2000; Baynes 2002; Gutmann and Thompson 2004; Hedrick 2010) and a number of different lists of criteria are in circulation.

In *Between Facts and Norms*, Habermas appropriates the set of criteria proposed by Joshua Cohen as, in his words, "a plausible characterization of the deliberative procedure" (Habermas 1996, 305). Cohen prescribes the following parameters for a legitimizing discussion: (a) rationality ("argumentative form"); (b) inclusivity and publicness (all who are possibly affected should have an equal chance to take part); (c) freedom from external coercion; (d) freedom from internal coercion (equality among the participants – their positions in the debate should yield only to "the unforced force of the better argument"); (e) revisability of the decisions made; (f) inclusivity concerning the subject matter of the deliberation (any issue that can be regulated in the equal interest of all can be discussed); and (g) inclusivity regarding interpretations of needs and wants (see Habermas 1996, 305).

If we are to simplify the picture a little bit, we may conclude that according to the proceduralist ideal of public legitimization presented in *Between Facts and Norms*, a norm or a social practice (such as a public policy) can be regarded as legitimate only if it is positively evaluated in a public discussion that is rational, open, free from coercion, and equal. Why do precisely these parameters apply, and not others? A number of authors claim, and I share their view, that the basic substantive assumption in this regard is that a social norm or practice is legitimate only if it is worthy of approval by a person who corresponds to the modern ideal of a human being, i.e., someone who makes a decision in an autonomous and responsible way (see, for example, Gripsrud 1999, 37). In other words, this understanding of public legitimization is modernist in character, just as is the Habermasian model of the public sphere as a whole.[1]

The key term in this respect is, in the opinion of certain writers, *agency* (see, for example, Muhlberger 2005). Put differently, a person cannot exercise her agency in approving or disapproving social norms and practices if she does not do so in accordance with her own will, for example, in situations of coercion, blind trust in someone else's opinion on the matter under consideration, and so forth. This would also be the case when she yields to certain emotions, to personal or group idiosyncrasies, or to communication that is not open to all possible relevant contributions. The type of communication whereby she is to be convinced that the norm or practice in question is justified in light of her beliefs must make available all relevant information on all relevant topics, and all possible interlocutors must be allowed to speak because each one, in principle, might be able to reveal certain truths that could weaken or undercut the force of otherwise legitimizing messages.

All this is not to say that recognition of the legitimacy of some norms or social facts cannot be wrong even when it is achieved and justified by a procedurally correct public debate. Even if a public that is most informed and competent about the issue under discussion arrives, in a procedurally perfect way, at the conclusion that a given norm or social fact meets its legitimacy criteria, it may turn out that the said norm or social fact will actually have detrimental consequences for the individuals and groups concerned. The proceduralist approach to legitimacy characteristic of the Habermasian model of the public sphere does not pretend to be a mechanism for "producing" absolute legitimacy. It is important, however, that even in the case of self-deception, this self-deception is on the part of the agent who decides what is or is not legitimate for herself. The agent may be incorrect about the correspondence between her beliefs and the actual norm or policy whose legitimacy she is assessing. The agent's own beliefs may also be wrong in view of her actual interests, as well as those of others. However, what is important to the legitimacy of a norm or social fact is whether or not the agent makes a decision in a responsible (in the modernist sense of the word) manner, or lets someone else decide what is legitimate or illegitimate for her.

This also holds true for the basic beliefs which serve, in the situation described here, as a frame of reference for assessing the legitimacy of norms or social facts. They, too, are subject to change under certain conditions, of course. Otherwise the model of legitimization discussed here would be characterized not by modernism but by simple dogmatism. In any case, however, any such change should be made in continuity with the overall set of beliefs of the agent, which constitutes the agent's identity. Such a change needs to take place as a successive step in the self-development of this set of beliefs so as not to impair its integrity. At the same time, the agent needs to recognize and be aware that she is changing (as a result of being under pressure from new experiences or because her basic set of beliefs has proved to be, under some circumstances, internally inconsistent) this frame of reference *herself*.

It is also important to note that another key element of the proceduralist approach to legitimacy is the revisability of all decisions that are made in a publicly-deliberative way (see Cohen's list of procedural criteria for the non-manipulation of public communication, noted above).

Of course, the question of the direction in which the will of the agent is leaning is also of critical importance. Is it possible to arrive at a legitimate collective decision through procedurally correct public communication if the participants evaluate the arguments used in the discussion (or, in other words, the criteria they apply in judging whether a proposal is acceptable to them) from positions that have been formed as a result of previous manipulative influences? Can the proceduralist approach to legitimacy be used to distinguish *bona fide* public communication from manipulative public communication if all, or at least some, of the participants in the debate, in order to assess legitimacy, start from frames of reference that are, for example, racist or religious-fundamentalist in their nature?

Here it is appropriate to note yet another significant limitation of the normative claims of the Habermasian model of the public sphere. It is relevant only to a liberal-democratic (or, as Rawls would say, "well-ordered" – see Rawls 1997, 765) society. This means that the object of legitimization (norms, practices) ought to be assessed by the public exclusively in the spirit of a Kantian-type deontological morality, i.e., not with a view to some teleological worldview beliefs[2] held by the assessors, but to the capacity of these norms or practices to balance the interests of the individual and group participants in the life of society. An undistorted legitimizing communication in Habermas's sense should – at least *prima facie* – correspond to the liberal principle of priority of the Right or of Justice with regard to the different, competing notions of the good life. The achievement of reasonable consensus on the legitimacy of norms and social facts should not be obstructed by differences regarding the ideals of the Good which, naturally, are professed in some way or another by all participants in the debates on publicly significant issues.

In fact, Habermas dissociates himself from the classical liberal methodology that distances political communication from "ethical" (in Habermas's terms) issues, i.e., from such issues concerning the self-understanding and the identity of the different groups participating in public life. Commenting on theses of Bruce Ackerman, Charles Larmore, and Nancy Fraser, the German philosopher proposes in *Between Facts and Norms* a procedurally "softened" version of the liberal approach to this problem:

> For this reason, we may assume that the know-how informing argumenta-
> tive practices represent a point of convergence where participants, however
> diverse their backgrounds, can at least intuitively meet in their efforts to
> reach an understanding. In all languages and in every language community,
> such concepts as truth, rationality, justification, and consensus, even if inter-
> preted differently and applied according to different criteria, play the same
> grammatical role. At any rate, this is true for modern societies that, with
> positive law, secularized politics, and a principled morality, have made the
> shift to a postconventional level of justification and expect their members to
> take a reflexive attitude toward their own respective cultural traditions.
>
> (Habermas 1996, 312)

Of course, the modernist ideal of the public sphere should not be used for evaluation of the normative rightness of the patterns of public legitimization in societies that differ, in a historical or cultural aspect, from modern ones. In other
words, we do not have sufficient reason to qualify norms and practices that are
de facto legitimate in certain societies as not genuinely legitimate just because
they have been and are still being justified by public communication that is
carried out in patterns which differ historically or culturally from those used in
modern society. It would be a manifestation of modernist naiveté and arrogance
to condemn as fictitious the legitimization of norms and practices in all non-
modern, or alternatively modern (if we accept Schmuel N. Eisenstadt's conception of "multiple modernities" – see Eisenstadt 2000) societies, because the
public communication which justifies them is not argumentative enough, and/or
is influenced more by the authority of the persons who participate in the debates
than by the quality of the arguments that they use, and/or is not really open, and
so forth.

On the other hand, however, the unquestionable fact that public legitimization
can be achieved in very different ways does not imply that all patterns of such
legitimization are morally acceptable in any cultural and social setting. It is true

that the criteria through which a distinction can be made between *bona fide* and manipulative public legitimization should match the cultural and social environment in which they are applied (in my opinion, the elaboration of such criteria for application outside "Western" societies would be a very fruitful track of research in the domain of the theory of multiple modernities[3]); however, this does not preclude the application of modernist criteria to the modernist model of the public sphere within modern societies.

Notes

1 "Modernist" is used here not in the sense of subject-centered reason as a point of reference (see Habermas 1987, 294), but in the sense of Modernity as an unfinished project (Habermas 1997).
2 Of course, the very modernist frame of reference of the assessment of norms and policies as legitimate or illegitimate, described here, presupposes certain substantive beliefs. Gripsrud, Muhlberger, and other authors associate with those beliefs the criteria for the procedural correctness of public communication of the sort proposed by Cohen and Habermas – in the sense that these criteria explicate, in a certain aspect, the modernist ideal of the human being. This also holds true for the mutual interpretations of the interests of the individuals and groups that are affected by the discussed norms and policies; these interpretations are of crucial importance in evaluating the convincing force of the arguments used in the debates on the legitimacy of the norms and/or policies in question. But I will deal specifically with the question of the proceduralist "purity" of the Habermasian models of the public sphere and of deliberative democracy in the next chapter. At this point it should be enough for us to conclude that the criteria for distinguishing *bona fide* from manipulative legitimizing public communication, applied in the models under review, do not in themselves carry a manipulative potential.
3 Especially worth noting in this respect is the research on the patterns of public legitimization in Muslim societies (see, for example, Eickelman and Anderson 2003; Salvatore and Eickelman 2006), some of which are even called by a number of authors the "Islamic public sphere" (see el-Nawawy and Khamis 2010; Salvatore 2010).

References

Azmanova, Albena. "Deliberative Conflict and 'The Better Argument' Mystique." *The Good Society* 19, no. 1 (2010): 48–54.

Baynes, Kenneth. "Deliberative Democracy and the Limits of Liberalism." In *Discourse and Democracy: Essays on Habermas's Between Facts and Norms*, edited by Rene von Schomberg and Kenneth R. Baynes, 15–30. Albany: State University of New York Press, 2002.

Benhabib, Seyla. "On the Public Sphere, Deliberation, Journalism and Dignity." *Interview by Karin Wahl-Jorgensen* (August 4, 2008), www.resetdoc.org/story/00000000965, accessed December 18, 2015.

Boggs, Karl. *The End of Politics. Corporate Power and the Decline of the Public Sphere.* New York: Guilford Press, 2000.

Bohman, James. *Public Deliberation.* Cambridge, MA: The MIT Press, 2000.

Breese, Elizabeth Butler, "Mapping the Variety of Public Spheres." *Communication Theory*, 21 (2011): 130–149.

Calhoun, Craig. *Habermas and the Public Sphere.* Cambridge, MA: The MIT Press, 1992.

Dahlgren, Peter. "Doing Citizenship: The Cultural Origins of Civic Agency in the Public Sphere." *European Journal of Cultural Studies* 9 (2006): 267–288.

Eckert, Stine and Kalyani Chadha. "Muslim Bloggers in Germany: An Emerging Counterpublic." *Media, Culture and Society* 35 (2013): 926–938.

Eickelman, Dale and Jon Anderson (eds.), *New Media in the Muslim World. The Emerging Public Sphere*. Bloomington: Indiana University Press, 2003.

Eisenstadt, Shmuel. "Multiple Modernities." *Daedalus* 129, no. 1 (2000): 1–29.

Eisenstein, Zillah. *Global Obscenities*. New York: New York University Press, 1998.

Eliasoph, Nina. *Avoiding Politics*. Cambridge: Cambridge University Press, 1998.

El-Nawawy, Mohammed and Sahar Khamis. "Collective Identity in the Virtual Islamic Public Sphere. Contemporary Discourses in Two Islamic Websites." *International Communication Gazette* 72 (2010): 229–250.

Elsadda, Hoda. "Arab Women Bloggers: The Emergence of Literary Counterpublics." *Middle East Journal of Culture and Communication* 3 (2010): 312–332.

Elster, Jon. "Introduction." In *Deliberative Democracy*, edited by Jon Elster, 1–18. Cambridge: Cambridge University Press, 1998.

Fishkin, James S. *When the People Speak: Deliberative Democracy and Public Consultation*. Oxford: Oxford University Press, 2009.

Fraser, Nancy. *Unruly Practices: Power, Discourse, and Gender in Contemporary Social Theory*. Minneapolis: University of Minnesota Press, 1989.

Garnham, Nicholas. "The Media and the Public Sphere." In *Habermas and the Public Sphere*, edited by Craig Calhoun, 359–376. Cambridge, MA: The MIT Press, 1992.

Greider, William. *Who Will Tell the People?* New York: Simon and Shuster, 1992.

Gripsrud, Jostein. "Scholars, Journalism, Television – Notes on Some Conditions for Mediation and Intervention." In *Television and Common Knowledge*, edited by Jostein Gripsrud, 34–52. London and New York: Routledge, 1999.

Gutmann, Amy and Dennis Thompson. *Why Deliberative Democracy?* Princeton: Princeton University Press, 2004.

Habermas, Jürgen. *The Philosophical Discourse of Modernity*, Cambridge, UK: Polity Press, 1987.

Habermas, Jürgen. *The Structural Transformation of the Public Sphere: An Inquiry into a Category of Bourgeois Society*. Cambridge, MA: The MIT Press, 1991.

Habermas, Jürgen. *Between Facts and Norms.* Cambridge, MA: The MIT Press, 1996.

Habermas, Jürgen. "Modernity: an Unfinished Project." In *Habermas and the Unfinished Project of Modernity: Critical Essays on The Philosophical Discourse of Modernity*, edited by Maurizio Passerin d'Entrèves and Seyla Benhabib, 38–58. Cambridge, MA: The MIT Press, 1997.

Habermas, Jürgen. "Political Communication in Media Society: Does Democracy Still Enjoy an Epistemic Dimension? The Impact of Normative Theory on Empirical Research." *Communication Theory* 16 (2006): 411–426.

Hedrick, Todd. *Rawls and Habermas. Reason, Pluralism, and the Claims of Political Philosophy*. Stanford: Stanford University Press, 2010.

Hess, Jacob Z. and Nathan R. Todd. "From Culture War to Difficult Dialogue: Exploring Distinct Frames for Citizen Exchange about Social Problems." *Journal of Public Deliberation* 5, no. 1 (2009): 1–14.

Hinsch, Wilfried. "Legitimacy and Justice." In *Political Legitimization without Morality?* Edited by Jörg Kühnelt, 39–52. Berlin: Springer, 2008.

Kant, Immanuel. *Perpetual Peace, and Other Essays on Politics, History, and Morals.* Indianapolis: Hacket Publishing Company, 1983.

Mccallum, Richard. "Micro Public Spheres and the Sociology of Religion: An Evangelical Illustration." *Journal of Contemporary Religion* 26, no. 2 (2011): 173–187.

McCann, Bryan J. "Queering Expertise: Counterpublics, Social Change, and the Corporeal Dilemmas of LGBTQ Equality." *Social Epistemology: A Journal of Knowledge, Culture and Policy* 25 no. 3 (2011): 249–262.

Muhlberger Peter. "Human Agency and the Revitalization of the Public Sphere." *Political Communication* 22, no. 2 (2005): 163–178.

Negt, Oskar and Alexander Kluge. *Public Sphere and Experience: Toward an Analysis of the Bourgeois and Proletarian Public Sphere.* Minneapolis: University of Minnesota Press, 1993.

Rawls, John. "The Idea of Public Reason Revisited." *University of Chicago Law Review* 64, no. 3 (1997): 780–807.

Rossi, Enzo. "Legitimacy, Democracy and Public Justification: Rawls' Political Liberalism versus Gaus' Justificatory Liberalism." *Res Publica* 20 (2014): 9–25.

Salvatore, Armando. *The Public Sphere: Liberal Modernity, Catholicism, Islam.* New York: Palgrave Macmillan, 2010.

Salvatore, Armando and Dale Eickelman (eds.). *Public Islam and the Common Good.* Leiden: Brill, 2006.

Sandel, Michael. *Democracy's Discontent.* Cambridge, MA: Harvard University Press, 1996.

Schiller, Herbert. *Information Inequality.* New York: Routledge, 1996.

Swaine, Lucas. "Deliberate and Free. Heteronomy in the Public Sphere." *Philosophy & Social Criticism* 35, no. 1–2 (2009): 183–213.

Wexler, Mark N. "Rachel Carson's Toxic Discourse: Conjectures on Counterpublics, Stakeholders and the 'Occupy Movement'." *Business and Society Review* 118, no. 2 (2013): 171–192.

Wilson, Terri S. "Civic Fragmentation or Voluntary Association? Habermas, Fraser, and Charter School Segregation." *Educational Theory* 60, no. 6 (2010): 643–664.

5   Legitimacy and public deliberation

What is "public deliberation"?

In the previous chapter, I addressed the question of how public deliberation can help protect legitimizing communication from manipulation. The distinction between *bona fide* and fictitious public legitimization is of crucial importance to this study as it considers the justification of minority claims as a means to influence minority policies so as to better align them with the needs and interests of minority communities. To use a term I introduced at the beginning of this book, the justification of minority claims can lead to the *communicative empowerment* of these communities, and may also offer an alternative to the political forms of their empowerment (the disadvantages of the political forms of empowerment were discussed in Chapter 3). Hence, if the legitimization of such claims is manipulated in some way, this will make the communicative empowerment of minorities impossible. That is why in this chapter I will focus in more detail on public deliberation, viewing it, above all, as a method of legitimate collective decision-making.

Undoubtedly, not every collective decision is legitimate from the perspective of those affected by it – even if it remains uncontested, that is, if it appears to be consensual. Let us imagine, for instance, a consensus on some issue that has been reached through a discussion at the office of an authoritarian boss, or through a spontaneous unanimous vote at some forum on the proposal of a charismatic speaker, or a decision made by a group of people to harm someone who is oblivious to their intentions. What are the conditions that must be followed in the decision-making process in order to guarantee that the decision made will be seen as legitimate by everyone affected – that is, everyone agrees to, approves of, and is willing to abide by it? In other words, what criteria should be met in the decision-making – or communication – process for a decision to be accepted as legitimate by everyone concerned?

One obvious possible way to answer this question is to start from the tautological formula that "a collective decision is legitimate if everyone concerned agrees to it." We have here nothing more than an "inverted" definition of legitimacy. This answer to the above question would make sense only if it is complemented with criteria regarding the way consensus is reached. In other words, if there are specific requirements that must be met for it to be real, rather than fictitious.

There is a difference of opinion in the literature on this topic. Some authors are more comprehensive in formulating such conditions than others. The general tendency is to seek an answer to the question, "What would motivate a rational person to freely accept a decision as legitimate?" Political philosophy offers different solutions to this problem. One of these solutions can be found in the model of deliberative democracy, and it stipulates that collective decisions made by the method of public deliberation may claim to be legitimate. What does this mean?

I will begin with a relatively brief interpretation on this issue. In his book *Public Deliberation: Pluralism, Complexity, and Democracy*, James Bohman (1996, 16) proposes the following conditions which he thinks are necessary for the "ideal procedure" of democratic deliberation:

> the inclusion of everyone affected by a decision, substantial political equality including equal opportunities to participate in deliberation, equality in methods of decision making and in determining the agenda, the free and open exchange of information and reasons sufficient to acquire an understanding of both the issue in question and the opinion of others, and so on.

Bohman obviously does not claim that this definition is exhaustive, but that it includes the main characteristics of public deliberation, which are also pointed out by other scholars. The "publicness" of this form of deliberation consists in its "openness," or in other words, its "inclusivity" – everyone who feels affected by the deliberated decision has the right to join in. This also presupposes publicness in the more elementary sense of the word, that is, that the debates are conducted "before the eyes" of the public, as it were. Everyone has the right to know what position each of the participants is defending and, more importantly, with what arguments. This is precisely what enables the inclusion, at any stage of the debate, of new participants who think that the issue being discussed affects them, so that their position must be taken into account in order to reach a legitimate consensus – provided, of course, that they can substantiate that this is indeed the case. Here – and Bohman makes this point perfectly clear – the individual participant's social status and other characteristics do not matter. Everyone is equal insofar as arguments are the only thing that matters, regardless of who presents them.

At the same time, the publicness of deliberation also presupposes that the arguments must be – or at least are meant to be – acceptable to all. That is, that they are made to address everyone and are formulated so as to be understood and accepted by everyone. Here, I will quote another philosopher who expressly points this out:

> On the standard conception of deliberative democracy, participants in the deliberative process are required not only to offer arguments but to offer

arguments persuasive to all: there is no presumption then that some members of the deliberating body do not count.

(Festenstein 2002, 91)

Joshua Cohen (1989) suggests a quite comprehensive list of the requirements that a debate must meet in order to have legitimizing functions. Cohen's list has already been mentioned in Chapter 4 of this book, and it includes seven such conditions. In my opinion, the first four (as listed in Cohen's essay) are the most noteworthy. As I summarized in the previous chapter, they are: rationality, openness (inclusivity), freedom from coercion, and equality of the participants.

The priority of the self-reflexivity of participation in these kinds of debates, as noted by Seyla Benhabib (1996, 72), is also very important. She presents public deliberation as a constantly self-evaluating and self-correcting (with a view to the relationship between its purposes and actual outcomes) activity:

> Very often individuals' wishes as well as views and opinions conflict with one another. In the course of deliberation and the exchange of views with others, individuals become more aware of such conflicts and feel compelled to undertake a coherent ordering.

(Benhabib 1996, 71)

Furthermore, guided by the need to publicly convince their partners in the process of deliberation, the participants must try to formulate their arguments in a way that is also acceptable from points of view that are different from their own: "This process of *articulating good reasons in public* forces the individual to think of what would count as a good reason for all others involved" (ibid.; emphasis in original). This leads to the development of what Seyla Benhabib, citing Hannah Arendt, calls an "enlarged mentality."

Moreover, through self-reflection public deliberation corrects itself as a procedure:

> A deliberative model of democracy suggests a necessary but not sufficient condition of practical rationality, because, as with any procedure, it can be misinterpreted, misapplied and abused.... Nonetheless, the discourse model makes some provisions against its own misuses and abuses in that the reflexivity condition built into the model allows abuses and misapplications at the first level to be challenged at a second, metalevel of discourse. Likewise, the equal chance of all affected to initiate such discourse of deliberation suggests that no outcome is prima facie fixed but can be revised and subject to reexamination.

(Benhabib 1996, 72)

In the literature on this issue, we also often encounter a laconic definition: public deliberation is a debate governed by "the unforced force of the better argument" (Habermas 1996, 306). In a sense, this definition replaces almost all other requirements that protect public communication from being manipulated. If the participants in a debate form their stances on the debated issues solely on the basis of reasoned arguments, then this means that they will not be influenced by coercion, authority or charisma, or any rhetorical means of appealing to their hearts and minds.

Differentia specifica of deliberative decision-making

A number of scholars distinguish this type of decision-making from other types, which are characteristic of democratic societies – that is, from decision-making through the "aggregation" of preferences and through "bargaining."

Joshua Cohen thinks that according to the aggregative understanding of democracy, it

> institutionalizes a principle requiring equal consideration for the interests of each member; or, more precisely, equal consideration along with a "presumption of personal autonomy" – the understanding that adult members are the best judges and most vigilant defenders of their own interests.... The natural method for giving such consideration is to establish a scheme of collective choice – majority or plurality rule, or group bargaining – that gives equal weight to the interests of citizens in part by enabling them to present and advance their interests. And that requires a framework of rights of participation, association and expression.
>
> (Cohen 1997, 411)

Actually, "aggregative" democracy does not exclude debates involving the exchange of reasons, discussed above. It also allows for transformation of the voter's standpoint. After all, this is what election campaigns are about. But the principle difference between aggregative and deliberative decision-making is that in the former, individuals determine their position and decide which option to support, exclusively with a view to their self-interest. The process of persuasion, which is usually involved in the struggle for votes, seeks to explicate the relationship between the different options on the table and the interests of voters – that is, it enables each of the addressees to realize what their best interest is and to decide which option is most preferable to them. Conversely, in deliberative decision-making the focus is on the relationship between the available options, on the one hand, and some values shared by all participants, on the other.

What follows from this difference? Whatever decision is made through a vote, i.e., through the numerical superiority of the preferences of some over those of others (hence the term "aggregation"), the losers in the "contest" will be unhappy with the outcome. They may accept it as legitimate to the extent that it is based on a democratic procedure, but it will not be *their* decision. They voted for something else, but got this instead. In such a situation it is difficult to expect that everyone affected by the decision will abide by it or enact it in good faith.

What about decision-making through bargaining? It is also consistent with contemporary democratic practices. In politics, agreements between parties – for example, an agreement to form a coalition, or to support a no-confidence vote against the government – are usually reached in this way. As Jon Elster (1998, 6) writes, a bargain is reached through the exchange of offers and counteroffers between the participants where the outcome is determined by the conditions under which the bargaining occurred, but above all by the parties' "resources that enable them to make credible threats and promises." The literature on this subject discusses various bargaining techniques, such as bluffing, using a "flamboyant opening gambit" to get the attention of the "Other Side" (for example, "take it or leave it" offers), blackmail, flaunting an allegedly better alternative to the deal being offered (that is, demonstrating to the other side that we are not particularly eager to reach an agreement with them because we have just as good of an offer from another potential partner), and so forth (see Susskind 2006, 278).

In contrast to aggregative democracy and bargaining, in public deliberation the focus is on transforming the participants' preferences – this is what persuasion is about. That is why these types of decisions are reached through a consensus. The process of mutual persuasion continues until all parties unite around one option. The latter becomes a unanimous decision, rather than a decision imposed by some on others.

The unforced force of the better argument

Undoubtedly, both the definitions of the deliberative model of democracy, as well as the criteria for public deliberation, presuppose integrity of the participation in the process of collective decision-making. If we are aware that the other side's reasoned objection to our argument is more convincing but do not admit it publicly and keep insisting on our position, we will block public deliberation. Public deliberation is possible only if the better argument always prevails. Recognition of the force of the better argument is viewed in public deliberation theory as the most important safeguard against the manipulation of public communication:

> So defined, deliberation presupposes a willingness on the part of the participants to listen to one another with an open mind rather than sticking doggedly to their own prior views and positions. Insofar as this presupposition holds, the agreements that they reach will be based not on the balance of advantage but on the balance of argument.
>
> (O'Flynn, 2015, 210)

What can make us evaluate in good faith all of the arguments presented in such communication, especially if "the better argument" is not in our own best interest? Is it at all possible to give up our selfishness in the name of the reasonableness of deliberative decision-making? Is such a methodology realistic?

Political philosophy and ethics propose various counterfactual models of social relations. For example, it can be argued that the way material goods are distributed is legitimate if everyone concerned agrees to it – provided that in the discussion on who should get what and how much, each person declares one's needs with utmost sincerity, that is, without trying to cheat one's partners. Of course, in all likelihood, not one actual method of the distribution of goods fully meets this condition, therefore none are fully legitimate in this sense. Yet, even so, the counterfactual model does have some merit because it can provide criteria for establishing which of the partially legitimate existing mechanisms for regulating social relations are more legitimate than others.

This is not the case with the model of deliberative democracy. In the words of Seyla Benhabib (1996, 84), the theory that gave rise to the model elucidates "the already implicit principles and logic of existing democratic practices." Among the latter, Benhabib includes what she calls "deliberative bodies" in democratic societies, the activities of parliamentary opposition, free and independent media (where and to the extent that they exist), and so forth (see ibid.). Later, I will also discuss Habermas's reconstructive method, with which Benhabib's above-quoted statement has a lot in common. In the last part of this chapter, I will also point out various other cases of real social interactions – institutional and informal – which many people think are early and imperfect, but are nevertheless realized applications of the deliberative model.

Some authors deny the very possibility that people may voluntarily admit that another's argument is right if it is not in their own best interest:

> The key question for those who believe that "differences" can be worked out through conversation is whether or not anyone can be convinced to do or support something that is not in their own best interest. It seems unlikely.
>
> (Susskind 2006, 274)

Still, most authors are of the opposite opinion and believe that the model of deliberative democracy can work in practice. One of their main arguments is that a completely effective motive to participate with integrity in public deliberation can be the subject's desire to keep and affirm their public authority, their legitimacy, and their reliability as a participant in democratic political life.

If the superiority of a given argument over the alternative ones is unquestionable in the eyes of the public, yet we refuse to admit it, we are likely to lose the public's trust. All the more so if we are invited to justify our position and have to resort to manipulative rhetorical devices that can easily be exposed as such by the parties concerned who have the right to take part in the debate (according to the criteria for public deliberation).

In a somewhat different context, Jon Elster (1998, 12) introduced a formula mentioned in the previous chapter of this book, which can also be used as a description of this type of motivation: the "civilizing force of hypocrisy." Naturally, here the question arises as to whether we are dealing with genuine participation in good faith or merely with an imitation of such. In discussing the differences between aggregation and transformation of preferences at the beginning of this chapter, we noted that a major flaw in the aggregative way of decision-making (through voting) is that there are always losers who very likely are not going to commit themselves morally to a decision that is not theirs, but which has been imposed on them. Even though they may formally consent to the will of the majority because of considerations such as those noted above, in all likelihood they will not contribute in good faith to the enactment of the decision in question. Is there a difference between this case and the one where someone joins a publicly-reached well-reasoned consensus only in order to avoid discrediting oneself in the public eye?

A number of authors who support this argument explain the "civilizing force of hypocrisy" to mean that it is very likely that someone who systematically participates in public deliberations in a correct manner, although originally guided by strategic (in the Habermasian sense), selfish motives, may, over time, sincerely come to embrace this correctness and transform her strategic attitudes into communicative ones:

> On this view public debate might generate psychological pressures toward "self-censorship." These pressures deter speakers from advancing claims that might be deemed "unreasonable" because they reflect a speaker's self-interest or because they articulate positions they suspect others consider morally objectionable. Such self-censorship expresses not so much genuine conviction as anticipation of disapproval or reproach. Yet, over time, something like dissonance reduction might induce such parties to actually adopt "reasonable" positions to which they earlier paid only lip service.
>
> (Johnson 1998, 171–172)

I will also cite another formulation, since in order to answer the question of whether this interpretation of the civilizing-force-of-hypocrisy argument is convincing enough, it is important that we know what conceptual assumptions it is founded upon.

> The second response is that in the long run a participant would be encouraged to mimic and perhaps ultimately to adopt the norms which guide deliberation. Since it is difficult to offer purely egoistic reasons for adopting a particular measure in a process of public discussion ("It's good for me" is unlikely to be a widely persuasive argument), she must frame them in the interest of all, and give reasons which all can appreciate. In this way, she must "launder" her egoistic preferences for public presentation. This in turn may carry with it a psychological corollary: lip service to the common good means that "one will in time be swayed by considerations about the common good."
>
> (Festenstein 2002, 97)

In my opinion, this understanding of the "civilizing force of hypocrisy" is not in the spirit of the theory of deliberative democracy. I have no objections against the historicism of this conception – namely, that the move from correct participation "out of necessity" to genuine correct participation in public deliberation cannot be done at once, by the "all or nothing" law. Indeed, it would be more realistic to expect that this is a process that has intermediate stages: nuanced states of the partially-this-partially-that type. But the reliance on psychological habituation to correctness conflicts with the rationalist-normativist spirit of the theory of deliberative democracy.

The possibility that ostensibly correct participation in public deliberation may be guided by hidden strategic motives indeed calls into question the model of deliberative democracy. However, I believe that the solution to this problem should be sought along the same lines as that of the very motive for demonstrating correctness, be it hypocritical or not. The desire to gain, maintain and continue to affirm public authority for ourselves does not have to "fade" over time. If our conduct is being watched by a critical public, it does not matter whether our motives are genuine or we are merely pretending. There would be a problem if we assume that the effect of the "civilizing hypocrisy" may be sporadic; that at a given moment we may pretend "for appearance's sake" that we are participating in decision-making in good faith, only to disregard, or even to obstruct, the agreed-upon decision when we are no longer being watched by anyone. However, in the theory of deliberative democracy there is no such assumption. On the contrary, it relies precisely on the constant, critical activity of the public.

Historicism plays a role here, too, but in a different way. A critical public sphere cannot be formed overnight; it is something that is developed over time. This is why the current existing models of deliberative democracy are far from the ideal of how the public sphere should function, and also why instances of "incorrect" decision-making through public deliberation are not infrequent. Later in this chapter I will refer to Habermas's reconstructive approach to the issue of the discrepancy between the ideal and the actual in this respect.

Concerning the said discrepancy, it should also be noted that the very core of the deliberative model – the motive to strive to meet the expectations of the public by respecting the arguments that it finds to be the most convincing – is bound to the procedures of classical representative democracy. Would one need public prestige and public trust if there were no elections or if power relations did not depend on the will of the majority? The proponents of the deliberative model themselves do not deny that at present it is a supplement to representative democracy:

> In other words, the deliberative democracy literature does not represent a direct refutation of the liberal democratic commitment to representative democracy. Rather it suggests that we could usefully supplement this practice with others, which encourage interactive debate and the transformation of preferences.
>
> (Squires 2002, 133)

Thus, in the final analysis, the "civilizing force of hypocrisy" turns out to be bound to the power mechanisms that do function in society. The most effective motive to safeguard and affirm the public legitimacy of our political conduct comes from our awareness that our "political fate" depends on the electorate. However, not all forms of public deliberation are directly related to the exercise of political power. The literature on this subject points out various patterns of the deliberation of publicly significant issues where certain procedural rules are observed in order to prevent the manipulation of public communication, which is necessary in order to reach legitimate decisions. Without claiming to be exhaustive, I will mention spontaneous grassroots networks, neighborhood councils, citizens' juries, consensus conferences (see Hendriks 2009, 173), deliberative opinion polls, focus groups (see Papadopoulos and Warin 2007, 445) and, of course, the multiple virtual discussion forums such as social networks and internet forums, as well as some forms of debates in the traditional print and broadcast media.

All these different forms of public deliberation can be classified into various typologies. One such option is to distinguish between experimental (for example, deliberative polls) and actual debates (see Papadopoulos and Warin 2007); another option is to distinguish between micro and macro public deliberations "which differ in terms of the scale and formality of deliberation" (Hendriks 2009, 175). Micro-discussions of this kind are well-structured in deliberative terms, deal with a specific issue, and the number of citizens participating in them is relatively small. Conversely, macro-discussions occur in a freer form, deal with larger-scale issues, and take place in the media, at forums organized by social movements, civil society associations and networks (see ibid.), on the internet, and so forth.

Abigail Williamson and Archon Fung divide public-deliberative forums into government venues for public deliberation (for example, New England town meetings, public hearings, citizen committees, collaborative forums, closed stakeholder processes, and neighborhood associations) and civic venues (conversation cafés, national issues forums, deliberative polling, and citizen juries) (see Williamson and Fung 2005, 2).

Another significant distinction is that between formal ("strong") and informal ("weak") publics, as proposed in Habermas's model of deliberative politics which "proceeds along two tracks" (Habermas 1996, 314). As noted in the previous chapter, this model provides for a sort of "division of labor," where the legitimate exercise of power requires two stages. At the first one, norms or policies are legitimized; at the second, binding decisions concerning their adoption or implementation are made within the institutions of political power. The link between these two stages is the exercise of what Jürgen Habermas terms "communicative power" through pressure from public opinion on the authorities and thanks to, as Jon Elster so eloquently puts it, the "civilizing force of hypocrisy":

> Communicative power is exercised in the manner of a siege. It influences the premises of judgment and decision making in the political system without intending to conquer the system itself. It thus aims to assert its imperatives in the only language the besieged fortress understands: it takes

responsibility for the pool of reasons that administrative power can handle instrumentally but cannot ignore, given its juridical structure.

(Habermas 1996, 486)

Let us return to the question of what motivates participants in public deliberation to recognize the force of the better argument – it would be strange if the participants' motives were the same in all patterns of this type of legitimizing communication. If we use Habermas's typology, in formal public deliberation at the level of a "strong" public the "civilizing force of hypocrisy" is unquestionably at work. However, it cannot be relied upon in informal deliberations in the public sphere. Yet it is precisely the legitimizing type of public deliberation that is important to this study.

What could make rank-and-file participants in a debate on a publicly significant issue admit the superiority of another's argument, which may not be in their own best interest, and which may require them, for example, to sacrifice something in the name of justice? Such ordinary citizens do not particularly need public prestige because they are unlikely to run in elections in the foreseeable future and do not particularly care what the other participants in the deliberation think about them. What could stop them, then, from denying the convincing force of an argument that they for some reason do not like, even though they cannot justify their position to the others?

Here I will venture to take a somewhat extreme position. In my opinion, unjustified refusals to recognize the validity of an argument should not be taken into account at all in informal legitimizing public deliberations. Such refusals can block only the "decision-making mode" type of deliberation (Ryfe 2005, 61), which occurs within the framework of "strong" publics. At the formal level, consensus is indeed a necessary condition for the legitimacy of decisions. But in informal legitimizing deliberations what is important is their effect on public opinion. A stubborn, unsubstantiated refusal to accept an obviously convincing argument should not be regarded by the public as compromising the consensus. Or, to put it in legal terms, such an unjustified refusal should be "null and void" for the public at large.

Some scholars of public deliberation have advanced such considerations, but in more general terms. Philippe Urfalino (2014, 321), for example, proposes a wider understanding of consensus, which he terms the "rule of non-opposition." According to this rule, if a proposal made in a debate is not contested, it should be considered as adopted by consensus. Meanwhile, Cristina Lafont takes a more articulate position on this subject. In her opinion, a participant in the deliberation who, for some reason, does not approve of the decision that is supported by the majority, still has a reasonable motive to accept it as legitimate if – and this is the crux of the idea – she judges that the argumentation of the proponents of the decision has been more cogent in the preceding discussion than the reasons presented against it. The participant might still think that the decision is not the best possible in the situation, or even that it is wrong. Nevertheless, if she is aware that for the time being she cannot prove this to the other participants, she must accept that the others are right to support it. Furthermore, such a "defeat" is not final. Every deliberative agreement is revisable, provided that ample argumentation for a revision is presented:

> Those participants in a process of deliberation that on a given occasion disagree with the agreement reached by the majority may still give their voluntary consent to it for the *deliberative* reason that their arguments failed to convince most members of the community that the decision is actually incorrect (unjust, inefficient, and so forth) and not only putatively so.
>
> (Lafont 2006, 20; emphasis in original)

We thus accept a decision that we consider to be incorrect, unjust, or ineffective not because we have agreed in advance that it should be reached by a majority vote, but because we accept that the better argument should always prevail. Consequently, if we are determined to overturn as soon as possible a decision that we view as "incorrect" because we believe that it is not in everyone's best interest, then we should concentrate our efforts not merely on winning more supporters for our cause. The danger in this course of action is that, on the one hand, the goal of winning more supporters can be achieved not only through deliberation, but also by using strategic and even immoral ways; on the other hand, this may even prove impossible to do if self-interests are involved. What we need to do, instead, is to put more effort into elaborating our argumentation, "enlightening" the "public," and so forth.

Our focus here is on the informal legitimizing deliberation taking place among a "weak" public within the framework of civil society. In my opinion, within the context of informal legitimizing deliberation, consensus should be viewed in a broader sense. The proof of the legitimacy of a decision is not necessarily in the fact that everyone affected agrees with it, as stated in most definitions of public deliberation, but, is rather in the absence of convincingly reasoned disagreement. In this case, the subjective willingness of the participants in the deliberation to recognize the superiority of the better argument does not matter. What matters is the ability of the public to evaluate the force of the articulated arguments themselves. If someone stubbornly insists that something that is seen by the public as white must be regarded as black, she will discredit herself in the public eye as someone whose theses are not worth consideration.

The model of deliberative politics which proceeds, in the words of Habermas, along two tracks, is very important to the concept of communicative empowerment of minorities that is advanced in this study. This model reveals and conceptualizes the possibilities for the exercise of "communicative power" by civil society. Those possibilities are not unproblematic, of course. But in my opinion, the main problem here does not have to do with the recognition of the force of the better argument, but with the readiness of the public to actually support deliberatively legitimized positions. Indeed, it is important that the public at large be capable of distinguishing between convincing and unconvincing arguments – in other words, the public's communicative competence matters. But an even more significant condition necessary for the exercise of communicative power is the mobilization of public opinion to exert pressure on the institutions of political power to make binding decisions regarding the introduction of regulations or the implementation of policies that have already been publicly legitimized.

Here I see a danger – and, to my mind, this is the most vulnerable point in the Habermasian model – of displays of "uncivilized hypocrisy," if we may thus paraphrase Jon Elster's popular formula. What I mean is that there exists the possibility that the public may generally recognize, or at least not contest, the legitimacy of a given claim, but may not take it to the next level and exert public pressure on the authorities to satisfy this claim. This possibility is very likely in the case of minority claims whose satisfaction requires certain sacrifices or efforts (for example, allocation of additional funds from the state budget) from society at large.

A leitmotif in the critiques of the concept of deliberative democracy (some of which have already been noted while others will be discussed below) is that it is not realistic and is merely wishful thinking. As one author puts it, many people think that public deliberation is "just talk" – that is, that "public deliberation generates acquiescence and/or skepticism rather than action" (Polletta 2008, 1; see also Cloud 1998; Tonn 2005). Admittedly, it is difficult to mobilize public opinion, particularly in support of minority claims. But the model of deliberative politics that is being discussed here is not utopian or counterfactual. It is a product, rather, of Habermas's reconstructive method and, in this sense, I see certain prospects for increasing the public's sensitivity to minority claims in a "well-ordered" society. I associate these prospects with the interest of the public in such a society to keep its self-awareness free from internal inconsistencies. If liberal-democratic self-awareness is burdened by discriminative attitudes, this undoubtedly undermines its self-consistency. Furthermore, the existence of or – in the worst case scenario – the intensification of internal conflicts in the self-awareness of a society endangers this society's integrity and, ultimately, its well-being. What more effective motive could there be for the public to respond positively to minority claims that have been publicly legitimized in a plausible way?

In addition to the above considerations, the specific characteristics of public opinion in Central and Eastern Europe also need to be addressed. Here, in this region, we often find displays of "civilizing hypocrisy" related to the processes of integration into the established democratic way of life of "the West." People in this part of the world are particularly sensitive to assessments of the political reality in their countries that come from "the outside" – that is, from the societies that still serve as role models in structuring public life – even though we are well aware that they themselves have problems. In this respect, it is justified to consider the question of legitimizing minority claims within the frame of reference of a transnational public sphere, which is already the subject of serious studies (e.g., Cammaerts and Audenhove 2005; Bohman 2007; Fraser 2007; Bee, Scartezzini, and Scott 2008).

Procedure as a safeguard against the manipulation of public communication

As repeatedly noted here, the legitimization of norms and social facts is viewed – within the framework of the model of the public sphere associated with the names of Kant and Habermas, above all – as the attainment of consensus on them, through "undistorted" public communication, by everyone affected. In public deliberation theory, the protection of communication against manipulation is achieved by applying a series of requirements to the process of mutual persuasion of the interlocutors. In the literature on the subject, this approach to legitimacy is characterized as proceduralist. A norm (or policy) is legitimate if it has been approved by everyone affected, according to the relevant procedure:

> Deliberative politics acquires its legitimating force from the discursive structure of an opinion- and will-formation that can fulfill its socially integrative function only because citizens expect its results to have a reasonable quality.
>
> (Habermas 1996, 304)

Of course, this is not the only way of attaining legitimacy. Max Weber, for example, famously identified three types of legitimate authority: rational-legal, traditional, and charismatic authority. In public deliberation theory, the substantivist approach to legitimacy is regarded as an alternative to the proceduralist one. A norm or social fact may be considered legitimate in the substantivist sense if the people affected accept it because it corresponds to their beliefs and their awareness of their interests. The main difference between the substantivist and the proceduralist approach to legitimacy is that the latter does not require such correspondence. It only requires that the people affected by the relevant norm (or social fact) reach agreement through undistorted communication. In this case, procedural correctness is the source of legitimacy in that it guarantees that the legitimizing communication has not been manipulated: "This deliberative model of democracy is proceduralist in that it emphasizes first and foremost certain institutional procedures and practices for attaining decisions on matters that would be binding on all" (Benhabib 1996, 73).

The proceduralist approach to legitimacy has at least one obvious advantage. It does not require that the subjects of legitimization in a given case have the same beliefs or interests: "members of a political community might agree on procedures, even where they disagree on matters of substantive value" (Gregg 2002, 742). A particular norm or social fact may be equally acceptable to the people affected by it even if they have very different beliefs and interests. A typical example of substantive legitimacy is the way members of a congregation regard the norms professed by their religion. An example of procedural legitimacy is that of a decision made through public deliberation by the residents of a town to oppose the construction of an industrial plant in the area. Their beliefs and interests regarding the construction project in question will most likely differ. But as a result of the deliberation, all of the residents have arrived at the conclusion that stopping it from going ahead would be in the best interest of everyone affected. The decisive factor for the legitimacy of the decision in this case is the guarantee – ensured by the observance of the relevant procedure – that the debate has not been manipulated.

The possibility to legitimize norms and social facts through procedurally correct public communication is valuable to liberal democratic societies above all because it is compatible with their pluralism. Citizens do not need to share the same religion or ideology in order to recognize the legitimacy of the laws and policies implemented by the authorities. The civic unity of society does not necessarily presuppose cultural and political consensus. Here, however, I will also examine another difference between the substantivist and the proceduralist approach to legitimacy which is relevant to the main task of this study – namely, finding possibilities for the communicative empowerment of minorities by promoting their capacities for the public legitimization of their claims.

In order to find a common language between the representatives of minority communities and the public at large – which is a necessary condition for mobilizing public opinion in support of minority claims – it is important to have ways to assess the latter's legitimacy from an external point of view, namely, from the positions of people who do not have to share the beliefs of the authors of those claims. If legitimacy is understood in substantivist terms, this is impossible. For example, how could we recognize the legitimacy of a claim made by the members of a religious minority calling for the introduction of the study of their faith for schoolchildren in their community if we think that the religion in question is a delusion and that it harms rather than helps people? Furthermore, how could we believe the statements of representatives of this minority that no matter how harmful their claim appears to be from an outsider's point of view, it is essential to the minority members as it brings meaning to their existence?

However, our position is bound to change significantly if the value of this religion to the members of the minority is justified through a procedurally correct discussion within their community. The correctness of the discussion should serve as a guarantee to the outsiders that the minority group's claim that their religion is important for their authentic human existence is genuine, and not the product of manipulation by their religious or political leaders. As for the procedural correctness itself, it is something we can evaluate, in the capacity of an external observer, without particular difficulty – for example, by applying the criteria for public deliberation.

Habermas's reasons for applying a proceduralist approach to the legitimacy of legal norms in *Between Facts and Norms* are by no means confined to the desire to combine the unity of public life with cultural and political pluralism. As we know, Habermas developed his conception of deliberative democracy by building upon discourse ethics – first elaborated by himself and Karl-Otto Apel – which, in turn, can be viewed as an attempt at dialogizing Kant's ethical formalism. In *Between Facts and Norms*, Habermas also attempts to go beyond the controversy between natural law and legal positivist interpretations of the legitimacy of legal norms. In this respect, it is particularly important to him to justify this legitimacy without recourse to metaphysical postulates, but also without taking extreme positivist positions. Habermas's proceduralism

> avoids metaphysics by not depending on rational intuitionism or natural rights, or any metaphysical or prepolitical account of the human subject, and yet it provides a normative basis for the justification of democratic constitutionalism that can withstand the withering scrutiny of objectivating approaches from the social sciences.
>
> (Hedrick 2010, 132–133)

In this regard, however, a number of authors have voiced serious doubts about the possibility of establishing the legitimacy of norms and social facts entirely on procedural grounds. Admittedly, it is tempting to accept a given norm or policy as legitimate solely because it has been approved by everyone affected following a discussion governed by rules which guarantee that there is no risk of manipulation. This understanding of legitimacy frees us from the need to require substantive consensus from the individuals or groups affected, as well as – if we view legitimacy not in descriptive but in normative terms – from the need to deal with the issue of whether or not we, ourselves, are capable of joining the substantive consensus in question.

However, it stands to reason that we should ask ourselves: isn't the general proceduralist criterion for legitimacy (at least as it is understood in this study) – that the agreement to the given norm or social fact on the part of those affected by it should be a result of reasonable and autonomous decisions – based on substantive grounds? Isn't this criterion the product of a modernist worldview that presupposes certain metaphysical assumptions? The same also holds true for the more specific standards for the procedural correctness of communication, such as the rationality and equality of the interlocutors. In the words of Joshua Cohen (see Cohen 1994, 591), we cannot view a fair procedure as a source of legitimacy without explaining what makes it fair, yet this will unavoidably engage us in substantive considerations. As other proponents of the substantive interpretation of proceduralism have noted, "No proceduralism can operate without introducing into itself at least a few, specific substantive norms" (Gregg 2002, 744), or "Procedural principles have substantive content, too" (Gutmann and Thompson 2004, 25). Even if the participants in a public deliberation do not bind the process of reaching a legitimate decision to substantive presuppositions, at the meta-level this seems unavoidable.

It is difficult to object to such critiques of the ideal of an absolutely proceduralist approach to legitimacy. Habermas himself proposes a more specific solution to this problem in the spirit of the reconstructivist methodology applied by him in *Between Facts and Norms*. He views the connection between undistorted communication and legitimacy as one that is necessarily founded on certain presuppositions which are related to communicative reason and make possible the linguistic forms of life, as well as, *eo ipso*, practices such as discourse and self-government (see Hedrick 2010, 129). "Whoever makes use of a natural language in order to come to an understanding with an addressee about something in the world is required to take a performative attitude and commit herself to certain presuppositions" (Habermas 1996, 4). It follows from this that those who do not agree with the proceduralist understanding of legitimacy do so not because they do not subscribe to the relevant modernist substantive presumptions but because they do not take into account some necessary presuppositions that make communication in public life possible.

Here, I will not address the issue of how convincing Habermas's response to the critiques against "pure" proceduralism is. In my opinion, what is more important in this case is that both the eminent German philosopher and his opponents situate the proceduralist approach to legitimacy in the context of a modernist worldview, thereby limiting – justifiably or not – its inclusivity in regard to cultural and political differences. More specifically, a number of publications on deliberative democracy and public deliberation give voice to apprehensions that, in their effort to safeguard legitimizing communication against manipulation, the "orthodox" proponents of this paradigm propose criteria for the procedural correctness of communication that would deprive broad circles of citizens of the possibility to publicly legitimize their claims. Moreover, this especially applies to members of minority groups and categories that are already disadvantaged in public life:

> In this way, taking deliberation as a signal of democratic practice paradoxically works undemocratically, discrediting on seemingly democratic grounds the views of those who are less likely to present their arguments in ways that we recognize as characteristically deliberative ... namely women; racial minorities, especially Blacks; and poorer people.
>
> (Sanders 1997, 349)

A number of authors concerned with gender and racial issues claim that such an approach is unjust with respect to communities and categories of people who are culturally predisposed to a type of communication that is more expressive, emotional, and rhetorical rather than dispassionate, impersonal, and argumentation based (see, for example, Young 1997; Williams 2000; Huspek 2007). As an alternative – or, rather, as a complement – to the deliberative form of legitimizing communication, Iris Marion Young, for example, has developed her own concept of inclusive political communication. In her book *Inclusion and Democracy*, she presents three modes of such communication: greeting, rhetoric, and narrative (see Young 2002, 53).

No one can deny that the predominant style of communication in many minority communities does not conform to the typical deliberative criteria. In this respect, I believe two issues need to be elucidated. One is that if we assume that public deliberation is an effective instrument for the protection of public communication from manipulation (and, consequently, as an important prerequisite for the public legitimization of norms and policies), this does not mean that we claim that there are no other ways to prevent abuse of the communicative power of civil society, provided that there is no room left for manipulation. For example, a passionate public speech by a charismatic minority leader who uses impressive rhetorical devices does not provide any guarantees in and of itself that its legitimizing messages are not meant to secure personal gains for the speaker, as well as, possibly, for his family and a group of close aides, rather than to help resolve the problems of the community.

The other issue is that we do not have to ascribe – in an essentialist manner – to various minorities any particular styles of communication as characteristic of all their members, and as predetermined and unchangeable. We should not underestimate the communicative diversity within minority communities, or the possibilities for change in the communicative competences of their members. In this spirit, Christian F. Rostbøll, in contrast to such scholars as Iris Marion Young, Melissa Williams, and Michael Huspek, regards the contingent character of the factors that in most cases shape the self-understanding of the members of cultural communities not as something to be reckoned with, but rather as a challenge. Rostbøll (2008, 156) observes that "Issues such as self-deception, adaptive preference formation, manipulation, ideological domination, and the like may all be contributing factors to the way in which people understand what is good for them." As a result, an important task of deliberative democrats is to encourage and provoke processes of self-reflection not only within, but also outside the public sphere (see ibid., 220).

These critiques against the public-deliberative approach to legitimization are made from positions that may be viewed as "internal" to the deliberative paradigm. Of course, critiques in this respect are also made "from the outside." I cannot examine them in detail here. I will only mention two of the most authoritative ones. One stems from the *agonistic* interpretation of the social role of conflict – that is, the understanding of public life as an arena of competition, an arena of contest that unavoidably entails conflict. From such a point of view, the consensual ideal of resolving social issues is not just unattainable and utopian; it is also misleading and steers political activities in a wrong, futile direction. More specifically, the agonistic model of public life is generally associated with the name of Hannah Arendt and her book *The Human Condition* (1958); currently, however, Chantal Mouffe's concept of agonistic pluralism is most commonly associated with this model:

> I contend that the belief in the possibility of a universal rational consensus has put democratic thinking on the wrong track. Instead of trying to design the institutions which, through supposedly "impartial" procedures, would reconcile all conflicting interests and values, the task for democratic theorists and politicians should be to envisage the creation of a vibrant "agonistic" public sphere of contestation where different hegemonic political projects can be confronted.
>
> (Mouffe 2005, 3)

The other critique which, I think, must be noted is directed against the argumentative element of the ideal of public deliberation. It comes from postmodernist positions or from positions related to postmodernism. It refers, above all, to the absolutization of "the unforced force of the better argument" – the assumption that an argument that is incontestable in a given situation must absolutely bind its addressees to agree with it and to transform their preferences accordingly.

Furthermore, in the spirit of this critique, if, for example, we look more carefully at the "intimate" mechanisms of argumentation, we will see that they are certainly not as independent from contingent factors as they are claimed to be by the proponents of rational communication as an exclusive means of public legitimization. According to one opinion that is characteristic of the postmodernist position, logic, itself, is nothing more than "the underlying assumptions, deeply held, often unexamined, which form a framework within which reasoning takes place" (Suddaby and Greenwood 2005, 37). Another author with similar views argues that "insofar as a theoretical representation is regarded as objectively true, it is viewed in that way because its methods of construction have become so familiar that they operate transparently" (Brown 1990, 188).

In other words, the argumentation of a given thesis which claims that it ensues from unquestionable facts in a perfectly logical manner, operates with presumptions and constructions that are in no way less dependent on contingent circumstances and private interests than any rhetorical attempt to influence the beliefs of a given interlocutor. Moreover, the defense of the position that rational communication should have a monopoly on public legitimization gives rise to suspicions that it aims at (or, at best, involuntarily contributes to) the domination of particular social circles over the public sphere.

What we have here is again a clash between two rival paradigms. I will not undertake to trace the course of this discussion, which is important and interesting in and of itself. I will only note that, in my opinion, it is not relevant to the role of public deliberation as a legitimizing factor in the two-track model of deliberative politics. The criteria for the procedural correctness of communication discussed here, which include rationality, are designed to minimize possible manipulation of legitimizing communication. In this sense, resorting to argumentation to convince the interlocutors simply enables them to compare the reasoned claim addressed to them with their beliefs and awareness of their interests, and to decide for themselves whether they have sufficient reasons to agree to the claim in question or not.

Here, the argument – however good as it may be – is not understood as a lever that automatically secures the agreement of its addressee by virtue of its cognitive merits, but as a form of communication that respects the autonomy of the interlocutor who is treated – in a communicative-modernist spirit – as an agent who is entitled to decide for herself whether, and how, to transform her preferences, beliefs, and/or awareness of her interests. In other words, the argument-based communication is regarded here as a form of communication that does not allow for someone to make the above-mentioned choices for someone else, only to then impose those choices on the latter by coercion, by virtue of an authority that deserves blind trust, or by the power of a charismatic speaker who has full command over their audience, and so forth.

References

Arendt, Hannah. *The Human Condition*, Chicago: The University of Chicago Press, 1958.

Bee, Cristiano, Riccardo Scartezzini, and Alan Scott. "The Development of a European Public Sphere: A Stalled Project?" *European Political Science* 7 (2008): 257–263.

Benhabib, Seyla. "Toward a Deliberative Model of Democratic Legitimacy." In *Democracy and Difference*, edited by Seyla Benhabib, 67–94. Princeton: Princeton University Press, 1996.

Bohman, James. *Public Deliberation: Pluralism, Complexity, and Democracy*. Cambridge, MA: MIT Press, 1996.

Bohman, James. *Democracy across Borders. From Démos to Démoi*, Cambridge, MA: The MIT Press, 2007.

Brown, Richard Harvey. "Rhetoric, Textuality, and the Postmodern Turn in Sociological Theory." *Sociological Theory* 8, no. 2 (1990): 188–197.

Cammaerts, Bart and Leo Van Audenhove, "Online Political Debate, Unbounded Citizenship, and the Problematic Nature of a Transnational Public Sphere." *Political Communication* 22, no. 2 (2005): 147–162.

Cloud, Dana L. *Control and Consolation in American Culture and Politics: The Rhetoric of Therapy.* Thousand Oaks, CA: SAGE, 1998.

Cohen, Joshua. "Deliberation and Democratic Legitimacy." In *The Good Polity: Normative Analysis of the State*, edited by Alan Hamlin and Philip Pettit, 17–34. New York: Basil Blackwell, 1989.

Cohen, Joshua. "Pluralism and Proceduralism." *Chicago-Kent Law Review* 69 (1994): 589–618.

Cohen, Joshua. "Procedure and Substance in Deliberative Democracy." In *Deliberative Democracy*, edited by James Bohman and William Rehg, 67–92. Cambridge, MA: The MIT Press, 1997.

Elster, Jon. "Introduction." In *Deliberative Democracy*, edited by Jon Elster, 1–18. Cambridge: Cambridge University Press, 1998.

Festenstein, Matthew. "Deliberation, Citizenship and Identity." In *Democracy as Public Deliberation*, edited by Maurizio Passerin d'Entrèves, 88–111. Manchester: Manchester University Press, 2002.

Fraser, Nancy. "Transnationalizing the Public Sphere. On the Legitimacy and Efficacy of Public Opinion in a Post-Westphalian World." *Theory, Culture & Society* 24, no. 4 (2007): 7–30.

Gregg, Benjamin. "Proceduralism Reconceived: Political Conflict Resolution under Conditions of Moral Pluralism." *Theory and Society* 31, no. 6 (2002): 741–776.

Gutmann, Amy and Dennis Thompson. *Why Deliberative Democracy?* Princeton: Princeton University Press, 2004.

Habermas, Jürgen. *Between Facts and Norms.* Cambridge MA: The MIT Press, 1996.

Hedrick, Todd. *Rawls and Habermas: Reason, Pluralism, and the Claims of Political Philosophy*. Stanford: Stanford University Press, 2010.

Hendriks, Carolyn M. "Deliberative Governance in the Context of Power." *Policy and Society* 28, no. 3 (2009): 173–184.

Huspek, Michael. "Normative Potentials of Rhetorical Action within Deliberative Democracies." *Communication Theory* 17 (2007): 356–366.

Johnson, James. "Arguing for Deliberation: Some Skeptical Considerations." In *Deliberative Democracy*, edited by Jon Elster, 161–184. Cambridge, UK: Cambridge University Press, 1998.

Lafont, Cristina. "Is the Ideal of a Deliberative Democracy Coherent?" In *Deliberative Democracy and its Discontents*, edited by José Luis Marti and Samantha Besson, 3–26. Burlington, VT: Ashgate, 2006

Mouffe, Chantal. *On the Political*. London and New York: Routledge, 2005.

O'Flynn, Ian. "Deliberative Democracy for a Great Society." *Political Studies Review* 13, no. 2 (2015): 207–216.

Papadopoulos, Yannis and Philippe Warin. "Are Innovative, Participatory and Deliberative Procedures in Policy Making Democratic and Effective?" *European Journal of Political Research* 46, no. 4 (2007): 445–472.

Polletta, Francesca. "Just Talk: Public Deliberation After *9/11*." *Journal of Public Deliberation* 4, no. 1 (2008): 1–14

Rostbøll, Christian. *Deliberative Freedom. Deliberative Democracy as Critical Theory*. Albany: State University of New York Press, 2008.

Ryfe, David M. "Does Deliberative Democracy Work?" *Annual Review of Political Science* 8 (2005): 49–71.

Sanders, Lynn M. "Against Deliberation." *Political Theory* 25 (1997): 347–376.

Squires, Judith. "Deliberation and Decision Making: Discontinuity in the Two-Track Model." In *Democracy as Public Deliberation*, edited by Maurizio Passerin d'Entrèves, 133–151. Manchester: Manchester University Press, 2002.

Suddaby, Roy and Royston Greenwood. "Rhetorical Strategies of Legitimacy." *Administrative Science Quarterly* 50, no. 1 (2005): 35–67.

Susskind, Lawrence. "Arguing, Bargaining and Getting Agreement." In *The Oxford Handbook of Public Policy*, edited by Michael Moran, Martin Rein, and Robert Goodin, 269–295. Oxford: Oxford University Press, 2006.

Tonn, Marie Boor. "Taking Conversation, Dialogue, and Therapy Public." *Rhetoric and Public Affairs* 8 (2005): 405–430.

Urfalino, Philippe. "The Rule of Non-Opposition: Opening Up Decision-Making by Consensus." *The Journal of Political Philosophy* 22, no. 3 (2014): 320–341.

Williams, Melissa. "The Uneasy Alliance of Group Representation and Deliberative Democracy." In *Citizenship in Diverse Societies*, edited by Will Kymlicka and Wayne Norman, 124–154. Oxford: Oxford University Press, 2000.

Williamson, Abigail and Archon Fung. *Mapping Public Deliberation. A Report for the William and Flora Hewlett Foundation*, Cambridge, MA: Taubman Center for State and Local Government, John F. Kennedy School of Government, Harvard University, 2005.

Young, Iris M. *Intersecting Voices: Dilemmas of Gender, Political Philosophy, and Policy*. Princeton: Princeton University Press, 1997.

Young, Iris M. *Inclusion and Democracy*. Oxford: Oxford University Press 2002.

6 The internet as a medium for public deliberation

How does "communicative power" work?

As I already noted, the concept of public legitimization of minority claims, proposed here, is based on the theory of communicative power as formulated by Jürgen Habermas. In works published after *Between Facts and Norms*, Habermas describes in more detail how he thinks civil society could "predetermine" public policies whose design and implementation are within the competence of the institutions of political power.

The influence that is exercised (or rather, that could be exercised under certain conditions) by public opinion on policy decisions originates as a public expression of opinions and ideas in all sorts of forms, or, in the words of Habermas (2006, 415), "wild flows of messages – news, reports, commentaries, talks, scenes and images, and shows and movies with an informative, polemical, educational, or entertaining content." The effect of these "wild flows of messages" on public opinion is shaped, weakened, or strengthened by "everyday talk in the informal settings or episodic publics of civil society" (ibid., 416) among friends, colleagues, or even with casual acquaintances. In the formation of public opinion on issues of common concern, though, an important role is also played by such influential "communicators" as journalists, politicians (insofar as they participate in public communication not from a position of power), lobbyists who represent interest groups, "advocates" of various causes, experts, "moral entrepreneurs," as well as authoritative and politically independent intellectuals who intervene in public discourse at crucial moments to defend the common interest (see ibid.). "These actors do not possess 'power', per se, but derive public influence from the 'social' and 'cultural capital' they have accumulated in terms of visibility, prominence, reputation, or moral status" (ibid., 418).

Of course, public opinion formed in the public sphere cannot, in itself, exercise "communicative power" with regard to the "strong public," that is, the institutions of political power which, in liberal democracies, have a monopoly on the creation and implementation of binding decisions. As noted in Chapter 4, according to Habermas's two-track model of deliberative politics, "communicative power" can be exercised only in a real representative democracy; or, in other words, only if the fate of political parties truly depends on the voters' will which, in turn, is influenced by public opinion:

> Actors of civil society articulate political interests and confront the state with demands arising from the life worlds of various groups. With the legal backing of voting rights, such demands can be strengthened by threatening to withdraw legitimation.
>
> (Habermas 2006, 417)

Up to this point, the account of Habermas's model that I have proposed is completely value-neutral. Certain citizens are persuaded, through public communication, that some norms and states of affairs are legitimate while others are not. The convictions that prevail among them form public opinion, which the power-holders reckon with in order to improve, not worsen, their performance in the next elections. Such an account does not deal with the question of which of these convictions are based on more or less true information and which ones correspond to the public interest, and which ones do not. Nor does it deal with the question of whether or not, in a particular case, "communicative power" works for the benefit of the public interest or of someone's private interest.

These are important questions, of course, and they are addressed by Habermas's model of deliberative politics, which also contains strong normative elements. As noted in Chapter 4, Habermas attaches great importance to the protection of public communication from manipulation, or, as he puts it, from "communication pathologies" (Habermas 2006, 416). The public sphere can facilitate the self-government of the citizenry in a modern society, but it can also obstruct it. That is why the German philosopher links his model to public deliberation as a methodology for discussing issues of common concern. He thinks it can "operate as a cleansing mechanism that filters out the 'muddy' elements from a discursively structured legitimation process" (ibid.).

The public sphere and the internet

Beginning in the 1990s, there began to appear publications dealing with the possibilities provided by the internet for exercising "communicative power" on the part of the citizenry. There were discussions, not only about the ways of conducting legitimizing public communication in a virtual format, but also about how to use the internet to activate civil society and to mobilize citizens to participate in the political process. There were great hopes that the new possibilities with which to exercise communicative influence on "the hearts and minds" of the public would lead to more effective forms of empowerment of the citizenry than those of traditional representative democracy (see, for example, Dahlgren 1991; Castells 1997; Alexander 1998; Hague and Loader 1999; Jordan 1999). These expectations were based on some of the characteristics of online public communication which made it more independent – as a factor dictating the behavior of citizens – from political power, from economic pressure, from institutional conditions, from the various formal and informal hierarchies existing in society, and so forth.

The possibility of communicating anonymously, that is, under a nickname or an assumed identity, was, and remains, of special interest in this respect. Anonymity allows participants in communication to express their opinions freely, or to disclose information that influential individuals or institutions want to keep secret from the public, without fear of sanctions – formal or informal (such as, for example, ridicule or ruining relationships that matter to the participant). In the early days of the Internet, it was generally assumed that anonymity would encourage:

> the contribution of ideas from those whose views were not being heard in the decision-making process and thereby increase the number of comments received, expand the range of constituencies that were heard, and broaden the topics on which respondents commented and, in addition, encourage greater and more truthful disclosures.
>
> (Haines et al. 2014, 766)

Of course, the authors who argue that anonymity can play a role in increasing "civic agency" (for example, Dahlgren 2012), also discuss the risks it poses for the quality of public communication. I will examine these risks later in this chapter. However, first I will take a look at some of the most widely discussed advantages of online communication in terms of empowering the citizenry.

One of them, and perhaps the most obvious, is that online communication vastly increases the political significance of "horizontal" social interactions, that is, of those conducted within the framework of civil society:

> An important attribute of the net (broadly understood) is its capacity to facilitate horizontal, or civic communication: people and organizations can link up with each other for purposes of sharing information, providing mutual support, organizing, mobilizing, or solidifying collective identities.
>
> (Dahlgren 2012, 30)

In addition, online participation is largely independent of the institutions of political power. There is no need to resort to any means of coercion to influence the hearts and minds of people on the internet. Moreover, the internet enables even single individuals to exert substantial influence on the public, and it therefore often plays an alternative and competitive role to the traditional media, which is controlled by interests wielding large amounts of political and economic power. A fact not to be ignored is that participants in the virtual public sphere are protected from possible sanctions on the part of the powers that be (mostly because of the possibility to hide the real identity of the writer on the internet). Furthermore, such contributions are independent of the sovereignty of the state in which they take place because of the wide freedom of virtual communication across national borders (see Farrell 2012).

Facebook and other social networks are not organized in hierarchical structures. Not only are they not governed by any external institutions of power, they also do not have any internal governing bodies. That is why virtual networks are flexible and easily adaptable to actual situations, as well as resistant to encroachment. If a political party or economic entity attempts to seize control of a part of the network in order to use it for its own purposes – as is sometimes the case with traditional print or broadcast media – it is bound to fail. Even if malicious participants (for example, trolls paid by a political party or company offering trolling services) were to join in the "game," they would not be able to take over a significant part of the network. Other participants can always intervene in the communication and thwart the organizers' plans. Such actions can, at worst, "muddy" online public communication, but they cannot bend it to someone's will.

Scholars share a unanimous opinion in that the internet offers possibilities for the emancipation of ordinary citizens from institutions and other "hard" social structures:

> The "many-to-many" nature of the Internet enables large numbers of people to circumvent costly, constricted, controlled corporate-owned media. This is highly conducive to decentralized, democratic participation.
>
> (Langman 2005, 55)

In this regard, Manuel Castells (2009, 4) has introduced the term "mass self-communication" to describe the transformation of users into "both senders and receivers of messages," which makes them less dependent on communications corporations. The internet has also made it possible to break through the hierarchies of institutions without investing substantial material resources. To draw public attention to some flaws in the operation of a local government, for instance, we no longer have to go door to door to get residents to attend a protest meeting and to rent a hall for the purpose. As Henry Farrell (2012, 37) writes, "this dramatic increase in ease of access would lead to the unseating of traditional elites and the democratization of public debate."

The rise of online communication has also cast new light on the issue of cultural hegemony, thematized by Antonio Gramsci (mentioned in Chapter 4). Specifically, the practice whereby a dominant class presents a particular worldview, which suits it best, in such a convincing way – thanks to its capacity to control the relevant discourse because of its dominant economic, as well as political position – that it is accepted by everyone, including the exploited class, as "common sense," and as the only possible way to view things. This makes the emancipation of oppressed classes impossible. However, the practically unlimited access to public communication provided by the internet allows the formation of alternative publics, including the so-called "counterpublics," which can promote their discourse in a much more convincing way than through traditional media. They no longer need the approval of the latter's management in order to make themselves heard, nor do they need substantial material resources to launch their own newspapers or broadcasting networks that can compete with the existing ones in terms of prestige or influence.

The internet contributes to the democratization of public communication in another aspect, too. It facilitates the access of marginalized groups to public communication. Although there are also certain limits in this respect, which are referred to in specialized literature by the term "digital divide" and which will be discussed in more detail later, the possibilities of people with low incomes and without much influence in society to impact the course of public debates are incomparably greater than they were before the rise of Internet communication. In this regard, scholars dealing with these issues have expressed great hope that "Internet communication might include multiple actors, especially those from civil society who, with comparatively few resources, may not have had (as much) access to the old media" (Gerhards and Schäfer 2010, 145; see also Dahlgren 2012, 33).

An interesting new phenomenon related to online communication has also been noted. The boundaries between private life and public communication have become "porous." A Facebook profile or a blog, for instance, belong both to their author's private sphere and to the public sphere. Individuals make public their intimate reflections and descriptions of intimate experiences, often intentionally seeking a public effect, at that. In this way, many people have become able to influence public communication without having a high social status or substantial material resources. "Highly porous boundaries are exemplified by a public sphere that is easily penetrated, especially by disadvantaged members of society (in terms, perhaps, of SES [socioeconomic status]), or by people who are otherwise less politically engaged" (Brundidge 2010, 1057).

The relativization of the difference between public and private communication on the internet is also important in regard to a very popular conception of the mechanisms of influencing the views of citizens. I am referring to the so-called "two-step flow theory of mass communication," developed by Elihu Katz and Paul Lazarsfeld (1955) in the late 1940s. According to this theory, mass media does not directly form the opinions of citizens on political issues. Its influence is mediated by "opinion leaders," that is, by people from the informal milieu of the addressees of political messages – some of their friends, relatives, colleagues – whom they personally trust. Ultimately, opinions are formed and affirmed in informal conversations. It is precisely these types of, so to speak, private-public discussions that are freely – and widely – conducted on the internet; furthermore, if we believe in this theory or in its successors represented by more recent concepts of multi-step flow models of mass communication (Straubhaar, LaRose, and Davenport 2013), then these types of private-public discussions ought to be especially effective in forming public opinion.

Online public communication is also more inclusive in terms of the topics of discussion. On the internet, attention can be drawn to issues which, for various reasons, have not been "in the spotlight" so far: perhaps they were not sufficiently attractive to the traditional media, or would discredit influential individuals, or simply the public did not realize that they were important. But as practice shows, in some cases it takes just a single individual to "blow the whistle" and alert the public, thus focusing its attention on the relevant issue.

In this regard, it is noteworthy that access to information through the internet is much easier than through print or broadcast media. Most of the information on the web is accessible to everyone and easy to find online. Information can also be generated by the participants in virtual communication. What is most important, however, is that the information available to users online is much more difficult to "filter," control and regulate than that in the traditional media. The best known example of this is WikiLeaks. Generally, "it is expected that alternative evaluations and interpretations will be presented online, and that the information available will be more differentiated on the Internet" (Gerhards and Schäfer 2010, 145).

Another widely discussed characteristic of internet communication is that it creates a peculiar type of "soft" or "weak" social ties. The virtual communities formed around shared interests, initiatives or causes are not characterized by stable, hierarchical organization. They do not require any discipline from participants. Participation in such communities is not seen as binding. Despite this, however, they are capable of very effective political mobilization. The factor that makes up for the lack of systemic organization and discipline is the ease of coordination on the web. For example, looser groups can organize the activities of their members via a form of coordination which is called "shared awareness": "the ability of each member of a group to not only understand the situation at hand but also understand that everyone else does, too" (Shirky 2011, 35).

It is widely assumed that civic movements such as those that led to the so-called Arab Spring or Occupy Wall Street would have been impossible without social networks (see, for example, Farrell 2012, 39). The formation of such loosely coordinated virtual groups also enables political agendas to be created at the grass-roots level, regardless of geographical distance and national or cultural boundaries at that. A telling example in this regard is the Anti-Globalization Movement (see Wall 2005).

* * *

The possibilities for using online communication to empower the citizenry have been the subject of a growing number of publications in recent years. Optimistic views, some of which are discussed above, prevail. Of course, there are also skeptical opinions. Here I will outline some of the main "sobering" arguments.

One of the obvious drawbacks of internet communication is that it has replaced some forms of domination in society with others. The critics do not deny that it has helped to weaken traditional hierarchical relations, but point out that they have been supplanted by others, leading to the so-called "digital divide." The internet has produced new inequalities. The members of society who can make full use of online communication prove to be in a sort of privileged position compared with those who, for various reasons, cannot. One of those reasons is poverty – even in the so-called Western societies there are still many people who cannot afford to buy a computer and/or to pay for internet access. Another reason is educational "deficiencies." To use the internet, one must be at least computer-literate. People who can barely write their name cannot take full advantage of online communication. Motivation for using the internet also matters. If you live in a ghetto-like minority neighborhood, for example, communicating on the web is unlikely to be within your cultural horizon. Thus, the development of online culture creates new elites and, hence, new hierarchies in society, and the longer-term consequences of this development are hard to predict (see McChesney 2013; Andreasson 2015).

Criticism is also leveled at another characteristic of online communication, which is generally seen as one of its advantages – namely, that it enables large-scale political mobilization of the citizenry, without any hierarchical organization. It is a fact that the internet can be used to disseminate petitions, to raise funds for humane causes, as well as to organize mass street protests. But if it turns out that political change requires taking more serious risks than, say, spending a night in police custody, then this type of civic activism proves to be insufficient. According to the critics, online communication cannot achieve significant political effects. In this regard, a new term has been coined – "slacktivism" – to refer to civic initiatives "whereby casual participants seek social change through low-cost activities" (Shirky 2011, 41).

Open access to online communication was discussed above as one of its advantages. But it has a downside, too. The fact that all sorts of people – with different levels of competence, different motives for participating in an online discussion, or even different degrees of civility – can express their opinions in the virtual public sphere, makes debates not just more inclusive and therefore more public, but also more vulnerable to "muddying" by incompetent, irresponsible, or even malicious intervention. Although it is true that most forms of online communication include tools for filtering out extremely offensive content, the overall picture remains problematic.

According to some authors (see, for example, Dean 2003), the virtual public sphere is bound to be regularly "contaminated" by destructive participation because it allows people to get involved in online discussions anonymously. Anonymity protects them from persecution for expressing their opinions, but it also allows them to behave irresponsibly. One of the most characteristic examples in this respect are the so-called "haters." Hiding under a nickname, participants in internet discussions can attack their opponents with offensive or even obscene language, trying to win the argument by discrediting their "victims" in the eyes of the public, by driving them to withdraw from the debate (no one likes to be insulted, especially if they are participating under their real name), or by provoking them to "respond in kind," that is, to resort to the same indecent, aggressive language. In all cases, however, such "victories" are "Pyrrhic" because they make the whole discussion unconvincing and undermine its ability to legitimize or delegitimize anything. In fact, online hating is more an expression of inferiority complexes than a consciously applied rhetorical tactic. As a social phenomenon, it is the subject of serious research (see, for example,

Strangelove 2010), but in all cases it is an activity that is harmful to the virtual public sphere.

In the literature on the subject, concerns have also been expressed that online public communication weakens social cohesion because the individuals participating in it are much less exposed to the uniforming influence of mass media and consume mostly personalized information. Although it is a positive that the internet makes it difficult for influential political and economic forces to control public opinion, it is also true that the internet threatens the public peace by increasing political polarization and strengthening extremism (Farrell 2012). It is a fact that mass brainwashing leads to the depersonalization of participants in public life and, to some extent, makes them subject to the control of institutions, corporations, and so forth. But, on the other hand, the mass media in democratic countries generally contributes to maintaining a social homeostasis, whereas internet communication creates more opportunities for individuals and small groups to exert significant influence on the public sphere, thus increasing the risk of social and political disruption.

Another serious drawback of internet communication, in its capacity as a mechanism for generating legitimacy, is that it is vulnerable to "trolling." In the literature, there are quite a few different definitions of this phenomenon (see Bishop 2013; Phillips 2015), some of which overlap with the definition of "hating." Generally, "trolling" is regarded as an activity that disrupts online discussions. Such an effect can also be produced unintentionally. Participants in a debate can be disruptive by obsessively defending – albeit in good faith – their opinions on the topic under discussion simply because they are deeply deluded and are not used to admitting that they may be wrong. But what is more dangerous for the quality of the virtual public sphere is its deliberate subversion or manipulation with the aim of "distorting" the picture created by the online discussion of a particular topic. In the most outrageous case, morally speaking, such abuses of the freedom and openness of the virtual public sphere are committed for political purposes – to embarrass a political opponent, to simulate public support for a given policy or practice, or, in a word, to *manipulate* public opinion. The paid services of companies specializing in such morally objectionable activities are used quite often in such cases.

As we can see, internet communication is far from the normative ideal envisaged in Jürgen Habermas's model of "communicative power." The internet is already an arena of all sorts of manipulation of public communication. Let me remind the reader that by "manipulation of communication" I mean changing someone's convictions in a way that is contrary to their own nature. In other words, the outcome is a change in people's convictions that they did not consciously make themselves through a rational decision, "in full awareness" of what they were doing. This understanding of manipulation is in tune with the modernist ideal of agency that underlies the model of the so-called "critical public sphere."

I believe it is in order here to return to the leitmotif of Jürgen Habermas's normative model of the public sphere – namely, binding the legitimizing capacity of public communication (and, respectively, the capacity of civil society to exercise communicative power with regard to the institutions of political power) to the protection of public communication from manipulation. Such protection is of paramount importance, as evidenced by practice, which has proven the falsity of the hopes of a number of theorists that the public sphere offers a large variety of possibilities for true, rather than fictitious legitimization of norms and social facts, which include patterns of legitimization that do not meet the admittedly rather demanding criteria for non-manipulation based on the Habermasian model. Recently, such hopes have been pinned on the development of various patterns of public legitimization in some Muslim societies, which certain authors attest to the formation of an Islamic public sphere and which attracted media and scholarly interest mainly in connection with the so-called "Arab Spring":

> Such a movement, though costing a certain loss in terms of the kind of political subjectivity that was typical of earlier uprisings of the modern and contemporary eras, seems to fulfill in unexpected ways the promises of the Habermasian theory of the public sphere, while also deeply unsettling its rigidly formal presuppositions. It did so, indeed, while being oriented to culturally specific views of the social body and of the common good that are largely ignored, or bracketed out, by Habermas and Habermasians.
>
> (Salvatore 2013, 225; see also el-Nawawy and Khamis 2010;
> Salvatore 2010)

However, as shown by the development of the events after the "Arab Spring," as well as by the boom in Islamic politico-religious online communication in the past few years (for example, here is a – by no means exhaustive – list only of some current websites where one can get a fatwa about every issue that one may be interested in: Ask Imam.com, Ask Imam.org, IslamOnline.com, Islam Question&Answer, FatwaIslam.com, Fatwa-online.com, Islamic-Fatwa.com, and SunniPath.com), the free sharing of opinions and views online can easily degenerate into indiscriminate indoctrination. This makes it even more important to apply the methodology of public deliberation to the internet, however demanding its criteria for procedural correctness of communication may appear to be, especially against the background of the prevailing spontaneity of expression of opinions online.

That being said, I would like to reiterate once again that the protection of public communication from manipulation, which is the purpose of the restrictive criteria applied in public deliberation, is justified only with regard to the legitimizing functions of public communication. Considering that public debates can serve a myriad of functions other than to legitimize communication, there is no reason to insist that the restrictions proposed by Habermas be imposed when public debates function in a capacity other than as a legitimizing tool, especially when they take place on the internet. In this sense, the reservations of some authors, such as the above-quoted Armando Salvatore, regarding the Habermasian "rigidly formal presuppositions," seem to me to be a moot point.

Public deliberation and the internet

Present-day forms of online communication are characterized by great diversity. The attempts to create sustainable platforms for public deliberation on issues of common concern for larger or smaller publics occupy a relatively modest place in this overpopulated "space." Still, the number of such sustainable platforms is not insignificant and has been growing in recent years; some of these platforms have even attracted considerable public attention. In the introduction to a book published in 2009, Todd Davies (2009, 5) provides the following examples from North America:

> the Deliberative Democracy Consortium and its online working group (the ODDC), the National Coalition on Dialogue and Deliberation (NCDD), the Canadian Community for Dialogue and Deliberation (C2D2), the International Association for Public Participation (IAP2), the Online Community Research Network (OCRN), and various initiatives associated with e-democracy pioneer Steven Clift (Publicus.net).

Referring to Europe, Davies (2009, 5–6) points out initiatives such as:

> the Towards Electronic Democracy (TED) program of the European Science Foundation, the Council of Europe's Ad-hoc Committee on E-Democracy (CAHDE), DEMO-net – the eParticipation Network of Excellence (funded by the European Commission), the eParticipation Trans-European Network for Democratic Renewal & Citizen Engagement (funded by eTEN), and the recently formed Pan-European e-Participation Network (PEP-NET).

Various publications discuss the experiences associated with the operation of public deliberation platforms, such as CODEPINK, which have a pacifist and feminist orientation (Simone 2006), PICOLA – Public Informed Citizen Online Assembly (Cavalier, Kim, and Zaiss 2009), Deme (Davies et al. 2009), E-Liberate (Schuler 2009), and YourView (van Gelder 2012) – this is by no means an exhaustive review of online public deliberation practices. There are also attempts being made to classify the types of online deliberation. One such classification was proposed by Seeta Peña Gangadharan (2009). Some forms of online deliberation are organized by the institutions of political power themselves (governmental agencies, municipalities) for the purpose of informing the citizens about issues of public interest. These are platforms such as online town halls and community computer networks (see Gangadharan 2009, 338). Another type of virtual public communication is represented by the various civic online discussion forums, which are managed mainly by nongovernmental organizations. A third type, according to Gangadharan, is related to the so-called online news media, that is, virtual spaces where users comment on news in various forms. Gangadharan identifies as a fourth type of online public deliberation the public-private sphere formed by social networking sites such as Facebook and

YouTube: "these virtual spaces contain design features that facilitate deliberative activity and that transform a virtual private sphere into a public square" (ibid.). Finally, the author classifies the freer forms of debate on issues of common concern, such as chatrooms and other forums, as a separate type of communication, and defines them as "*general purpose* online deliberation" (ibid.; emphasis in original).

Many publications are devoted to discussing the advantages and disadvantages of the internet in its capacity to serve as a medium for public deliberation. Without claiming to be exhaustive, I will mention some of these advantages and disadvantages, beginning with the characteristics of online communication that have given rise to optimistic expectations. An article by a group of authors (Davies et al. 2009), entitled "An Online Environment for Democratic Deliberation: Motivations, Principles, and Design," lists several parameters of this type of communication that facilitate collective debates. It points out that conducting public communication online eliminates those organizational difficulties that would have otherwise reduced the effectiveness of face-to-face deliberation. The first of these difficulties is ensuring the physical attendance of the representatives of all stakeholders at meetings, which often proves to be impossible because of various obligations or engagements of the participants and makes the results of the face-to-face debate insufficiently representative. There are no such difficulties in online deliberation. The latter also ensures an adequate frequency of discussions on a particular issue, as well as good communication between the discussion "sessions" (see Davies et al. 2009, 278).

In online debates, it is easy to access and contribute information. As this is more difficult in face-to-face meetings, some participants may find themselves in a disadvantaged position or the debate itself may take a wrong turn. Besides, when the issue discussed is of great complexity and there is a large number of participants who have to split into groups in order to discuss all aspects of the issue, then the online format makes coordination easier. Record-keeping and access to records of previous debates is also much easier in online deliberation. Furthermore, online debates allow greater transparency. If deemed necessary, they can be streamed live or uploaded to be made available to everyone with internet access, thus becoming truly public (see Davies et al. 2009, 279).

The possibility to participate anonymously in any kind of virtual public communication was discussed above as a factor contributing to the freedom of expression and equality in such interactions. Anonymity in online public deliberation, in particular, can be even more productive:

> The quasi-anonymity and text-based nature of electronic group discussion, for instance, might actually reduce patterns of social dominance. Studies demonstrate that online discussions are generally much more egalitarian than face-to-face encounters, with reduced patterns of individual dominance and increased contributions by low-status participants.
>
> (Price 2009, 42)

Anonymity clears the way, so to speak, for the manifestation of the superiority of the better argument, which is the main condition for non-manipulated legitimization through public deliberation.

Comparative studies of the way disagreement is expressed and perceived in online and face-to-face deliberation have yielded interesting results. Some respondents have pointed out that they are more prepared to express disagreement with their opponents in discussions over the internet, "because it felt to them more comfortable and less dangerous" (Price 2009, 43). If the discussion is conducted anonymously, we would expect that participants would be more frank and outspoken (see Christopherson 2007). Some studies have shown, however, that disagreement is actually expressed less frequently and more cautiously in an online environment than in face-to-face discussions. The proposed hypothesis is that the insufficient coherence in online communication "seemed to make it more difficult for participants to sustain disagreements" (Stromer-Galley, Bryant, and Bimber 2015, 15). Of course, in making general conclusions on such important issues one must also bear in mind how the real-life organizational and social-psychological settings in which the respective experiment or survey was conducted may affect online deliberation.

In addition to the opportunity to participate anonymously in virtual public deliberation, a number of other parameters of online debates which attest to the deliberative quality of communication are discussed in the literature. In his study entitled *Promises and Limits of Web-deliberation,* Raphaël Kies (2010), examines some characteristics of online debates, such as reciprocity, plurality, empathy, reflexivity, and justification. These characteristics are not specific to this type of deliberation, but its online format allows them to be "measured." The degree of *reciprocity*, for instance, can be measured by "the proportion of posts that are part of a thread versus the ones that initiate a thread" (Kies 2010, 99), that is, by the readiness of the participants to join in a discussion initiated by others. Reciprocity can also be measured by assessing "the extent to which a post takes into consideration arguments and opinions of a preceding posting" (ibid.). The degree of plurality is measured by studying the diversity in the content of the expressed opinions, the range of the topics under discussion, and the sociodemographic profiles of the users (ibid.). The degree of empathy is measured by the ratio between the messages that were insulting, ridiculing or injurious, on the one hand, and those that were respectful, as well as those "… that revealed concerns for the opinions and needs of fellow citizens" (Kies 2010, 100), on the other. The degree of reflexivity is assessed on the basis of the extent to which online debates have influenced the initial opinions of their participants (ibid.), and so forth.

As the above-quoted publications show, conducting public deliberation online helps eliminate a number of possibilities for the manipulation of this type of public communication. However, some doubts about the quality of online deliberation itself, as a means of exercising communicative power by the citizenry, have also been expressed, and in a fairly convincing manner, at that.

A number of these doubts concern the possibilities of making binding decisions through online public deliberation. Jürgen Habermas (2014) himself, in a relatively recent interview, pointed out that "What these communicative spaces (closed in themselves) are lacking is an inclusive bind, the inclusive force of a public sphere highlighting what things are actually important." Another author who has contributed to the promotion of the public deliberation paradigm, Seyla Benhabib (2008), also in an interview, criticized the idea of "Internet democracy" because it "confuses information and exchange of views with action commitments that need to be made over a long period of time."[1] I will not discuss these concerns here as this study deals mainly with the possibilities for using public communication to legitimize norms and social facts (which of course is quite different from "just talk," see above).

According to some authors, conducting public deliberation online has not only positive but also negative effects on its legitimizing capacity. As such debates are conducted in an unstructured environment, without the help of a facilitator, their quality is questionable:

> It is unrealistic to assume that online users in a self-managed environment will sufficiently understand and appreciate the inherent value of deliberation to sustain their involvement in resolving tough issues through respectful discourse, often with unlike-minded others.
>
> (Hartz-Karp and Sullivan 2014, 1)

Nor are there any guarantees for the representativeness of a debate that is open for participation to everyone where the participants are not selected on the basis of specific criteria by organizers who are responsible for the debate's correctness. "Finally, unlike the careful elicitation of representative participation in face-to-face deliberation, online deliberation has a self-selection bias" (Hartz-Karp and Sullivan 2014, 2). These risks can be avoided only by online deliberation platforms that are used by "long-term communities of interest, devoted to specific topics" (ibid.).

Another concern about conducting public deliberation online in a virtual environment is about the effect this could have on the public. Since a well-informed public has a good understanding of how this method of legitimizing norms and social facts works, it should have no reason to distrust messages that meet its criteria for credibility and fairness – especially if the discussions producing such messages are open. If everyone can ask for or provide further information that sheds new light on the topic under discussion, question some of the arguments of other participants, and so forth, the internet seems to be a particularly favorable environment for conducting public deliberation. However, some characteristics of online communication that conflict with this ideal model have also been pointed out. According to Azi Lev-On and Bernard Manin (2009, 118), "for users highly committed to a given cause, the Internet offers the opportunity to build their own effective echo chamber, therefore not enhancing, and even possibly impairing, their deliberative capabilities." For his part, Matthew Hindman fervently questions the widespread view that the Internet democratizes public communication. In his study entitled *The Myth of Digital Democracy*

(2009), he focuses on the difference between who speaks and who gets heard in cyberspace: "On the Internet the link between the two is weaker than it is in almost any other area of political life" (Hindman 2009, 17). The fact that everyone can express an opinion on any issue on the internet certainly does not mean that this opinion will be heard by the public and will have any real effect on it. Or, as Hindman (2009, 17) puts it, "online speech follows winner-take-all patterns."

Even more serious concerns about the quality of online deliberation have been voiced by Cass Sunstein. In his book entitled *Republic.com*, Sunstein (2001) claims that the internet is conducive to "enclave" communication between like-minded people, thereby leading to greater polarization and hardening of attitudes and ultimately hindering rather than facilitating the achievement of reasonable consensus on the debated issues. I will return in more detail to the issue of "enclave deliberation" in the final chapter of this book.

The contradictory assessments of the capacities of the internet as a medium for conducting public deliberation make the issue of the design of platforms for online debate all the more important. In the rest of this chapter, I will discuss some attempts to design websites that seek to take full advantage of the freedom, democratic nature and inclusivity of online communication while minimizing the possibilities to abuse anonymity. I will focus on projects that give priority to the argumentativeness of debates. As noted above, recognizing the superiority of the better argument largely has the same effect as the application of a number of other criteria for safeguarding public communication against manipulation (see, for example, Chapter 4). If a debate has been resolved by force of the better argument, this means that no coercion was involved and that someone's authority, charisma, or rhetorical skills have not influenced the outcome.

Here I will follow the anthropological approach to argumentation. As is well-known, this approach binds the power of arguments to their consistency with the audience's frame of reference:

> certain arguments have the force to persuade an audience as due to the beliefs that specific audience has – in other words, by referring to the general *epistemic background* in its widest sense that the target audience is considered to share with the arguer.
>
> (Van Eemeren and Grootendorst 2004, 15; emphasis in original)

Linking the power of arguments to the beliefs of their addressees, which is characteristic of the anthropological approach, is consistent with a significant trait of the model of the public sphere used here – namely, the fragmentation of the public sphere into separate publics. Furthermore, this approach is also consistent with the modernist normative understanding of legitimization that I follow here, according to which people should not be led to agree with norms or social facts that conflict with their beliefs or with their awareness of their own interests, as this would mean that they would not be making these types of important decisions independently, that is, by exercising their agency (see Chapter 4).

Even if someone is using arguments to motivate one's audience to change its initial beliefs, this should be done by revealing the inconsistencies in the very system of those beliefs, or between them and facts which the addressees of the arguments themselves recognize as existing. In other words, from a modernist perspective, such an exogenous change in someone's beliefs should take the form of a development characterized by continuity between the old and the new state of affairs, not of the destruction of one system of beliefs and its substitution by another. The latter case would involve coercion or manipulation – two phenomena that are common in real public life, the fight against them being a priority of morally oriented theories of public legitimization such as the public sphere model associated with the philosophy of Jürgen Habermas.

I will now briefly present several platforms for online public deliberation whose design provides for special "mechanisms" to safeguard the deliberative quality of online communication, especially by giving priority to persuasion through arguments. I will begin with PICOLA (Public Informed Citizen Online Assembly), a project developed at Carnegie Mellon's Center for the Advancement of Applied Ethics and Political Philosophy (see Cavalier, Kim, and Zaiss 2009, 73). According to Cavalier et al. (ibid.), "PICOLA delivered a multimedia environment designed for enabling online structured dialogue." The platform allows users to participate in debates at three levels. At the education phase, they can learn about the issue at hand in an online reading room with customizable content. The discussion phase is where the actual debate takes place, with the possibility to present questions to an expert panel. At the highest level, the reflection phase, "participants can think about the issues further, continue discussions in the asynchronous forum, and take a survey to express their opinions on the topic" (see ibid., 74–75).

In an article in the *Journal of Public Deliberation*, Tim van Gelder (2012) presents an Internet platform called YourView, designed by him. According to van Gelder (2012, 1), its main task is "to 'cultivate' better deliberation." This should be done by "providing an opportunity for citizens to easily access key arguments on major issues, take a stand on those issues, and help shape the 'collective wisdom' – the considered collective view" (ibid.). More specifically, this is done by allowing users to "vote" for one position or another on the public issue under discussion and present arguments for their vote. The platform thus "provides succinct distillations of key arguments pro and con on each issue, so anyone can easily ascertain what those arguments are" (ibid., 6). An important tool designed to make the platform more attractive is its system for evaluating the credibility of participants. This evaluation depends on their actions in the forum and the responses of the other participants:

> achieving higher and higher credibility scores in a challenging environment is intrinsically rewarding. Further, credibility scores appear alongside participants' usernames, so credibility is highly visible.

> (Van Gelder 2012, 8)

In this regard, I believe we should also consider the question of the "attractiveness" of such forms of public deliberation on issues of common/general interest. Practice shows that strictly argumentative discussions are not particularly popular among web users. This is also one of the reasons for skepticism about the ability of the internet to serve as a medium for public deliberation. As Hartz-Karp and Sullivan (2014, 1) point out: "Moreover, the culture of the open web is aimed at instant gratification, antithetical to the goals and processes of public deliberation." To my mind, if an awareness of the need to prevent manipulation becomes an inalienable part of the culture of public opinion formation in a society, as well as a cornerstone of civic activity on the web, then this would solve the problem. In such a case, the desire to impose one's personal view of the discussed issue, i.e., to "defeat" the opponents – one of the main motives for participating in internet discussions at present – would be increasingly replaced by the desire to impose "the truth" one believes in. A motivation of the latter kind can definitely prompt participation in seemingly boring exchanges of arguments online, especially if the design of the respective platform highlights their cultural and social relevance rather than obscures them.

In *The Deliberative Democracy Handbook*, Michael Weiksner (2005) presents another such forum, the website e-thePeople.org.[2] In what sense is this website designed so as to attract, foster and facilitate argumentative communication?

First of all, posts are arranged not chronologically but by conversations. That is, if someone posts a comment on an article published on the website, the comment appears next to the article. Using this format makes the online discussions easy to follow. In addition, there is a system that allows for the self-moderation of the website by the participants. Its most distinctive element is that each item has a view count, a "rating" of relevance, and a feedback rating showing the number of positive and negative comments. Hence, users can choose whether to read only the most popular items, or the less popular ones too, and so forth. In other words, users are able to navigate the confusing abundance of posts (many of which may be irrelevant or of poor quality) that often makes people avoid online discussion forums.

The EU-funded Project IMPACT (Integrated Method for Policy Making Using Argument Modelling and Computer Assisted Text Analysis) is an example of an approach to online deliberation that gives top priority to argumentation. This is a European Framework 7 project that was launched in 2010. Its aim is to design an argumentation toolbox for deliberation on public policies. The project has developed methods and instruments such as the *Argument Visualization Tool* and *Argument Reconstruction Tool*:

> The intention is to integrate tools that contain knowledge about the problem domain and can perform reasoning to suggest solutions to the problem with argumentation tools described as sense-making systems which typically do not support reasoning but rather structure the problem, by using visualization techniques.
>
> (Benn and Macintosh 2011, 61)

One of the more specific objectives of the project is to facilitate – by developing adequate tools – the reconstruction of formal arguments based on the analysis of unstructured texts from various information sources (see ibid., 60). Another objective is to produce large Web-based argument maps that can be used in policy modeling and analysis (see ibid., 61).

As even this brief overview of just several attempts to develop online deliberation platforms shows, there are enough possibilities to configure their design so as to combine the freedom, spontaneity, inclusivity and egalitarianism of virtual communication with the unforced force of the better argument. Admittedly, this is not a simple task, but the worldwide efforts made in this respect are already yielding results that give us reason to be optimistic. Thus, we can hope that public deliberation – as a means for making binding decisions and for legitimizing norms, as well as policies and other social practices – now has a new and promising medium for effective realization that is the internet.

Notes

1 The format of the two interviews published on the internet makes it impossible to cite the exact page number.
2 Here I present the various designs of online deliberation platforms as described in publications. The question of which of these platforms are still operating and how effective they are requires an empirical investigation that would be very helpful in elucidating the capacity of the internet to serve as a medium for public deliberation, but is beyond the scope of this study.

References

Alexander, Cynthia (ed.). *Digital Democracy.* New York: Oxford University Press, 1998.
Andreasson, Kim (ed.). *Digital Divides: The New Challenges and Opportunities of e-Inclusion.* Boca Raton, FL: CRC Press, 2015.
Benhabib, Seyla. "On the Public Sphere, Deliberation, Journalism and Dignity." *Interview by Karin Wahl-Jorgensen* (August 4, 2008), www.resetdoc.org/story/00000000965, accessed December 18, 2015.
Benn, Neil and Ann Macintosh. "Argument Visualization for eParticipation: Towards a Research Agenda and Prototype Tool." In *Electronic Participation*, edited by Efthimios Tambouris, Ann Macintosh, and Hans de Bruijn, Third IFIP WG 8.5 International Conference, ePart 2011, 60–73. Heidelberg: Springer, 2011.
Bishop, Jonathan (ed.). *Examining the Concepts, Issues and Implications of Internet Trolling.* Hershey PAM: IGI Global, 2013.
Brundidge, Jennifer. "Toward a Theory of Citizen Interface with Political Discussion and News in the Contemporary Public Sphere." *International Journal of Communication* 4 (2010): 1056–1078.
Castells, Manuel. *The Power of Identity.* Malden, MA: Blackwell Publishers, 1997.
Castells, Manuel. *Communication Power*, Oxford: Oxford University Press, 2009.
Cavalier, Robert, Miso Kim, and Zachary Sam Zaiss. "Deliberative Democracy, Online Discussion, and Project PICOLA (Public Informed Citizen Online Assembly)." In *Online Deliberation. Design, Research and Practice*, edited by Todd Davies and Seeta Peña Gangadharan, 71–82. Stanford: CSLI Publications, 2009.

Christopherson, Kimberly. "The Positive and Negative Implications of Anonymity in Internet Social Interactions: 'On the Internet, Nobody Knows You're a Dog.'" *Computers in Human Behavior* 23 (2007): 2028–2056.

Dahlgren, Peter. "Introduction." In *Communication and Citizenship: Journalism and the Public Sphere*, edited by Peter Dahlgren and Colin Sparks, 1–26. London: Routledge, 1991.

Dahlgren, Peter. "Reinventing Participation: Civic Agency and the Web Environment." *Geopolitics, History, and International Relations* 2 (2012): 27–45.

Davies, Todd. "Introduction: The Blossoming Field of Online Deliberation." In *Online Deliberation. Design, Research and Practice*, edited by Todd Davies and Seeta Peña Gangadharan, 1–22. Stanford: CSLI Publications, 2009.

Davies, Todd, Brendan O'Connor, Alex Cochran, Jonathan J. Effrat, Andrew Parker, Benjamin Newman, and Aaron Tam. "An Online Environment for Democratic Deliberation: Motivations, Principles, and Design." In *Online Deliberation. Design, Research and Practice*, edited by Todd Davies and Seeta Peña Gangadharan, 275–292. Stanford: CSLI Publications, 2009.

Dean, Jodi. "Why the Net is not a Public Sphere." *Constellations* 10, no. 1 (2003): 95–112.

El-Nawawy, Mohammed and Sahar Khamis. "Collective Identity in the Virtual Islamic Public Sphere. Contemporary Discourses in Two Islamic Websites." *The International Communication Gazette* 72, no. 3 (2010): 229–250.

Farrell, Henry. "The Consequences of the Internet for Politics." *Annual Review of Political Science* 15 (2012): 35–52.

Gangadharan, Seeta Peña. "Epilogue: Understanding Diversity in the Field of Online Deliberation." In *Online Deliberation. Design, Research and Practice*, edited by Todd Davies and Seeta Peña Gangadharan, 329–358. Stanford: CSLI Publications, 2009.

Gerhards, Jürgen and Mike S. Schäfer. "Is the Internet a Better Public Sphere? Comparing Old and New Media in the USA and Germany." *New Media Society* 12 (2010): 143–160.

Habermas, Jürgen. "Political Communication in Media Society: Does Democracy Still Enjoy an Epistemic Dimension? The Impact of Normative Theory on Empirical Research." *Communication Theory* 16 (2006): 411–426.

Habermas, Jürgen. "Im Sog der Gedanken." Interview published in the *"Feuilleton" of the "Frankfurter Rundschau"* of June 14/15, 2014. www.resetdoc.org/story/00000022437, accessed October 5, 2015.

Hague, Barry N. and Brian Loader (eds.). *Digital Democracy*. London: Routledge, 1999.

Haines, Russell, Jill Hough, Lan Cao, and Douglas Haines. "Anonymity in Computer-Mediated Communication: More Contrarian Ideas with Less Influence." *Group Decision and Negotiation* 23 (2014): 765–786.

Hartz-Karp, Janette and Brian Sullivan. "The Unfulfilled Promise of Online Deliberation." *Journal of Public Deliberation* 10, no. 1 (2014): 1–15.

Hindman, Matthew. *The Myth of Digital Democracy*. Princeton: Princeton University Press, 2009.

Jordan, Tim. *Cyberpower: The Culture and Politics of Cyberspace and the Internet*. London: Routledge, 1999.

Katz, Elihu and Paul Lazarsfeld. *Personal Influence*. New York: The Free Press, 1955.

Kies, Raphaël, *Promises and Limits of Web-deliberation*. New York: Palgrave Macmillan, 2010.

Langman, Lauren. "From Virtual Public Spheres to Global Justice: A Critical Theory of Internetworked Social Movements." *Sociological Theory* 23, no. 1 (2005): 42–74.

Lev-On, Azi and Bernard Manin. "Happy Accidents: Deliberation and Online Exposure to Opposing Views." In *Online Deliberation. Design, Research and Practice*, edited by Todd Davies and Seeta Peña Gangadharan, 105–122. Stanford: CSLI Publications, 2009.

McChesney, Robert W. *Digital Disconnect: How Capitalism is Turning the Internet Against Democracy*. New York: The New Press, 2013.

Phillips, Whitney. *This Is Why We Can't Have Nice Things: Mapping the Relationship between Online Trolling and Mainstream Culture*, Cambridge, MA: The MIT Press, 2015.

Price, Vincent. "Citizens Deliberating Online: Theory and Some Evidence." In *Online Deliberation. Design, Research and Practice*, edited by Todd Davies and Seeta Peña Gangadharan, 37–58. Stanford: CSLI Publications, 2009.

Salvatore, Armando. *The Public Sphere: Liberal Modernity, Catholicism, Islam*. New York: Palgrave Macmillan, 2010.

Salvatore, Armando. "New Media, the 'Arab Spring,' and the Metamorphosis of the Public Sphere: Beyond Western Assumptions on Collective Agency and Democratic Politics." *Constellations* 20, no. 2 (2013): 217–228.

Schuler, Douglas. "Online Civic Deliberation with E-Liberate." In *Online Deliberation. Design, Research and Practice*, edited by Todd Davies and Seeta Peña Gangadharan, 293–302. Stanford: CSLI Publications, 2009.

Shirky, Clay. *Here Comes Everybody: The Power of Organizing Without Organizations*. New York: Penguin, 2009.

Shirky, Clay. "The Political Power of Social Media: Technology, the Public Sphere, and Political Change." *Foreign Affairs* 90, no. 1 (2011): 28–43.

Simone, Maria. "CODEPINK Alert: Mediated Citizenship in the Public Sphere." *Social Semiotics* 16, no. 2 (2006): 345–364

Strangelove, Michael. *Haters, Spammers, and Other Deviants*. Toronto: University of Toronto Press, 2010.

Straubhaar, Joseph, Robert LaRose, and Lucinda Davenport. *Media Now: Understanding Media, Culture, and Technology*. Boston: Wadsworth Publishing, 2013.

Stromer-Galley, Jennifer, Lauren Bryant, and Bruce Bimber. "Context and Medium Matter: Expressing Disagreements Online and Face-to-Face in Political Deliberations." *Journal of Public Deliberation* 11, no. 1 (2015): 1–24.

Sunstein, Cass. *Republic.com*. Princeton, NJ: Princeton University Press, 2001.

Van Eemeren, Frans H. and Rob Grootendorst. *A Systematic Theory of Argumentation. The Pragma-Dialectical Approach*. Cambridge, UK: Cambridge University Press, 2004.

Van Gelder, Tim. "Cultivating Deliberation for Democracy." *Journal of Public Deliberation* 8, no. 1 (2012): 1–11.

Wall, Derek. *Babylon and Beyond: The Economics of Anti-capitalist, Anti-globalist and Radical Green Movements*. London: Pluto, 2005.

Weiksner, Michael. "e-thePeople.org: Large-Scale, Ongoing Deliberation." In *The Deliberative Democracy Handbook*, edited by John Gastil and Peter Levine, 213–227. San Francisco: Jossey-Bass, 2005.

7 Is intercultural public deliberation possible?

The challenges of communication across cultural barriers

As has been was mentioned more than once in this book, I use here the Habermasian model of the public sphere as a frame of reference for developing patterns of public legitimization that could help minority groups win the support of public opinion for their claims. These claims should be formulated as a result of an "ethical-political" (in Habermas's terms) discourse within the group; that is, through a discussion among like-minded people in substantive terms, which deals with the good life, collective identity, and the interpretation of needs of the group and which constitutes a means for its "hermeneutic self-understanding" (Habermas 1996, p. 163). As a second step, they should be justified within a "moral" (in the same author's terms), universalistic discourse, involving everyone actually or potentially affected, which should meet the criteria of public deliberation in order to minimize the risk of manipulation. It is at this point that the major theoretical problem to be addressed by this study arises. How can the public be convinced that the claims of a minority group that are *pro* or *contra* certain norms or policies are legitimate? As was discussed earlier, the criteria for procedural correctness that are characteristic of public deliberation can provide a guarantee against the manipulation of public communication. Are they applicable, however, to *intercultural* communication?

A number of authors have pointed out that public deliberation is not amenable to cultural diversity (see Galeotti 2010; Lovett 2010; Hayward 2011; Olson 2011). In more specific terms, the rationalistic approach to the legitimization of policies by communicative means appears to encounter difficulties when issues involving cultural differences are at stake. The problem is that the general public is not able to evaluate as justified or not justified those claims concerning minority policies that are rationally substantiated by referring to the cultural needs of the members of the respective minority group. But if such claims are not acknowledged to be legitimate, they cannot contribute to the formation of a public opinion that could, in turn, exert communicative pressure on the relevant legislative and executive institutions. How, then, could these institutions be able to design and implement minority policies that will work, according to Habermas's model, in the equal interest of all individuals and groups that are affected by them? Briefly stated, under such circumstances, the voices of the members of minority groups would not reach the authorities who have the power to decide their fate.

The difficulty with applying public deliberation as a tool for legitimizing certain minority policies is that it is impossible for an "outsider" to judge whether or not members of a minority have, in reality, the cultural needs to which they refer when substantiating policy claims. This is due primarily, but not solely, to cultural differences. For example, how can I know that when a member of an ethnic or linguistic minority insists that it is necessary for her children to study all subjects at school in their mother tongue and not in the national language, that this is truly the case? Of course, it would not help to judge from the position of being from the "mainstream" group whose mother tongue is also the official language. Besides, from the vantage point of the majority, a minority's language could simply be offered as a separate subject that could be studied as either a mandatory or elective course. It could also be taught only at private schools or as an extracurricular activity. The best option for a given region or country depends on the specific circumstances – the state of intercultural and political relations, as well as the agenda of the minority's members (this agenda may differ between different subgroups within the minority according to their priorities at a given moment and many other factors). As Melissa S. Williams (2000, 125) maintains, "whether or not citizens will recognize others' reasons *as* reasons may be a socioculturally contingent matter" (emphasis in original).

The debates on minority policies and legal norms that regulate relations between minority groups and society at large concern the degree and range of satisfaction of the cultural needs of minorities – that is, the conditions for the reproduction of their collective cultural identities over time. The means of guaranteeing the correct implementation of already legitimized norms and policies are also the subject of debate. What do I mean here by "degree and range of satisfaction"? To the above example regarding the varying degrees of significance of the role of the mother tongue in the education of schoolchildren from ethnic minorities, I will add the analogous difference in the degree to which it could play a general role in the overall lives of the members of the respective community. In the extreme case, the use of minority languages may be prohibited entirely. In other cases, it may be prohibited only in public places, but not in informal, private conversations. There may be a prohibition on the use of minority languages in public political statements (for example, conducting election campaigns in a language other than Bulgarian is prohibited in Bulgaria, see Election Code, Article 181 (2), *Durzhaven vestnik* [*State Gazette*], no. 19, March 5, 2014). The use of minority languages in the media may or may not be permitted; if it is permitted, there may or may not be a requirement that it be accompanied by a translation in the official language. A minority language may be recognized as a second official language in those regions of a country where the respective minority is a majority, or in the whole country. This means that every citizen will have the right to communicate with public administration officials, with the police and the judiciary in either of the two languages.

There are, therefore, many options, and they can be combined in all sorts of ways. I would like to add another example regarding an issue that has become particularly problematic in recent years – the issue of public expression of religious identity. As is well known, this is particularly relevant to Muslim communities in the "Western" world, especially with regard to Muslim women's dress. Should Muslim women be allowed to wear a headscarf, hijab, chador, niqab, or burka in public places (and especially in state institutions)? Where should the lines be drawn between acceptable and unacceptable expression of religious identity? If such expression is allowed to a certain extent, what would justify setting limits on it? If we decide that Muslim women should be allowed to wear a headscarf because this is in keeping with the norms of their religion, how could we justify banning them from wearing a burka, for example? Isn't one and the same thing at stake in both cases – the observance of a religious norm? What arguments could justify drawing the line between them?

As for the range of cultural needs that merit satisfaction, in my opinion it is important first and foremost to consider the specific sensibility of the members of minority groups which comes from their cultural traditions, religious norms, and historical background. One element of the cultural life of a country that is taken for granted by the mainstream population may be perceived as offensive by some minority citizens. More so – as is often the case – at some point in time this same element may *actually turn out to be* offensive. I have in mind cases in which some element of the cultural environment, which has not been regarded as problematic by anyone for centuries on end, suddenly comes to be seen as insulting to the members of some religious or ethnic community. Let us take, for example, the issue of displaying crucifixes in classrooms in some predominantly Catholic countries. Why, at some point in time, does this turn out to be a problem for non-Christian schoolchildren and their parents, considering that it was not seen as disrespectful to anyone before that? Could the reason be that, until that point, those "affected" were in an oppressed position and had kept their indignation to themselves? Or could it be that an immoderate policy of the recognition of the value of their minority identity by the authorities has raised the self-confidence of the members of the non-Christian minorities to the point of arrogance and they are now trying to pressure society at large into satisfying whatever demands they might choose to make? Or could it be that some of their leaders have found out that objecting to crucifixes in classrooms is one way, among many others, for them to demonstrate their concern for the well-being of their community and to assert, *eo ipso*, their political significance by waging yet another "battle" for more – in this case, maybe entirely unnecessary – rights and liberties?

As we can see, the nuances in the degree and range of satisfying the cultural needs of minorities are not only important; they also pose a huge challenge to politicians, scholars, and the public as a whole. How can this degree and range be "calibrated" so as to be optimal for every particular case, for every minority group, for every country, and for every specific situation? In this regard, it is tempting to seek the solution in a legitimizing pattern of public communication

that is maximally protected from manipulation by applying the public deliberation method. But then we will have to resolve the already mentioned fundamental problem: how can interlocutors who belong to different publics convince
one another?

The challenges that argumentative communication faces in having to overcome cultural "barriers" are interpreted in various ways depending on the methodology that is applied in the efforts to articulate and understand them. Certain
scholars claim, for instance, that since rationality cannot be dissociated from the
cultural tradition that informs it (MacIntyre 1988), any argument whatsoever can
only be valid within its own cultural frame of reference. Others question the
applicability in public discourse of reasons provided by "comprehensive doctrines" insofar as they refer to assumptions characteristic of the respective doctrine that, as such, are not accepted by the general public (Rawls 1993; 1997).
Anne Phillips investigates the importance of the specific experiences of cultural
communities that are not shared by non-members and, as we have seen (in
Chapter 4 of this book), she draws the conclusion that the "politics of presence"
is preferable to the "politics of ideas" with respect to how the interests of minorities are represented in the institutions of the state (see above). Melissa S. Williams argues in turn that marginalized and privileged groups attach alternative
social meanings to one and the same practice. As a consequence:

> the reasons that undergird marginalized groups' critique of the practice *do
> not function as reasons for members of privileged groups*, because the social
> meaning of the practice for the marginalized group is (at least initially)
> inaccessible to them.
>
> (Williams 2000, 138; emphasis in original)

Williams (2000, 138) illustrates this point by referring to a debate that took place
in the United States Senate in 1993 concerning approval for a design of the
insignia of an NGO called the United Daughters of the Confederacy. Because
the insignia included an image of the Confederate flag, the African-American
senator Carol Moseley-Braun argued against approval and substantiated her
position by pointing to the social meaning of this flag as an emblem of slavery.
A number of white senators from Southern states offered an alternative interpretation of the Confederate flag in the insignia, arguing that it served as a remem-
brance of sacrifices made for the homeland. The Senate ultimately voted in favor
of Moseley-Braun's proposal, but it was clearly not a consensual decision.
Moseley-Braun did not succeed in convincing her Southern opponents in a
publicly-deliberative manner that they should change their preferences because,
from their different perspective on the issue, her argument simply had no weight.

Which of the two competing interpretations of the Confederate flag is true and
which is false? The case would have been difficult enough if the Senate had to deal
with two sincere accounts of the ways in which two categories of citizens make
sense of one and the same symbol. Since this was not an epistemological issue but,
rather, a matter of deep conviction, neither of the two possible decisions – to

approve or not to approve the design of the insignia – could be in the equal interest of all "parties" concerned. This meant, however, that neither of the decisions could be legitimate according to the criteria of public deliberation.

But the situation was even more complicated. According to Williams' (2000, 140) analysis, there was a reasonable doubt as to whether Moseley-Braun's interpretation was "a valid representation of the distinctive experience of African Americans or an attempt to score political points by choosing to take offence at an innocuous piece of legislation." There are also other factors that may, in principle, cast doubt on the legitimacy of cultural minority claims in general, including cultural incommensurability, as well as both strategic and manipulative elements. Such issues make it really difficult to determine whether or not either side in the Senate debate could legitimize its claims, even if they were in fact presented in earnest.

Seyla Benhabib (2002) provides an impressive example of the complexity of this issue in her book *The Claims of Culture*. Referring to the notorious headscarf affair (*l'affaire foulard*) in France, she asks:

> But what exactly is the meaning of the girls' actions? Is this an act of religious observance and subversion, or one of cultural defiance, or of adolescent acting-out to gain attention and prominence? Are the girls acting out of fear, out of conviction, or out of narcissism?
>
> (Benhabib 2002, 117)

It is obvious that the way in which the general public judged the behavior of the students in this matter would have been different in each of these three cases. Demanding the right to wear a headscarf on the basis of religious conviction could claim public legitimacy in some way and to some extent, but this would clearly not be the case when doing so out of fear or narcissism. But how could an external observer discern one's true motives in this situation? Benhabib (ibid.) recommends that the actors in such cases should be given the opportunity to speak for themselves, that is, to state what has actually driven them to perform a given action. But this, in my opinion, would not be sufficient to resolve the problem concerning the legitimacy of their claims or practices. For example, what if they were in fact not quite aware of their own motives and/or their motives were mixed? What if not only cultural defiance (Benhabib's favorite alternative) was at play in the headscarf affair, but a degree of both religious sentiment and narcissism as well? Moreover, why should we assume that all of the students involved thought and felt about their actions in the same way? It may be that different students acted for different reasons.

In addition, the challenge of differentiating between publicly legitimate and illegitimate minority claims becomes even greater if we take into account the possibility that some of the actors involved might be motivated by false consciousness. To illustrate this situation, Ranjoo Seodu Herr (2008) presents some interesting examples in her article "Cultural Claims and the Limits of Liberal Democracy." Herr reflects on cases in which minority women support cultural practices that are discriminatory towards them (at least according to liberal standards), but which are – in their own opinion – valuable for their communities. Is this a manifestation of false consciousness, as an "orthodox" feminist would say, or is it an expression of deep cultural commitment? Such a person may derive her self-respect and an awareness of her own worth as a human being not from her individual merits, but from her sacrifices for the community's good. How could an external observer discern what is really the case in such a situation? As Andrea Baumeister (2009, 260) points out, "Although established cultural and religious practices are frequently at odds with a liberal conception of gender equality, many women strongly identify with the traditional way of life of their community."

Also, if a minority group presents a claim to the general public and the state authorities that certain rights be recognized and/or certain policies be changed or introduced in order to satisfy certain cultural needs of the minority's members, then some very pertinent questions arise. For example, who may speak on behalf of the group in such a case? What guarantees are there that the voice of the de facto speaker is in fact the voice of the group? Is it not possible that the demands express the will or interests of only some part of the minority group? Even in countries where the representation of minority groups in state institutions is legally regulated, people often criticize certain minority claims as intended to satisfy not so much the cultural needs of the group's members as a whole, but, rather, the private interests of its representatives and their associates. In many cases the tension between legal norms and public policies, on the one hand, and the cultural practices and claims, on the other, "are strategic or political in character, reflecting interests and power relations both within the community and between the community and the wider society" (Baumeister 2009, 267). Consequently, in order for public recognition of the legitimacy of such claims to be possible, the extent to which they are representative of the interests and will of the greater part of the members of the minority must, at least to some degree, be clear.

In summary, it is very difficult, for a number of reasons, for an external observer to rationally judge which cultural minority claims are legitimate and which are not. For example, the reasons presented by the minority in support of their claims may well be culturally "intransparent" for such an observer in the sense that they refer to traditions, mores, and beliefs that she regards as alien, which is why an outsider might not take the claims seriously. In addition, the very reference to the alleged cultural needs of the group's members might be deceptive in the sense that those presenting the claims might in fact be pursuing their own private interests and inventing or "constructing" cultural needs that either do not exist at all, or are regarded as unimportant by the people to whom they are ascribed. Such claims may also be substantiated by public expressions of support by members of the given minority who do so not freely, but out of conformism or even fear. It may also be the case that claims are substantiated on the basis of actual convictions of minority members, which may, however, not merit respect because they are the result of indoctrination, brain washing, deceit, ignorance, and so forth. Furthermore, not only might the claims in question correspond to the needs of only a part of the group, but it might even be the case that some of the members of the group actually consider the policies designed to satisfy their needs as undesirable for some reason. And the list continues.... In the literature devoted to communication problems of this kind, some authors use the term "deliberation in divided societies" (Dryzek 2005; O'Flynn 2006; Kanra 2012).

In light of this complexity concerning cultural claims, it appears overly optimistic to believe that their argumentative legitimization for the general public can take place through intercultural dialogue. Yes, an "enlarged mentality" in Arendt's (1982, 43) sense, or a Gadamerian "fusion of horizons" would be helpful in this respect, and intercultural understanding might clearly improve the communication between minority groups and society at large. Certain beliefs and mores that contrast with those that prevail among the general public can be made comprehensible for people who do not share them if they are explained with respect to the particular historical circumstances that have contributed to their formation, and if their self-consistency and pertinence to the living conditions of the group are revealed. However, we have also seen that, in addition to cultural differences, a number of other factors are relevant to whether and how the general public might evaluate the legitimacy of claims for minority rights and corresponding policies.

Even a very *"complex cultural dialogue,"* such as the one favored by Benhabib (2002, 22), would not suffice to untangle such a series of "knots."

Solutions proposed

In his article entitled "The Idea of Public Reason Revisited," John Rawls (1997) proposes an answer to the question about whether or not reasons that aim to de/legitimize political (public) norms and practices can be convincingly presented from non-public positions. Rawls (1997, 784) states in the form of his well-known "proviso" that:

> reasonable comprehensive doctrines, religious or nonreligious, may be introduced in public political discussions at any time, provided that in due course proper political reasons – and not reasons given solely by comprehensive doctrines – are presented that are sufficient to support whatever the comprehensive doctrines introduced are said to support.

One of the few examples that Rawls provides to illustrate this idea concerns Patrick Henry's arguments in favor of introducing school prayer in public schools in Virginia in the mid-1780s. Henry did not refer to the intrinsic virtues of Christianity, but rather to its ability to "correct the morals of men, restrain their vices, and preserve the peace of society" (cited in Rawls 1997, 795). His opponent, James Madison, did not deny the merits of Christianity as a religion, but simply maintained that civil society did not need the help of the religious establishment in order to function in an orderly fashion (see Rawls 1997, 784). Rawls (ibid.) concludes that the example of school prayer shows that public reason does not concern particular policies:

> Rather, it is a view about the kind of reasons on which citizens are to rest their political cases in making their political justifications to one another when they support laws and policies that invoke the coercive powers of government concerning fundamental political questions.

Rawls's "proviso" has been the subject of much discussion. One of the most influential criticisms against it focuses on its allegedly overly demanding requirements in regard to the adherents of comprehensive doctrines, particularly religion. For example, Habermas, along with certain other critics of Rawls, claims that it is not morally justifiable, with respect to the participation of religious communities in public discourse, to place the entire burden of the "translation" of doctrinally-specific into universally accessible arguments onto the members of the communities in question.[1] Habermas argues that:

> The liberal state must not transform the requisite *institutional* separation of religion and politics into an undue *mental and psychological* burden for all those citizens who follow a faith. It must well expect them to recognize the principle that any binding legislative, juridical or administrative decision must remain impartial with regard to competing world views, but it must not expect them to split their identity into public and private components as long as they participate in public debates and contribute to the formation of public opinions.
>
> (Habermas 2005, 5; emphasis in original)

Such criticism is justified from a certain point of view. It is true that Rawls does not simply claim that doctrinally-independent ad-hoc equivalents of doctrinally-specific reasons should be sought in each specific case in an opportunistic, "advocate-like" style. He does insist that there should be some logical link between a doctrinally-specific reason and a universally acceptable reason that leads to the same conclusion as the former. Moreover, this link should be provided on the basis of an articulate political conception. Rawls (1997, 778) observes that we should not try to directly supplement a doctrinally based reason by an appropriate universally acceptable one.

> Instead, we are required first to work to the basic ideas of a complete political conception and from there to elaborate its principles and ideals, and to use the arguments they provide. Otherwise public reason allows arguments that are too immediate and fragmentary.

Put otherwise, we should not arbitrarily look for some doctrinally-independent reason that might happen to support the claim that we originally substantiated by reasons pertaining to our comprehensive doctrine. We should, instead, consider an already existing complete conception concerning political justice and endeavor – systematically and rationally – in order to find elements that do the same job. This is a very demanding task. I agree with Wolterstorff and Habermas that it is not fair to place such a burden on the adherents of, for example, a comprehensive religious doctrine, while leaving their secular opponents to face no such challenge. In more general terms, it is difficult to object to Clarissa Hayward (2011, 469) who maintains that if:

> minority group members are constrained to advance claims and arguments, and to justify their political preferences in terms the dominant majority might accept, this requirement places an unfair, and a democratically unacceptable, burden upon them.

Nevertheless, I do not share Habermas's negative evaluation of the alleged "split" in the identity of people of faith into public and private components, which Rawls appears to recommend. My objection is that in "well ordered societies" (Rawls 2001, 27) – Rawls maintains that only they can host a liberal political order – religious people are also citizens with all the rights and duties that follow from this fact. In this respect, a certain degree of "dualism" involving their cultural (private) and civic (public) identities is inevitable. This, in fact, points to the cause of one of the differences between adherents of reasonable and unreasonable comprehensive doctrines according to Rawls's theory of political liberalism. That is to say, a fundamentalist Christian or Muslim will take seriously only those duties that follow from her faith, not those that follow from her civic allegiances.

In principle, Rawls sees no problem in a split within a person's identity in the manner that Habermas does. Rawls (1997, 791) states that:

> As citizens we have reasons to impose the constraints specified by the political principles of justice on associations, while as members of associations we have reasons for limiting those constraints so that they leave room for a free and flourishing internal life appropriate to the association in question.

Such dual identity in respect to adherents of reasonable comprehensive doctrines is, in fact, one of the conditions in Rawls's theory of political liberalism that make possible the so-called "overlapping consensus."

The relationship between one's cultural and civic selves can, of course, be quite problematic. However, tensions of this sort comprise a challenge that should be dealt with and not simply declared to be undesirable. It is my position that the twofold identity of members of cultural communities – and in one way or another we all belong to this category – is a promising resource for efforts to reduce and even eliminate the tensions between their "lifeworlds" and society at large. Habermas (2004, 18) himself writes in another publication from the same period that:

Citizens are equally empowered to develop what is for them their cultural identity and might appear to others as cultural idiosyncrasies, but only under the condition that all of them (across boundaries) understand themselves to be citizens of one and the same political community.

How can we view the problem which Rawls and Habermas address – namely, how can claims that originate from non-public social environments be "translated" into universally accessible ones – within the frame of reference provided by Habermas's two-track model of deliberative politics? As noted above, according to this model, legislative, executive, and judicial state institutions design, enforce, and implement binding norms and public policies that are legitimate insofar as they correspond to the requirements of public opinion. In this sense, society exercises "communicative power" with respect to its institutions (Habermas 2006, 359).

Public opinion, in turn, is formed as a recapitulation of the results of the discourses that take place in the public sphere. These debates transform the various messages that are generated in a lifeworld into universally accessible reasons that legitimate certain claims, thereby rationally shaping public opinion on issues of common concern. This transition from particularistic to universalistic considerations and forms of communication involves two distinct types of discourse, namely, ethical-political[2] and moral discourses. The former are of an intra-group nature, and they are aimed at articulating the self-understanding of the respective group and defining the common good of its members (Habermas 1996, 163). Argumentation proceeds here primarily on a substantive basis, that is, the reasons refer to interests and beliefs that are shared by the group's members. Moral discourses, in contrast, are universalistic. They aim at legitimizing norms and practices as being in the equal interest of all individuals and groups that are affected by them, whatever their interests and beliefs. The argumentation characteristic of this type of communication refers not to what is substantively common for the participants but, rather, to justice. As Habermas (2008b, 18) remarks, "For moral discourse allows all those concerned and affected an equal say and expects each participant to adopt the perspectives of the others when deliberating what is in the equal interest of all."

What, then, is the place of cultural minority claims within this frame of reference? As stated above, they should be considered as products of ethical-political discourses (see Habermas 1996, 308). However, in my opinion, they should not be regarded as formulated solely out of teleological considerations. It is true that they address certain cultural needs of the community's members which are related to their self-understanding, as well as their understanding of the community's good. But, on the other hand, these claims concern norms and policies that are binding for *all* citizens. That is why I think that if we are to qualify – in moral terms – minorities' claims, such as they are made in the real world, we should regard them as having both teleological and deontological grounds.

The problem which we have been discussing up to this point – how can such claims gain public recognition? – would then be transformed into: how can these claims be substantiated within a universalistic moral discourse? Insofar as such claims are an expression of the particular cultural needs of the members of a particular community, they can be justified only by referring to those needs. However, this type of justification cannot be recognized as valid in a universalistic discourse. For example, if an obligation to pray five times a day is derived from the norms of Islam, the need to have the appropriate conditions for doing so at one's workplace cannot be substantiated for non-Muslims by referring to the Holy Quran. Even if the latter are generally tolerant persons, others' religious norms cannot be binding for them.

How does Habermas deal with this challenge? To the best of my knowledge, he pays it no particular attention. Indeed, the two-track structure of his model helps him downplay the difficulties associated with the transition from particularistic to universalistic forms of argumentation. The latter are exclusively characteristic of deliberations on the part of what Habermas (1996, 307) terms "arranged" or "strong" publics, that is, those which function in the domains of political and legal institutions, where the deliberations conducted aim at binding decisions that concern society as a whole. The informal public sphere, on the other hand, is the territory where "weak" publics generate public opinion. Habermas (ibid.) argues in this regard that "opinion-formation uncoupled from decisions is effected in an open and inclusive network of overlapping, subcultural publics having fluid temporal, social and substantive boundaries." He ascribes an "anarchic structure" to the general public sphere that he (ibid.) terms "a 'wild' complex." It is as if such characterizations of the environment in which the transition from particularistic to universalistic patterns of communication – that is, from ethical-political to moral discourses – somehow relieves him of the obligation to indicate how it is possible to overcome the difficulties associated with granting public validity to decisions that have been justified by reference to contingent particular circumstances.

Habermas (2005, 2008a, 2008b) does, in fact, discuss one problem of this type – the role of religion in public life, particularly in the public sphere – but he does not generalize the solution that he proposes. The conceptual difficulty that has to be overcome in this case is, in my opinion, a specific instance of the more general problem that we are addressing. It concerns how culture-specific reasons, which refer to values and norms that are particular to a given religion, can be "translated" into a universally accessible language so that the claims they substantiate can receive public recognition.

Since Habermas regards the public sphere as functioning in a two-track fashion, he states that such culture-specific reasons need to be translated into generally accessible language only before they enter "the institutionalized decision-making process at the parliamentary, court, governmental and administrative levels" (Habermas 2008a, 8). In contrast, they can be discussed in any mode within the informal public sphere. This means that the task of translation constitutes a challenge shared both by those who put forward such claims, and also by the general secular public. As such, it should be a cooperative undertaking and comprise an element of complementary learning processes (see ibid., 9).

However, Habermas (ibid., 8) provides no specific explanation of how this can take place. Although he maintains that "a shift from the traditional to a more reflexive form of religious consciousness" on the part of religious communities, as well as a reciprocal process of the revision of the attitudes of secularists toward their religious fellow citizens, are necessary conditions for this type of translation, he goes into no further detail. Habermas presents a small number of examples of what he has in mind, one of which indicates a possible way to translate the monotheistic conception that human beings are sacred – insofar as they have been created by God – into the universally accessible idea that they have an inherent dignity and the right to self-determination. This might win, for instance, public support for an argument against granting parents the right to intervene into the genome of their as yet unborn child, even if this position has been generated within a religious cultural context (see Habermas 2003, 114).

But this approach, which relies on the communicative attitudes of both religious and secular citizens, leaves a very important question unanswered. What are we to do in the case of pressing issues, for example? What about the controversial claims of Muslim minorities about wearing the headscarf, chador, or burka in public; or the appeals of large religious groups that their children receive religious education at state and municipal schools; or demands that citizens professing certain religious affiliations be exempt from specific legal requirements? If the institution to which such claims are addressed replies that they can be considered only after the religious group involved and the public at large come to a consensus – if and when they find a common language in which to discuss the respective problem in a rational manner – then the decision would be postponed indefinitely. But many minority claims of this type do indeed require an urgent response by the authorities. An official response that refers to a "complementary learning process" would most probably not only be regarded by the minority group as a mockery, but also contribute to a deterioration in relations between it and the state.

In addition, the appeal that members of different publics make a mutual effort to work toward a mutual understanding leaves open the question of the balance between these efforts. Who should make more concessions? However well-intended and cooperative the mainstream public may be toward particular minority claims, how can it distinguish between reasonable and unreasonable ones, considering that both sides do not have mutually recognized criteria for reasonableness?

The general idea that claims put forward from non-public positions (as in the case of claims for changing legal norms and public policies so as to make them more conducive to the preservation and reproduction of the cultural identities of minority groups over time) may rely on public legitimization only if they are formulated in universally accessible terms is supported by other authors, too. In his conception of political tolerance, Rainer Forst proposes two criteria for the acceptability of reasons that justify certain liberties or restrictions on liberty; in other words, criteria that can serve to "measure" tolerance – that is, to distinguish between what is tolerable and what is intolerable in a liberal political environment. The two criteria are reciprocity and generality. What does the German philosopher mean by that?

> Reciprocity ... means that one cannot refuse to grant another person certain demands that one makes for oneself (reciprocity of contents) and that one must not assume that others share one's evaluative conceptions and interests – especially not by appeal to "higher truths," which are precisely *not* shared (reciprocity of reasons).
>
> (Forst 2014, 72; emphasis in original)

Regarding the other criterion, that of generality, Forst posits that the regulations that govern a kind of social relation must be justifiable by reasons which are shareable by all of those affected. Forst calls tolerance "a discursive *virtue of justice*" (Forst 2014, 72; emphasis in original).

Forst's conception of tolerance (developed in more detail in other publications, see Forst 2013) is thorough and elaborate but, in my opinion, it cannot help solve our problem. In justifying claims that concern norms and policies by appealing to the cultural needs of minority groups it is in principle impossible to apply either the criterion of reciprocity or that of generality. Each of these two criteria presupposes commensurability both of the actual and of the potential demands of the interlocutors – something that is absent in the relations between cultural minorities and society at large. What "reciprocity of contents" could there be, for example, in claims for providing mother tongue education for children from a given minority in municipal and state-owned schools, or for establishing minority-language television channels? And how could reasons that are based on culture-specific needs of the members of some minority be shareable between them and, say, representatives of government institutions?

Other scholars who work within the paradigm of deliberative democracy discuss various modifications of Habermas's model that would supposedly render it more appropriate for legitimizing minority claims in the public sphere. It should be noted that there is a clear tendency among such proposals to seek solutions at the cost of minimizing requirements for the deliberativeness of the discourses through which cultural claims would be justified to the general public. Four of the most prominent conceptions in this respect are those put forward by James Bohman (2000, 2003), Bohman and Richardson (2009), Jorge Valadez (2001), Michael Rabinder James (2004), and Monique Deveaux (2006).

In his book, *Public Deliberation*, James Bohman (2000) proposes a minimalist approach to public deliberation as a means of reaching agreements that can be accepted as legitimate by all parties concerned, even if they have different cultural values and attitudes. He discusses the possibility that an agreement may be accepted as legitimate by all parties insofar as it fosters mutual respect among the participants, and not because it is based on reasons that they all accept to be true. Bohman (2000, 6) maintains that:

> What is reasonable is not the shared content of political values but the mutual recognition of the deliberative liberties of others, the requirements of dialogue, and the openness of one's own beliefs to revision.

In this sense, Bohman argues against Habermas's idea that the consensus achieved through rational persuasion must be based on identical reasons that are acceptable to all parties and that legitimacy may derive solely from consensus, as well as that the parties that are not guided by shared principles cannot achieve anything more than a compromise (see Bohman 2000, 88).

Bohman proposes a somewhat different view of compromise, claiming that in some cases it may be the only way to reach an agreement that is regarded as legitimate by all parties. This is the case, for example, when the parties involved have to resolve a deep conflict stemming from significant cultural differences between them. An agreement that the participants have accepted for different reasons can still help settle intercultural disputes in a publicly deliberative way.

In a more recent article, co-authored by James Bohman and Henry Richardson (2009), the criteria for the legitimacy of the political process are relaxed even further, and the very demanding condition that "each of the participants aims to provide the others with reasons that all can accept" is replaced with the expectation that the participants "engage forthrightly with the others' arguments and respond open mindedly to them" (ibid., 273). This last criterion would be sufficient even if it is impossible to reach a comprehensive agreement (ibid.).

Jorge Valadez's conception of public deliberation is presented in his book, *Deliberative Democracy, Political Legitimacy, and Self-Determination in Multicultural Societies* (2001). Valadez claims that the classical deliberative-democratic model of decision-making does not need to be revised substantially in order to make it applicable to a multicultural environment, but he does not deny that argumentative communication across cultural boundaries is difficult to achieve. Valadez (2001, 6) points out that argumentative communication can be impeded not only by cultural incommensurabilities, but also by "significant and persistent cultural group differences in socioeconomic and political power."[3]

Despite this, Valadez argues that intercultural deliberation is still possible if two changes are introduced. First, the requirements regarding public deliberation should be relaxed – that is, public deliberation should not necessarily be expected to lead to consensus in multicultural situations. He claims that "in the more difficult cases of intercultural disagreement, it will suffice that participants believe they have equitably influenced the deliberative process and agree to continue to cooperate in good faith in future deliberations" (ibid., 5).[4]

Valadez defines his second proposal as "epistemological egalitarianism." By this he means a set of measures designed to partly compensate for the inequalities in communicative capacities stemming from inequalities in socioeconomic and political status. These measures should also facilitate communication between people with different cultural identities. The most important one of them is to ensure equal access to the epistemological resources that are indispensable for effective participation in public deliberation, as well as to adapt the methodology of public deliberation to multicultural environments. In this regard, priority should be given to providing

> equal access to information and information technologies, equal educational opportunities to develop the critical thinking abilities for analyzing and evaluating that information, and equal access to the social and material means necessary for the intracultural and intercultural exchange of information.
>
> (Valadez 2001, 6–7)

Also necessary is "the expansion of deliberative forums to include brief biographical and cultural narratives, exercises in empathetic imagination, and other means by which participants can gain greater mutual affective understanding" (ibid., 7).

Michael Rabinder James (2004) introduces the concept of "plural polity" in his book, *Deliberative Democracy and the Plural Polity*, as a means for conceptualizing the deliberative decision-making method in a new way that makes it applicable to a multicultural environment. He does not use the traditional terminology because he takes an entirely constructionist approach to cultural identity, where terms such as "plural deliberation" and "complex legitimacy" are key in his theory. James claims that in a *plural polity* there can only be *complex legitimacy*, access to which requires "*plural deliberation*." Whether or not a deliberation is plural should be determined on a case-by-case basis, according to four criteria: "the scope of deliberation, the relationship between understanding and criticism, the link between deliberation and decision-making, and conditions governing the deliberative and aggregative fairness of institutions and processes" (ibid., 52).

It is noteworthy that in James's account, plural deliberation is compatible both with agonistic and activist challenges to existing institutions. This is consistent with his endeavor to make the model of deliberative democracy more inclusive with regard to cultural diversity (see ibid., 81).

Monique Deveaux is even more inclined than Valadez and James to relax the criteria for legitimization through public deliberation. In her book, *Gender and Justice in Multicultural Liberal States* (2006), she argues that negotiation, bargaining, and compromise may be used in public deliberation whenever necessary, especially in cases of cultural conflict. As I understand it, her theory is that win-win and win-lose types of approaches can be applied together, or, in Habermas's terms, that communicative and strategic action can be performed simultaneously. Deveaux contends that if certain procedural criteria are met, collective decisions made in this eclectic way can be accepted as legitimate by everyone concerned. Or, in other words, that negotiation, bargaining, and compromise, on the one hand, and public deliberation, on the other, can be mutually complementary. According to Deveaux (2006, 111),

> In the context of deliberations which strive to give equal political voice to participants, and in which participants can openly challenge the rationale

(and purpose) behind cultural assertions and make claims about the benefits and harms of social practices, strategies of negotiation and compromise can signal the recognition that stakeholders have valid concerns, differences, and interests which are nonetheless irresolvable at the level of moral agreement.

Furthermore, Deveaux (2006, 112) maintains that decisions made solely on the basis of strategic considerations may eventually become morally justified:

> [S]ome interest-based agreements and compromises can come to take on a settled normative status over time: the decision to reform African customary law so as to permit women to inherit property, even if forged out a balancing of interests, may eventually (for many) come to enjoy normative acceptance, and indeed, to be viewed as more just than previous arrangements.

Deveaux admits that claims which allegedly concern the satisfaction of legitimate cultural needs of minority groups may in fact be driven by selfish interests of some of their members. But she sees a way to counter such manipulation through public deliberation on conflicts related to cultural practices. According to her, if the participants in such debates are selected so as to represent all relevant interests – namely, community leaders, representatives of women from the communities involved (Deveaux's study is focused on the gender aspect of public communication), experts and government policy-makers – this would make it difficult to camouflage strategic actions as communicative ones. This kind of debate would enable critical reflection upon the interests of the participants, therefore "those who simply seek to maintain control over vulnerable members of their community ... will be hard pressed to disguise their motive or find a legitimate justification for it that cannot be revealed as cynical window-dressing" (Deveaux 2005, 349–350).

I have reservations about this hypothesis. They are based on the considerations regarding argumentative communication across cultural "barriers" which I discussed at the beginning of this chapter. In a situation such as the one described by Deveaux, the claims of some representatives of the cultural community involved (let us say, its leaders who want to keep their control over vulnerable members of the community) are bound to be met with counter-claims by other members of the same community (let us say, representatives of the women from the community, who denounce the leaders' claims, revealing the selfish interests behind their seemingly noble concern for the protection of the community's cultural identity). In such cases the role of arbitrator in this dispute falls upon representatives of society at large (let us say, experts and government policy-makers). The latter, however, do not belong to the lifeworld of the community in question, they do not share its historical experience, nor do they have the same sensibility and cultural attitudes as its members. So how could they possibly judge who is sincere and who is not?

The claims of one party to the dispute that those of the other party are driven by selfish interests do not, in themselves, prove that this is indeed the case. In most cases, the other party will claim the opposite: that it is its opponents who are manipulating the public for their own gain. Such disputes are common in countries where the interests of ethnic minorities are represented by their own ethnic political parties which compete for their votes. Each party accuses the other of using cultural claims to promote its selfish interests while pretending to be concerned solely about the community's identity. In such cases, the public at large does not have criteria to help it decide, in an informed and rational way, who is telling the truth.

All four conceptions discussed above, which are designed to modify Habermas's model in order to facilitate the implementation of public deliberation in a multicultural environment, seek to resolve the problem of argumentative communication across the barrier of cultural differences by expanding the criteria for legitimization through public deliberation. This is certainly not an isolated tendency in the development of deliberative democracy theory. Numerous authors have argued for an "expanded understanding of deliberation" (see Mansbridge et al. 2010, 67) that can more adequately address the challenges of cultural diversity, as well as many other difficulties in the practical implementation of the theoretical model of deliberative democracy. Some call for a more inclusive approach to self-interest and power (Mansbridge et al. 2010), while others propose using non-discursive forms of communication such as rhetoric and story-telling (Bächtiger et al. 2010).

But although applying wider, less demanding criteria for procedural correctness of legitimizing public communication can indeed facilitate dialogue between different publics, including between minority communities and society at large, it does not solve the major problem – how to guarantee that public communication will not be manipulated. Indeed, it is very tempting to assume that a claim is legitimate even if we cannot really judge whether it is justified – which would be the case if the cultural environment in which it is reasoned and to which it refers is "intransparent" to us. But then, don't we risk being misled into agreeing to a demand that conflicts with our own convictions?

Although we undoubtedly need more realistic models of deliberative democracy, I believe that the potential of the "classical" model introduced by Jürgen Habermas in *Between Facts and Norms* has not yet been exhausted. Furthermore, the forms of public deliberation that do not fit into the narrow normative framework of this model are yet to demonstrate their capacity to produce legitimate agreements. That is why I will take a very different approach to the problems in deliberative democracy theory that stem from cultural diversity.

Notes

1 Another example of such criticism is provided by Nicholas Wolterstorff (Audi and Wolterstorff, 1997, 105).
2 Habermas differentiates between ethical-political and ethical-existential discourses. Both deal with questions of the good life, but the former concern the good life of a group or polity while the latter concern the good life of individuals.

3 On this point, Valadez's view is in tune with the critiques against the standard approach to deliberative democracy as voiced by Nancy Fraser (1989; 1997) and Iris Young (1997).
4 Valadez thereby largely agrees with Bohman's view and refers to him further on in his study (see Bohman 2000, 138).

References

Arendt, Hannah. *Lectures on Kant's Political Philosophy*. Brighton: Harvester Press, 1982.
Audi, Robert and Nicholas Wolterstorff. *Religion in the Public Square: The Place of Religious Convictions in Political Debate*. Lanham, MD: Rowman and Littlefield, 1997.
Bächtiger, Andre, Simon Niemeyer, Michael Neblo, Marco R. Steenbergen, and Jürg Steiner. "Disentangling Diversity in Deliberative Democracy: Competing Theories, Their Blind Spots and Complementarities." *The Journal of Political Philosophy* 18, no. 1 (2010): 32–63.
Baumeister, Andrea. "Gender, Culture and the Politics of Identity in the Public Realm." *Critical Review of International Social and Political Philosophy* 12, no. 2, (2009): 259–277.
Benhabib, Seyla. *The Claims of Culture*. Princeton: Princeton University Press, 2002.
Bohman, James. *Public Deliberation*. Cambridge, MA: The MIT Press, 2000.
Bohman, James. "Reflexive Public Deliberation. Democracy and the Limits of Pluralism." *Philosophy and Social Criticism* 29, no 1 (2003): 85–105.
Bohman, James and Henry Richardson. "Liberalism, Deliberative Democracy, and 'Reasons that All Can Accept'." *The Journal of Political Philosophy* 17, no. 3 (2009): 253–274.
Deveaux, Monique. "A Deliberative Approach to Conflicts of Culture." In *Minorities within Minorities: Equality, Rights and Diversity*, edited by Avigail Eisenberg and Jeff Spinner-Halev, 340–362. Cambridge, UK: Cambridge University Press, 2005.
Deveaux, Monique. *Gender and Justice in Multicultural Liberal States*. Oxford: Oxford University Press, 2006.
Dryzek, John S. "Deliberative Democracy in Divided Societies: Alternatives to Agonism and Analgesia." *Political Theory* 33, no. 2 (2005): 218–242.
Durzhaven Vestnik [*State Gazette*], no. 19, 2014.
Forst, Rainer. *Toleration in Conflict. Past and Present*. Cambridge, UK: Cambridge University Press, 2013.
Forst, Rainer. "Toleration and Democracy." *Journal of Social Philosophy* 45, no. 1 (2014): 65–75.
Fraser, Nancy. *Unruly Practices: Power, Discourse, and Gender in Contemporary Social Theory*. Minneapolis: University of Minnesota Press, 1989.
Fraser, Nancy. *Justice Interruptus. Critical Reflections on the Postsocialist Condition*. London: Routledge, 1997.
Galeotti, Anna Elisabetta. "Multicultural Claims and Equal Respect." *Philosophy and Social Criticism* 36, no. 3–4 (2010): 441–450.
Habermas, Jürgen. *Between Facts and Norms*. Cambridge, MA: The MIT Press, 1996.
Habermas, Jürgen. "Faith and Knowledge." In *The Future of Human Nature*, edited by Jürgen Habermas, 101–115. Malden, MA: Polity Press, 2003.
Habermas, Jürgen. "Religious Tolerance – The Pacemaker for Cultural Rights." *Philosophy* 79 (2004): 5–18.

Habermas, Jürgen. *Religion in the Public Sphere*, lecture presented at the Holberg Prize Seminar. 2005. www.holbergprisen.no/images/materiell/2005_symposium_habermas. pdf#nameddest=habermas, accessed October 5, 2015.

Habermas, Jürgen. "Political Communication in Media Society: Does Democracy Still Enjoy an Epistemic Dimension? The Impact of Normative Theory on Empirical Research." *Communication Theory* 16 (2006): 411–426.

Habermas, Jürgen. *A "Post-Secular Society" – What Does that Mean?*, paper presented at the Istanbul Seminars organized by Reset Dialogues of Civilizations, Istanbul. (2008a). www.resetdoc.org/EN/Habermas-Istanbul.php, accessed October 5, 2015.

Habermas, Jürgen. *Between Naturalism and Religion. Philosophical Essays*. Cambridge, UK: Polity Press, 2008b.

Hayward, Clarissa Rile. "What Can Political Freedom Mean in a Multicultural Democracy? On Deliberation, Difference, and Democratic Governance." *Political Theory* 39, no. 4 (2011): 468–497.

Herr, Ranjoo Seodu. "Cultural Claims and the Limits of Liberal Democracy." *Social Theory and Practice* 34, no. 1 (2008): 25–41.

James, Michael R. *Deliberative Democracy and the Plural Polity*. Lawrence, KA: University Press of Kansas, 2004.

Kanra, Bora. "Binary Deliberation: The Role of Social Learning in Divided Societies." *Journal of Public Deliberation* 8, no. 1 (2012): 1–15.

Lovett, Frank. "Cultural Accommodation and Domination." *Political Theory* 38, no. 2 (2010): 243–267.

MacIntyre, Alasdair. *Whose Justice? Which Rationality?* Notre Dame: University of Notre Dame Press, 1988.

Mansbridge, Jane, James Bohman, Simone Chambers, David Estlund, Andreas Føllesdal, Archon Fung, Cristina Lafont, Bernard Manin, and José Luis Martí. "The Place of Self-Interest and the Role of Power in Deliberative Democracy." *The Journal of Political Philosophy* 18, no. 1 (2010): 64–100.

O'Flynn, Ian. *Deliberative Democracy and Divided Societies*. New York: Palgrave Macmillan, 2006.

Olson, Kevin. "Legitimate Speech and Hegemonic Idiom: The Limits of Deliberative Democracy in the Diversity of its Voices." *Political Studies* 59, no. 3 (2011): 527–546.

Rawls, John. *Political Liberalism*. New York: Columbia University Press, 1993.

Rawls, John. "The Idea of Public Reason Revisited." *University of Chicago Law Review* 64, no. 3 (1997): 780–807.

Rawls, John. *Justice as Fairness*, Cambridge, MA: The Belknap Press of Harvard University Press, 2001.

Valadez, Jorge. *Deliberative Democracy, Political Legitimacy and Self-Determination in Multicultural Societies*. Oxford: Westview Press, 2001.

Williams, Melissa. "The Uneasy Alliance of Group Representation and Deliberative Democracy. In *Citizenship in Diverse Societies*, edited by Will Kymlicka and Wayne Norman, 124–154. Oxford: Oxford University Press, 2000.

Young, Iris M. *Intersecting Voices: Dilemmas of Gender, Political Philosophy, and Policy*. Princeton, NJ: Princeton University Press, 1997.

8 The communicative empowerment of minority groups

Ethical-political discourses as instances of public deliberation

As we search for a solution to our problem, namely, how can minority claims gain public recognition in spite of cultural differences, I would like to explore the possibilities provided by the most emblematic feature of the model of deliberative democracy – proceduralism. While this may also be one of the more controversial features of the model (see Cohen 1994; Kirshner 2010; Gledhill 2011), I do not wish to address proceduralism as such, but rather investigate it as an instrument capable of resolving the issue at hand. For this reason, I will focus on the proceduralist answer to the question, "What is the criterion for the public legitimacy of a collective decision?"

The answer from the proceduralist perspective is that all individuals and groups who may be affected by the decision in question, whether it concerns the approval of a norm, policy, or the like (see Benhabib 1996; Cohen 1997; Bohman 2000), must give their consent. This may at first seem to be an analytic statement, but the non-trivial elements of the theory, as pointed out in Chapter 5, concern the requirements for the procedure through which such consent is obtained. Specifically, the discussion leading to the decision must conform with certain criteria which guarantee that the consent is genuine and not a result of factors such as fear, momentary emotion, or blind trust in somebody else's opinion. If the decision is made in a procedurally correct way then it should be in the equal interest of all persons affected – not in the sense that someone else decides that this is the case, but because those affected themselves accept the outcome of the deliberation. Moreover, they do this as responsible people who are fully aware of their actions, not simply because they just happen to agree. As was stated above, the following four criteria for such agreement stand out from those discussed within the theory of public deliberation: freedom from coercion, rationality, equal standing of the interlocutors, and openness of the communication.

Of course, some of the participants in procedurally correct public deliberations, and perhaps even all, might be wrong in agreeing upon a certain decision. Some or all of them might have insufficient or false information concerning the situation, be guided by assumptions and values that they might subsequently reconsider, and so forth. The decision might turn out to be in fact unjust in regard to the interests of some of the parties involved. It might, also, lead to consequences that are at odds with the intentions of the participants. However, its procedural correctness also presupposes its *revisability* if someone presents ample argumentation for a change.

In this sense, the decision would be legitimate insofar as it is procedurally correct, rather than for substantive reasons. For example, the decision reached might, in fact, not be conducive for realizing a specific ideal concerning what is good for the community or for attaining some other concrete goal, but it may still be legitimate if it has been produced by "undistorted" (in Habermas's sense) public communication. However, this does not mean that an ethical-political discourse whose subject-matter concerns the common good of a group cannot be procedurally correct provided that all the deliberative criteria are met.

Let us now presume that all of these criteria have been met by an ethical-political discourse within a minority group – a discourse that addresses its cultural needs, as well as the respective claims for legal norms and public policies that would be advanced from its side into the public sphere. In other words, let us presume that this ethical-political discourse is a procedurally correct instance of public deliberation.

In this case, cultural "intransparency" should not prevent the general public from evaluating the legitimacy of a minority's cultural claims because one would not need to make any judgments about the substance of the argumentation that shapes the collective awareness of the group's members concerning their cultural needs. One would not have to share the cultural attitudes and beliefs of the members of the group in question because only the procedural correctness of the deliberations within the group – the deliberations that produced the collective decision to present these particular claims and no others – is what matters for evaluating the legitimacy of the claims presented.

Furthermore, the risk of strategic manipulation within the group would also be minimized because, if the criteria for deliberation are met, the members of the group who are not involved in an attempt at manipulation would have every opportunity to expose it through criticism based on convincing argumentation. The same is also valid concerning possible power struggles within the group since freedom from coercion and recognition of the "force" of the better argument are among the most important criteria for public deliberation. In addition, insofar as "false consciousness" is concerned, rational and free debate among equals provides opportunities to foster sound self-reflection among the participants. Finally, the representativeness of the claims put forward would be guaranteed by a procedurally correct public deliberation since every voice will be heard in a discussion that meets the deliberative criteria.

It thus appears that as far as the realm of models, ideals, and hypotheses is concerned, we have found an answer to the question, "How can cultural minority claims obtain public recognition?" While it may not be the only plausible resolution, it is, in my opinion, the one that best fits the frame of reference in respect to the Habermasian model of deliberative democracy. That is to say that if the claims put forward are the outcome of an ethical-political discourse within the respective minority group that meets the procedural criteria of public deliberation, then they should be regarded as legitimate by the general public, as well. Culture-specific attitudes and beliefs, strategic intra-group machinations, false consciousness of some or all group members, and so forth, cannot hinder the empirical evaluation of the procedural correctness of an intra-group discussion by the public at large. Rationality, freedom from coercion, equality of the interlocutors, and openness to all who can convince the others that they are, or could be, affected by the decision being discussed, and so forth, are all parameters of the procedural correctness of intra-group deliberation that are universally accessible.[1]

Is such a model of public legitimization of minority claims feasible, though? In order to demonstrate that it is not one of the so-called counterfactual normative conceptions, I will briefly examine two case studies of intra-group discussions that largely meet the criteria for ethical-political discourses. One is presented by Mohammed el-Nawawy and Sahar Khamis (2010) in their article, "Collective Identity in the Virtual Islamic Public Sphere. Contemporary Discourses in Two Islamic Websites." It is a review of the discussions conducted on the websites Islamonline.net and Islamway.com, which are described by the two authors as "popular" and "mainstream" for the Muslim public (see ibid., 230).

What gives me reason to claim that the discussions in question meet Habermas's criteria for ethical-political discourses? As el-Nawawy and Khamis (2010, 230) note, the two websites provide "a platform for argumentation, debate and exchange of ideas between the various participants around issues of common concern, as well as spreading knowledge and awareness of the Islamic faith." Furthermore, they expressly point out that these discussions contribute to "shaping the subjectivities and identities of current and future Muslim generations" (ibid.). The two authors definitely take a constructionist approach to identity. Although many of the discussions on the two websites are about what it means to be a true Muslim, how a true Muslim should behave in particular situations, and how the participants are looking for answers to these sorts of questions in Islamic scripture, el-Nawawy and Khamis do not view these discussions as an attempt to reveal or rediscover the enduring objective essence of "Muslimness" but, rather, as a process of the reproduction of Muslim identity over time:

> We perceive the process of collective identity formulation as a flexible and intersecting process of self-definition and self-representation, which is shared by a group of people, who inhabit similar or overlapping identity positions and identity-related discourses.
>
> (El-Nawawy and Khamis 2010, 239)

The authors point out the following specific mechanisms of the (re)construction of Muslim collective identity: the acceptance or refutation of "identity signifiers" that may be formulated both within the group and by "outsiders," that is, by the "Others"; promoting "a sense of religious communalism and collectivism that allows members of the Muslim *umma* to (re)construct their identities as members of the same community of faith" (ibid., 230); "discovering the differences among themselves and demarcating themselves from non-Islamic practices and life-styles" (ibid.).

El-Nawawy and Khamis pay special attention to the possibilities provided by the internet for (re)constructing collective identities as "imagined communities." The web allows the creation of "imagined worlds, that is, the multiple worlds that are constituted by the historically situated imaginations of persons and groups spread around the globe" (ibid., 234).

But could claims born of discussions such as those on the two websites win the support of public opinion in a liberal democratic society? Can we assume that a public which is guided by liberal democratic values would accept that a collective identity constructed and demonstrated in this way merits recognition and should be ensured adequate conditions for its sustainable reproduction over time? This would entail, among other things, that ethical-political discourses of this sort should leave no room for doubt in the minds of external observers that they might be a mere expression of collective emotions or, say, a means to promote someone's self-serving interests.

El-Nawawy and Khamis do not deal explicitly with this issue, but their con-siderations about another one shed light on it as well. They ask themselves whether the discussions on the two websites have a place in a Habermasian public sphere. To some extent, these discussions may be assumed to fall into the category of undistorted public communication because views are exchanged and consensus is reached on many of the issues discussed. A number of other authors quoted in the article see these and other such debates as instances of communi-cative action, characterized by free consultation and equality in thinking and expression of opinion (see, for example, Abu-Nimer 2006, 159). El-Nawawy and Khamis, however, think that, as a whole, the discussions in question do not meet the criteria of public deliberation. The viewpoints on which the participants reach consensus are not determined by the force of the better argument but by the interlocutors' unconditional identification with one of the parties to the con-flicts under discussion (especially in the case of the Palestinian–Israeli conflict). In addition, participants use emotion and assertiveness rather than reason (see el-Nawawy and Khamis 2010, 244). Considering these points made by Mohammed el-Nawawy and Sahar Khamis, we may conclude that the claims produced by such ethical-political discourses cannot win the support of public opinion in a liberal democratic society.

The other case study that I would like to say a few words about is an article by Valery Novoselsky (2015) entitled "Internet as a Tool of Change and the Role of Roma Virtual Network in a Process of Roma Empowerment" and published on the Roma Virtual Network (RVN) website. The article presents the RVN as a grass-roots initiative, implemented by volunteers that aims to provide information on Roma issues in 20 languages via the Internet. The RVN was established in 1999. Its audience includes EU-level policy-makers, civil servants, human rights activ-ists, and media, as well as a total of over 10,800 email addresses.

V. Novoselsky presents the RVN in the context of a network of public com-munications – mostly websites and social networks – that help form a self-awareness of the multiple Roma communities as a transnational ethnic group. "For some Roma the Internet, due to its relatively easy access and low costs, has been advertised as an emancipatory tool to open up channels of informational exchange and an innovative political space" (Novoselsky 2015, 8). For the pur-poses of my study, I will view these communicative interactions as ethical-political discourses.

According to Novoselsky's article, most of the discussions conducted in this virtual communication network deal with issues related to the common origin of the Roma, their shared cultural heritage and common goals. Emphasis is placed on "Romani traditions, music, dance, history, cuisine, films" (ibid., 6), thereby forming a particular ethnic image of this transnational community. Efforts are made to construct a common identity using the classic in-group/out-group opposition (see ibid., 7). National differences among the Roma communities are also downplayed in various ways and the possibilities for creating a unified non-territorial nation are discussed (see ibid.).

These ethical-political discourses also have a significant interethnic com-ponent. The various activities of Roma organizations are usually conducted in partnership with non-Roma ones. Photos of various events posted on websites that are part of the RVN usually show Roma and non-Roma participants together. These websites often feature articles and interviews by mainstream, non-Roma journalists specializing in interethnic relations. Public initiatives, such as petitions on Roma issues, always seek support from eminent non-Roma public figures and organizations.

Communication within this network of websites, blogs, Facebook profiles, etc. is also an important factor for the creation of a Roma intellectual elite. The network provides information about topical issues, events, activities, possibilities for participation in public forums, employment opportunities, contacts, and information about financial grants and other forms of sponsorship. "The variety of virtual platforms, representing various views on this world and universe, indeed helps to create the strata of Roma population able to think at more advanced intel-lectual level" (ibid., 9). According to Valery Novoselsky, the internet has already helped to create a circle of Roma intellectuals capable of exerting significant influ-ence on the international audience via public diplomacy and the media (see ibid.).

Here I will again raise the question: how can the public, both at the international and national levels, be assured that the claims raised through the vehicle of the RVN Internet platform regarding changes in legislation and public policies express the genuine cultural needs of the Roma? How can the public be assured that these are the real claims of the Roma and have not been fabricated to be used as a means to promote the interests of some Roma leaders and their associates, or as a "weapon" in the struggle for influence between Roma clans, or as a pretext to ask for funding for unnecessary or sham activities of nongovernmental organizations, or even as an attempt to realize a utopian project concocted by a group of enthusiasts who have lost touch with reality?

In my opinion, the adequacy of such claims can be warranted – to a great extent – by the procedural correctness of ethical-political discourses, which ensures a balance of the interests of all parties concerned (at least in the way that they themselves understand their interests), and, most importantly, which can be evaluated as such also from the outside. As far as the normative aspect of public deliberation is concerned, from a liberal point of view, every agreement that is the result of undistorted (in the Habermasian sense) communication – that is, every agreement that meets the liberal criteria of procedural correctness – is legitimate.

In Chapter 2 of this book, "The Complexity of Minority Issues," I presented my approach to these types of issues, which entails viewing each one of them within a three-dimensional coordinate system whose axes denote the degree of importance of the following three types of factors in every specific case: *cultural differences*, *group solidarity*, and social *and political factors*. In this regard, I also examined various typologies of social relations, focusing particularly on the typology proposed by Amy Gutmann (2003) – that of identity groups and interest groups – which is most relevant to the subject matter of my study. However, everything in the further course of this study showed that Gutmann's typology is a strong idealization. In reality, identity groups do not exist in pure form. Within ethnic, religious, and national communities, we find not only instances of mutual identification of their members with one another, but also cases of behavior driven by self-interest. There are also examples of behavior motivated by self-interest that is "disguised" as identity-driven. I think that the term "entrepreneurs of identity," introduced by the authors of a recent study on the psychology of leadership (Haslam, Reicher, and Platow 2011, 137), which I will discuss below, is very telling in this respect.

One of the factors that casts a reasonable doubt on minority cultural claims is the possibility of manipulating public opinion, whereby political interests are pursued through demands for satisfying alleged cultural-identity needs of the members of minority groups – needs that are non-existent, or are not what they are claimed to be, or at least are not as urgent as they are claimed to be. As practice shows, such manipulation is usually done by leaders of the community, or by groups within it that are fighting for influence, or by representatives of external political forces who are trying to use minorities to their own ends.

This kind of manipulation of public opinion usually presupposes manipulation of communication within the minority group itself. Someone ascribes to its members cultural needs which may not necessarily be recognized as such, or exactly as such, by the members themselves. That is why ensuring the procedural correctness of the communication through which the community's identity is reproduced over time would increase the credibility of claims that may be put forward and articulated through intra-group discussions of this kind.

Let us imagine that these discussions are conducted in the format of public deliberation, namely: without the coercion of participants (any attempt at exerting pressure can be exposed by the person targeted and this would discredit the discussion as a whole); the outcome of the discussion of every issue is decided by the force of the better argument; no one can be prevented from contributing their relevant arguments to the debate. In this case, it would be very difficult to make claims regarding norms and policies on which there is no reasonable consensus in the community. Any attempt to motivate the group members to support such claims may be contested by any one of them and is likely to fail. In this sense, binding the chances for public legitimization of minority claims to the public-deliberative procedural correctness of the ethical-political discourses that "produce" these claims would help to distinguish the promotion of a genuine identity "cause" (which may rely on recognition in a liberal democratic society) from the pursuit of self-serving social and political ends.

In this regard, the possibilities provided by the internet for conducting ethical-political discourses in the format of public deliberation are noteworthy. Of course, the traditional forms of public communication are also welcome, but the internet has definite advantages. As I mentioned in Chapter 6, the opportunity for participating in public discussions under a hidden identity minimizes the chances for exerting coercion over participants. Even the most non-violent forms of pressure such as verbal abuse or mockery will not have a significant effect if a person who has decided to use the web to reveal truths that are inconvenient for someone else does this under a nickname or fake identity. In this case the message will appear on the web independently of its true author. Besides, such a form of communication helps to ensure the equal standing of the interlocutors – it is irrelevant whether or not the author of the message enjoys high social prestige if the addressees do not know who the author actually is. What matters is the plausibility of the message itself. And, lastly, the fact that the communication is conducted remotely – not face-to-face – minimizes the role of the participants' rhetorical skills and charisma.

Ethical-political discourses as enclave deliberations

However, one of the parameters of ethical-political discourses seems quite problematic, as far as the public-deliberative correctness of this kind of communication is concerned – namely, their *exclusivity*. In this frame of reference a decision cannot be considered legitimate if persons (individuals, groups) who would be affected by its realization are excluded from the discussion. Ethical-political discourses are exclusive, in a way, because they proceed mainly on a substantive basis. As discussed in the previous chapter, an "outsider" cannot even evaluate the cogency of the arguments that are used, let alone participate in the debates, which is why this type of discourse falls into the category of so-called "enclave" deliberations (see Sunstein 2002a; Karpowitz et al. 2009).

This term has acquired a somewhat pejorative meaning in recent discussions, with a number of scholars indicating the various risks that ensue from the not properly public nature of this type of deliberation. These include such issues as the prioritization of the group's interests at the expense of the public good, the pitfalls of "groupthink" (particularly the risk of group polarization), and the inevitable limitation of the diversity of views taken into account (see Sunstein 2002a; Karpowitz et al. 2009, 580).

In this respect, the most serious difficulty would arise if we could not answer the simple question: how are the interests of society to be represented in a given ethical-political discourse? Claims that certain minority cultural needs must be satisfied are, in fact, demands that certain public policies be implemented, and the content and scope of such policies are a matter of importance not only for the members of the minority in question, but also for society at large. Will material resources be utilized for such purposes, and if so, in what amounts? Will a public administration accept additional significant obligations, such as the introduction of official bilingualism in a region with a substantial minority population? How seriously might a country's cultural space be fragmented if minority-run media are allowed to function? Should minority educational institutions be established? These are all questions that concern a given society as a whole.

The interests of society should thus be represented in the intra-group public deliberation which concerns the reproduction of the cultural identity of the minority over time. There is no doubt that society as a whole is one of the parties potentially affected by the outcome of such deliberations. If decisions concerning the identity in question are made "behind the back" of any such party, they cannot claim legitimacy as a result of public deliberation.

What would the problem of the representation of the interests of society at large in minority ethical-political discourses look like if we were to view it within the framework of the debate on "enclave deliberations"? A number of empirical studies, mostly in social psychology (some of the most authoritative ones are mentioned in Sunstein 2002a), give us reason to question the deliberative quality of discussions conducted in groups of "like-minded people" (a cliché often used in this debate – see ibid., 176). The main shortcoming of enclave deliberations with regard to the credibility of their results in the eyes of the "outside" public, is the so-called "group polarization," meaning that "the members of a deliberating group predictably move toward a more extreme point in the direction of their pre-deliberation views" (Sunstein 2002b, 120). In a later article, Sunstein (2007) also uses the term "ideological amplification" to refer to a special case of group polarization in which deliberation in like-minded groups tends to lead people to move "toward a more extreme point in the ideological direction to which the group's members were originally inclined" (Sunstein 2007, 274).

How can we explain this phenomenon of mutual "incitement" in cases of deliberation among like-minded people – for example, people with a shared identity? Undoubtedly, this is very important as it has a direct bearing on the question of whether or not ethical-political discourses may produce claims that merit the trust of the public at large. Sunstein identifies three factors that contribute to "ideological amplification." One is the specificity of the argumentation in such deliberative settings. According to the critics of "enclave deliberation," argumentation in such settings is inevitably distorted. When the majority of the arguments are skewed in a particular direction, participants are psychologically inclined to trust these arguments more than those that contradict them:

If the group's members are already inclined in a certain direction, they will offer a disproportionately large number of arguments going in that same direction, and a disproportionately small number of arguments going the other way. As a result, the consequence of discussion will be to move people further in the direction of their initial inclinations.

(Sunstein 2007, 275)

One could object that, if the criteria for public-deliberative correctness of the debate are met, then the frequency of usage of particular types of arguments should not matter. However, what does matter in this case is that if the discussion is not fully open, there is a danger that the arguments will be one-sided in terms of the content of the viewpoints presented in them: "the central factor behind ideological amplification is the existence of a *limited argument pool*, one that is skewed (speaking purely descriptively) in a particular direction" (Sunstein 2007, 275; emphasis in original).

The other two factors identified by Sunstein are of a psychological nature. One, which the author terms "social comparison," is based on people's desire to be perceived favorably by the other group members, as well as to perceive themselves favorably. This desire leads to conformity in discussions: "Once they hear what others believe, they often adjust their positions in the direction of the dominant position" (ibid.). The third factor is trust in the opinion of like-minded interlocutors. People are inclined to "become more confident after learning that others share their views" (ibid., 276). This psychological factor is all the more important when the participants in the deliberation share the same identity. In such cases, "persuasive arguments are likely to be still more persuasive; the identity of those who are making them gives them a kind of credential or boost" (ibid.).

The phenomenon of "enclave deliberations" is particularly prevalent on the web, according to widespread opinion. This is because participants in such communication have greater freedom to choose where to get their information from, whom to communicate with, and which discussions to take part in. Unlike traditional print and broadcast media, on the web people can configure the set of their sources of information and interlocutors as they prefer. Which blogs they read, which websites they visit, which forums they participate in, which friends they choose on Facebook – these and all other such decisions are up to individual users: "The internet is seen as increasingly giving users the ability to 'filter' information and interactions and so 'self-select' what they wish to be exposed to" (Dahlberg 2007, 829). As a result, they surround themselves almost exclusively with like-minded people and this leads to enclave deliberations, and hence, to group polarization and ideological amplification:

We find that blog readers gravitate toward blogs that accord with their political beliefs. Few read blogs on both the left and right of the ideological spectrum. Furthermore, those who read left-wing blogs and those who read right-wing blogs are ideologically far apart. Blog readers are more polarized

than either non-blog-readers or consumers of various television news programs, and roughly as polarized as US senators.

(Lawrence, Sides, and Farrell 2010, 141)

However, other empirical studies contradict these findings. Lincoln Dahlberg
(2007, 829) refers to publications on internet democracy, whose authors, such as
Jack M. Balkin, Jennifer Stromer-Galley, and David Weinberger, claim that on
the web "people are meeting difference and engaging in debate with others of
opposing positions." They argue, writes Dahlberg (2007, 830), "that research
shows that, as well as helping people find groups of similar interest and identity,
the internet is being used by many people encounter difference that they would
not normally encounter in everyday life."

The various types of virtual communication offer empirical evidence in
support of both of these opposing views. What is important in our case, however,
is the danger that ethical-political minority discourses conducted on the Internet
may erupt into flows of self-catalyzing, escalating grievances and demands
addressed at the general public and the institutions of political power – all of this
being done without any self-reflection and self-criticism whatsoever.

On the other hand, however, some of the authors working in this field point
out that enclave deliberations can play a positive role, too. They argue that deliberations of this sort enable members of groups and categories of citizens, whose
voice is unlikely to be heard in universally accessible discussions, to work out,
articulate, and justify their positions on issues that affect their interests, thus
raising their chances of exerting influence on public opinion, and ultimately – on
the institutions of political power.

Why is it assumed that some voices will be stifled in the "general chorus"?

The central empirical point here is that in deliberating bodies, high-status
members tend to speak more than others, and their ideas are more influential
– partly because low-status members lack confidence in their own abilities,
and partly because they fear retribution.

(Sunstein 2007, 277)

A number of authors even use, in a somewhat Gramscian spirit, the term "false
consensus" (Simone 2010, 124) to refer to public debates in which the positions
of some "subaltern publics" are not represented – not because these publics have
no objections against the proposed decisions, but because they were unable to
formulate and articulate them in a way that is sufficiently convincing for the
public at large.

In this sense, enclave deliberations may be a source of ideas and arguments
that would otherwise not appear in mainstream public communication. Thus,
they may help protect public communication from one-sidedness – that is, precisely from the flaw which quite a few authors ascribe to them. In the words of
their most outspoken critic, Cass R. Sunstein (2007, 277), enclave deliberations
can "greatly enrich the social 'argument pool'." As a whole, the discussion on

this kind of deliberation overlaps, in many respects, with the one on counterpublics mentioned in Chapter 4. Counterpublics may be viewed precisely as "territories" in which enclave deliberations are conducted. In both cases, however, the question remains as to how these only partly public deliberations can be included in the public sphere proper in a way that protects them, at least to some extent, from manipulation. For if we judge from the means by which public influence is exercised in practice by counterpublics such as the African-American, feminist, or gay and lesbian ones, this is done with the help of propaganda, public protests and political methods – that is, in ways that provide no guarantee whatsoever against possible distortions of public communication in the sense of pursuing individual or group self-serving interests on the pretext of fighting for justice.

In this regard, some authors propose possible forms of mediation between enclave deliberations and the general public – forms which, in essence, would not be foreign to public deliberation, especially when it comes to internet communication. Cass R. Sunstein (2001, 11) mentions "general interest intermediaries," which may play a role on the web that is analogous to that of national newspapers and broadcasters in traditional media. Maria Simone (2010, 131) proposes that the connection between the "shared nodes" and the "enclave nodes" on the web be effected by "highly connected individuals." Neither Sunstein nor Simone, however, explain how they believe these intermediaries should resolve the difficult problems that stem from the contrast between the two types of debate – deliberation within a limited circle of interlocutors who have relatively equal standing and "speak the same language," and deliberation that is open to all sorts of participants.

What do the criticisms of enclave deliberations entail for the hypothesis discussed here – namely, that the communicative empowerment of minorities could be achieved by aligning the ethical-political discourses, through which their cultural identities are reproduced over time, with the public-deliberative criteria of procedural correctness? These criticisms show, in a convincing manner, what happens when deliberations do not meet one important criterion related to their legitimizing capacity: their inclusiveness with regard to the position of everyone who is, or may be, affected by the decision under discussion. In the case of ethical-political minority discourses, this concerns society at large – it seems that its interests are not represented in these discourses in any way. This circumstance gives us reason to fear that even if the other three criteria are met in a discourse of this kind – namely, that it is free of coercion, that it is rational, and is conducted between participants on an equal footing – it may produce evaluations and positions regarding the community's cultural needs that are detrimental to the interests of society at large. I have in mind, above all, excessive, maximalistic claims regarding the norms and public policies that concern the conditions for the functioning of the community's identity.

In this regard, however, I would also like to point out some limitations of the debate on enclave deliberations. Judging from the publications devoted to it, to the best of my knowledge, a distinction is not made between types of enclave deliberation that differ in significant ways. Let us ask ourselves, for example, whether the group dynamics that account for the peculiarities of enclave deliberation are influenced (and if so, exactly how) by possible overlap between two kinds of self-identification of the participants in the debate. In one respect, these people identify with their like-minded interlocutors, for sure. However, is it not possible that in certain types of debates they, or at least some of them, may happen to also share an identity with other citizens who are also affected by the issue that is being discussed, but in a different way? By and large, the authors of these publications base their criticism of the flaws of enclave deliberation on instances when an issue is being discussed by interlocutors who have determined their position on it freely, guided exclusively by their civic consciousness. This circumstance practically rules out the possibility that a participant in an enclave deliberation may have a substantially ambivalent attitude toward the issue that is being discussed. If someone happens to be torn between two mutually exclusive positions concerning the subject matter of such a deliberation she will simply not join this particular debate.

The situation of people whose position on some issue is bound to their objective identity (even though, if we regard it from a constructionist point of view, it may be subject to development, redefinition, renegotiation, and so forth) is entirely different. In these cases, participants in a debate on such an issue cannot decide freely which group of "like-minded people" they will join. If they identify for some reason with more than one group or category of people, they may turn out to be in a contradictory position regarding the issue under discussion. Formulated in the terms of social identity theory, it may turn out that these individuals belong in some respect to a particular in-group, but in another respect to a different group that is an out-group in regard to the former one. In Chapter 2, I mentioned that in Central and Eastern Europe there are plenty of cases where people share an ethnic identity with one group and a religious identity with another, which means that to them the same individuals are representatives of both their in-group and an out-group. To a Muslim of Turkish ethnicity in Bulgaria, for example, a fellow Muslim may be an Other in another respect (if he or she is an ethnic Bulgarian or Roma). This holds true, of course, for the relationship between any minority identity and the national one. Furthermore, how would an enclave deliberation on, say, religious issues develop if the participants in it are of the same religion but differ by ethnicity or race? Would the group dynamics be the same as those of, for example, a gathering of environmentalists discussing the efficacy of woodland preservation?

Prima facie, it appears that the decisive factor in such a situation is the relative salience of the two overlapping and, in some cases, competing identities. Which one of these will the participants in the enclave debate choose to "heed" in determining their position, and which one will they choose to "ignore"? What will their choice depend on? It seems unlikely that people will be making such an important decision on a whim. However, such ambivalent situations leave a lot of room for manipulation of the debate by "entrepreneurs of identity."

Another criterion by which cases of enclave deliberation can be differentiated is the nature of the discussed topic – by whether or not the issues under discussion are of a teleological or a deontological nature. In other words, does the discussion aim to elaborate a collective position that concerns the attainment of some common goal, the realization of some project, or is the discussion focused on the achievement of a balance of the interests of all parties concerned in some problematic situation? I will discuss this issue in more detail later. At this point, I will only note that the bias stemming from the only partly public character of enclave deliberations is bound to be expressed to a different degree in the elaboration of teleological or deontological collective positions.

There is one more criterion by which enclave deliberations can be differentiated – by whether or not the debates are conducted anonymously. This issue has become all the more important with the rise of internet communication as a means of influencing public opinion. The effect of anonymity on group polarization has been actively studied in social psychology. A number of empirical studies devoted to it are presented in the articles, "The Positive and Negative Implications of Anonymity in Internet Social Interactions: 'On the Internet, Nobody Knows You're a Dog'" by Kimberly M. Christopherson (2007), and "Anonymity in Computer-Mediated Communication: More Contrarian Ideas with Less Influence" by Russell Haines, Jill Hough, Lan Cao, and Douglas Haines (2014).

I cannot discuss these in detail here. I will only note one of the results of an experiment conducted by the authors of the second article, which, in my opinion, confirms common-sense expectations: anonymity in discussing ethically relevant issues helps to reduce the conformism of viewpoints expressed by the participants but, at the same time, intensifies extremist tendencies in the discussion (see Haines et al. 2014, 779). This means that anonymity reduces group polarization in one respect but increases it in another. However, this publication, as well as many others in the field of social psychology that are devoted to this topic, does not discuss the argumentation of viewpoints expressed by participants in enclave deliberations – what reasons they give, how they justify their agreement or disagreement with others' opinions, what arguments they think are convincing and why they think so, and so forth.

Of course, the rationality of enclave deliberations is beyond the scope of social psychology studies. However, this issue is very important with regard to the credibility of the outcomes of such debates in the eyes of the public at large. In my opinion, the reduction of conformism and the intensification of extremism, which are phenomena characteristic of anonymous debates, are expressed to a different degree when these debates are conducted in a rational manner. The conformism-driven withholding of relevant arguments or counter-arguments has a significant impact on the quality of the debate, while the expression of extremist viewpoints is difficult to rationally justify to a public that holds liberal democratic views.

The dual identity of minority group members

Now, let us return to the question of how the interests of society at large could also be represented in an ethical-political discourse conducted within a minority community. This is a necessary condition for bringing ethical-political discourses into accord with the criteria of procedural correctness, that is, for ensuring the "undistorted-ness" of communication. As I pointed out at the beginning of this chapter, here I examine the possibility that the procedural correctness of an intra-group discussion of a minority community's cultural needs may serve as a guarantee to an external public that the claims produced by this discussion will present "to the world" genuine, legitimate needs of the community, and are not merely advancing the self-interests of particular individuals and/or groups. If, however, the interests of society at large are not represented in such an ethical-political discourse, it will "degenerate" into an enclave deliberation with all of the ensuing consequences for its reliability as a means of identifying, articulating, and justifying the respective minority's cultural needs to the general public.

I will try to answer this question by examining another possibility. Could the minority group members *themselves* represent the interests of society at large in such ethical-political discourses and, if they could, under what conditions? Does the fact that they participate in such discourses as "insiders," that is, as sharing beliefs and interests with their fellow minority members, preclude their participation in another capacity as well, namely, as citizens whose best interests involve the good of society as a whole?

Members of minorities are, with exceptions such as newly arrived immigrants, citizens of the country in which they live. It should be in their interest, therefore, that not only their community has the best conditions possible for the reproduction of its identity over time, but also that society as a whole prospers. It is clearly the case that the members of a minority community cannot benefit from any right that their community might enjoy if the country as a whole has been reduced to ruin as a result of their "successful" struggle to attain the recognition of their rights. History presents us with numerous examples of counterproductive fights for racial, ethnic, and religious rights that have achieved only Pyrrhic victories. That is to say that they in fact degraded the conditions of the very people whose good they sought to foster precisely because of the disruptions they caused in the broader social order. In this sense, there are sound reasons to assume that the identity of members of minority groups is dual – both cultural and civic. But why does history show that the behavior of such persons is usually driven more by their identity as members of a minority than as citizens? Why are they more inclined to identify themselves with the members of their community than with the rest of their fellow-citizens?

As I have repeatedly noted in this book, I view minority issues within a coordinate system with three "axes": cultural differences, group solidarity, and social and political interests (see Chapter 2). Put in terms of social identity theory, the above question would sound as follows: why do members of a minority community usually see themselves as an in-group and society at large as an out-group, considering that society should also be an in-group for them? In fact, one would expect such persons to have a dual identity, identifying themselves with both of these interacting groups.

Multiple identities have been studied in social psychology for decades, especially the conflicts within them.

> When identities are in conflict, the individual perceives them as incompatible or in opposition to each other. In contrast, when identities facilitate each other – that is, enactment of one identity makes enactment of the other identity easier, then identity harmony, or identity integration occurs.
>
> (Settles and Buchanan 2014, 170)

In the case of minority issues, most of them involve conflicts within minority identities, i.e. between the cultural and the civic "self" of the minority group members. Various models have been developed to describe the ways in which individuals cope with the tensions between the different "components" of their identities. For example, Sonia Roccas and Marilynn Brewer have proposed a model of "multiple identity complexity" (Roccas and Brewer 2002), which comprises four possible patterns of reconciling two distinct identities within the same individual. One of them is the so-called "unique compound group, e.g., middle-class lesbian" (Settles and Buchanan 2014, 171). Another one is merging the two identities in an additive manner – e.g. middle class and lesbian (see ibid.). A third opportunity is to suppress one of them (e.g. lesbian). And the fourth opportunity is the so-called "compartmentalization," which means that only one of the identities is activated at a time, depending on the situation (see ibid.). Another group of authors (see Amiot et al. 2007) proposed a model of resolving conflicts between identities in two ways. "The individual could develop a superordinate identity that reconciles the conflicts or the individual could recognize that the 'conflicting' components of each identity contribute positively to her sense of self" (Settles and Buchanan 2014, 171).

So, how can social identity theory help us explain the obvious fact that the cultural "component" of the identity of a minority group member tends to prevail over its civic "counterpart," thereby keeping the minority ethical-political discourses in the "track" of enclave deliberations and hindering the public legitimization of minority claims? An important factor for the unbalanced relationship between the civic and the cultural "sides" of a minority member's identity is, in my opinion, the intra-group dynamics of the minority community. If the relations between such a community and society at large are of the win-lose type, participants in ethical-political discourses will compete with each other in defending in-group interests at the expense of out-group ones, thereby contributing to the group polarization, ideological amplification, "groupthink" (Janis 1982), and so forth. In a win-lose setting, the reputation and the self-conception of a group member (see Sunstein 2002a: 177) are positively correlated with her contribution to the group's success in its competition with out-groups.

Group leadership plays a significant role in steering the interactions between minority communities and society at large in a win-lose direction. Some recent studies in the field of Social Identity Theory and Self-Categorization Theory have yielded interesting results. According to the authors of the monograph, *The*

New Psychology of Leadership: Identity, Influence, and Power, "effective leadership is always about how leaders and followers come to see each other as part of a common team or group – as members of the same *in-group*" (Haslam, Reicher, and Platow 2011, XXI; emphasis in original). This study, which I think sheds new light on the dynamics of intra-group relations, identifies several roles of group leaders that explain to a great extent the confrontation of minority groups with society at large.

One of them is the role of the in-group prototype. The more the leaders personify the identity of the group, the more effective they are:

> First, the effectiveness of leaders is tied to their in-group prototypicality; second, that in-group prototypicality is not a set characteristic of "us" but rather a function of how "we" relate to "them"; third, as the nature of "them" changes, so does the in-group prototype and hence the qualities that mark out a person as a leader.
>
> (Haslam, Reicher, and Platow 2011, 84)

This hypothesis is in agreement with the results of empirical studies which show that if the group is locked into overtly confrontational relations with an out-group, leadership positions in it are taken by members with more extremist attitudes (see ibid., 91). More generally, confrontation with an "external adversary" makes it easier for leaders to control the group. Other authors working in the paradigm of social identity theory claim that group conflicts in principle "not only create antagonistic intergroup relations but also heighten identification with, and positive attachment to, the in-group" (Tajfel and Turner 1986, 8). This peculiarity of group dynamics gives minority community leaders one more motive for putting forward maximalistic claims for rights and freedoms.

Another role that distinguishes a member of the group as its leader is that of "in-group champion" (Haslam, Reicher, and Platow 2011, 109). By this the authors mean that members expect their leaders "to promote the group interest *in the terms specified by the group's own norms and values*" (ibid., 132–133; emphasis in the original). The in-group champion usually demonstrates fairness in her relations with members of the in-group, and favors them over people in the out-group (see ibid., 132). Another important role of leaders is that of "entrepreneur of identity" (ibid., 137). This role implies the active participation of leaders in defining the boundaries of the group and the content of its identity (which beliefs and values are shared by its members, what distinguishes them from all others, and so on). In other words, successful leaders are able to "steer" the processes of group identity construction in accordance with their own interests: "Our argument is that, precisely because definitions of identity have such important social and political consequences, leaders will seek to mold these definitions to their own purposes rather than accept them as given" (Ibid., 146). Besides, it is very important that they do so in a subtle manner. As the authors point out, identity entrepreneurship actually involves a double labor. On the one hand, considerable work is involved in crafting a definition that is both plausible and appropriate to one's purposes. On the other hand, an equal amount of work is involved in hiding all this labor and making one's accounts of identity seem obvious, effortless, and "natural."

(Ibid., 146–147)

The final (as listed by the authors) role of leaders from the point of view of social identity theory and self-categorization theory, is that of "embedder of identity" (ibid., 165), which comprises their functions as an artist, impresario, and engineer of identity.

I have ventured to discuss this study in greater detail because it convincingly demonstrates the effects that group leaders' actions have on group dynamics. The question of what group leadership may consist of is important and complex in its own right and I cannot deal with it here. I will only note that the leadership of a minority community may be formal (in the context of legally regulated political empowerment of minorities in a given country, or of recognized collective minority rights), as well as informal, while functions such as those described in the above-quoted book can also be performed by activists – especially by militant activists – of the group. In all cases, however, such actions lead to confrontation between minority communities and society at large by the logic of in-group/out-group competition and of a zero-sum game. It is only natural that in such situations it will be difficult to sustain the "duality" of the identity of minorities' members – as members of such communities and as citizens. Consequently, the civic "component" remains in, so to speak, a latent state.

Leaders often create confrontation between minorities and society at large not only indirectly, by influencing group dynamics, but also in a more direct way – by subordinating their community's identity "cause" to their own political interests. In Chapter 2 of this book I examined these two components of minority issues, paying special attention to the possibility that one type of relations and action can be "disguised" as the other. By this I specifically mean the cases in which claims that are allegedly related to conditions for the proper reproduction over time of community identity are, in fact, used to promote the self-interests of a particular leader or group within the community. Attempts by members of the group, who belong to its elite, to gain nationwide political influence through some decisive interventions in situations of strained relations between the community and society at large are especially characteristic in this respect. Let us take, for instance, the cases in which the advancement of minority rights is accompanied by measures to provide political guarantees for their observance, which in turn improves prospects for minority leaders to be integrated into the political elite of the country. More generally, political interests – including those of political formations outside the minorities themselves – can also contribute to the exacerbation of tensions between minority communities and society at large. Nationalist tendencies in the political life of a given country, for example, predictably lead to the defensive mobilization of minorities.

What possibilities are there for achieving, by ideological and public-political means, a balance between the cultural and civic components of the identity of minority members, that is, between group solidarity and civic solidarity? A general solution is proposed by the "orthodox" liberal approach to minority issues, according to which public life should be guided exclusively by universal values, while the influence of cultural ones should be limited only to the private life of individuals (see, for example, Chapter 2). Concepts of universalistic solidarity are also discussed in the literature on this subject. Some authors have developed a theory of civic solidarity. According to Benjamin Barber (1998, 116), for example, the civic voice "speaks in terms that reveal and elicit common grounds, cooperative strategies, overlapping interests, and a sense of the public weal." Other authors, such as William Rehg, John Rawls, Thomas Scanlon, and Charles Larmore, abide by a concept of moral solidarity:

> Citizens who maintain moral solidarity are thus motivated by a sense of duty to justify themselves to others; this is a necessary condition for being a moral agent. While some conflicts ultimately may prove intractable, this does not disrupt the obligation to be civil to others in the public sphere.
>
> (Smith 2011, 6)

Still others, such as Charles Taylor or Shane O'Neill, point to the possibility of justifying universalistic solidarity by the multiculturalist principle of recognition based on the understanding of its reciprocity in the sense that it is not just us who owe others recognition but also others who owe us recognition; therefore, everyone stands to benefit in their self-realization from the universal granting of recognition (see Smith 2011, 7). Jürgen Habermas also acknowledges the balance between the two types of solidarity as a condition for recognizing the cultural rights of members of minority communities. As mentioned above (see Chapter 7), in his article, "Religious Tolerance – The Pacemaker for Cultural Rights," Habermas argues that citizens may be empowered to develop their cultural identity only under the condition that they do this as citizens of their political community (see Habermas 2004, 18).

Here I will take a substantially different approach to the issue of how to achieve a balance between the two components of the identity of minority group members, an approach that is consistent with the ultimate objective of this study – namely, to find possibilities for legitimizing minority claims in the eyes of a broader public that does not share the lifeworld of the minority community and therefore cannot judge in a substantive manner the validity of these claims. In the course of the study, we identified one such possibility – justifying such claims by referring to the procedural correctness of the ethical-political discourses through which they are articulated and substantiated. This procedural correctness, which guarantees that the claims are not the product of manipulated communication and therefore express legitimate cultural needs of the members of the community, can also be evaluated by external observers because it has parameters that can be empirically ascertained. In this way the claims produced by ethical-political discourses can be made convincing to the public eye.

But, as we already know, one of the conditions for the procedural correctness of ethical-political discourse is that the interests of society at large must also be represented in it, in order to prevent it from developing into an enclave deliberation. In my opinion these interests may be represented by the participants in the discourse *themselves*, provided, however, that they also identify themselves with the rest of their fellow-citizens, not just with each other. In other words, I see the balance between the cultural and the civic component of the identity of minority community members as a necessary condition for the public-deliberative correctness of ethical-political discourses.

In the course of this study we also arrived at the conclusion that the confrontation of minority communities with society at large – or, in other words, relations of the win-lose type – are a major obstacle to achieving such a balance. How can we deal with this challenge? I claim that it would be enough if the ethical-political discourses through which the self-understanding of such communities is articulated (and *eo ipso* their cultural identities are reproduced over time and claims addressed to the public and the institutions of political power are formulated and justified) are brought into conformity with the main criteria of public-deliberative correctness – freedom from coercion, rationality, equality, and openness.

What are my reasons for this line of thinking? The tension that exists between minority communities and society at large is due to certain factors. In this chapter, we examined the role of the social psychological factor "group leadership" and of the political factor "pursuit of individual and group *power* interests on the pretext of defending cultural identity." Of course, these are hardly the only sources of confrontation, but I believe they are the most important ones. If the communication between minority communities and society at large, through which the cultural needs of minority members are legitimized, is reframed so as to be immune to the influence of these two factors, the causes of tension between these communities and the wider society will most likely be eliminated, or at least minimized.

In other words, if the minority claims for legislation and public policies which would be favorable for the proper reproduction of minority identities over time are produced by ethical-political discourses that take place in a "territory" where leadership and politics are irrelevant, this interaction between minority communities and society at large would not be confrontational. It would be an interaction of a wholly cultural nature, without the involvement of group rivalries and political interests. In my view, all of this is possible if the claims in question are produced through "horizontal," not "vertical," communication – that is, if the outcomes of the discourses are determined by the force of the better argument, not by psychological manipulation or power pressure.

In such a case, the outcomes of these discourses would not affect anyone's status as a leader or political figure, and no one would stand to gain from exaggerating or minimizing claims related to the conditions for the reproduction of the cultural identity of minorities over time. Of course, bringing the ethical-political discourses in question[2] into alignment with the requirements of public deliberation is not incompatible with group leadership in minority communities, or with their participation in political life. What I am proposing here is only that the discussion of cultural minority claims be performed according to the rules of public deliberation, which protect it from manipulative influences motivated by considerations that have nothing to do with the safeguarding of minority identities.

However, a conceptual clarification is in order here. By proposing that cultural minority discourses may be distanced from the struggles of leaders' and political interests, I do not mean that participation in such discourses must not be motivated by any self-interest. This would simply be impossible, as shown by a series of convincing arguments against such an idealization of public deliberation that can be found in a keynote article by Jane Mansbridge and eight other eminent representatives of the public-deliberative paradigm (Mansbridge et al. 2010). Many of the participants in ethical-political discourses are motivated not only by an appreciation of their own cultural (ethnic, religious, national) identity, but also by various self-interests. If, for example, the issue under discussion is the use of the mother tongue in the education of children that belong to an ethnic minority, then teachers of this language will be an interested party in the debate. The same holds true for debates on the study of religion in state-owned and municipal schools. If the issue under discussion is the existence and operation of minority media outlets, one of the factors influencing the course of the debate will inevitably be the interests of the journalists who work, or would work, in such media outlets. This also applies to debates on the status of minority cultural institutions such as theatres and folk ensembles, and so forth.

Unlike the influence exerted in the course of such discussions by actual or aspiring minority leaders and politicians, participation in these discussions of rank-and-file members of the minority community who are motivated by individual or group self-interest would not lead to confrontation with the society at large, as long as the discussions are conducted in the format of public deliberation. Even if the self-interest of some of the participants drives them to make claims aimed at achieving self-serving ends, during the course of public deliberation the relative "weight" of their interests can always be compared – through the exchange of arguments related to shared culture-specific attitudes and values – with that of the interest of the other participants. Using alleged minority cultural needs as a cover for private self-interests can fool the general public, but not the members of the same cultural community.

On a more general level, the observance of the criteria of public deliberation by the participants in ethical-political discourses does not exclude self-interest as a motive for participation. For example, what would motivate us to agree with arguments that we cannot refute by presenting more convincing ones, even if this is against our interest? If our participation in such a discourse is driven by the common cause of our minority community to legitimize its claims in the eyes of the general public, then the answer to this question is obvious. Even if we have to make concessions regarding our immediate self-interest, in the longer term we stand to gain more from participating in the life of a community that enjoys good relations with society at large, rather than suffer discrimination, humiliation, and even repression as a participant in an ethnic, religious, or other conflict of this sort. If the procedural correctness of the ethical-political discourse is the price the community has to pay for the recognition of its claims for improvements in the norms and public policies that affect it, its members would benefit more from paying this price than from pursuing their immediate individual self-interests.

Relations of this sort between the individual members of a minority community and the general public would be guided by the "civilizing force of hypocrisy" discussed by Jon Elster (see Chapter 4). Unlike the influence exerted by this force over a politician, however, what is to be evaluated in our case is the correctness, not of an individual behavior, but of a discourse – in the sense that it is being protected from manipulation and, hence, in the sense of its credibility. Of course, such a configuration of the relations in question presupposes an adequate deliberative disposition on the part of the general public itself, that is, a capacity for evaluating the procedural correctness of minority discourses and readiness to comply with the claims they "produce" if these claims are judged to be legitimate. An appropriate illustration of such deliberative rapport between authors and addressees of claims is provided by a case study of communication between citizens and the local public administration in Sweden. This study focuses on the degree to which arguments are used in complaints about public school issues from citizens to the local authorities, and finds that they are used fairly often The explanation proposed is that in justifying their claims, the authors of the complaints are guided by their notions of the mentality of Swedish civil servants (assumed to be relatively rational and pragmatic) and seek to formulate their claims in a way that would help them achieve the desired effect on their addressees:

> If this is true, it might very well be the case that we are dealing with self-reinforcing processes: citizens behave more deliberatively – state opinions clearly supported by reason – if they know that it pays off in the context in which they participate (cf. Gambetta 1998).
>
> (Öberg and Uba 2014, 420)

* * *

How can such a methodology for the public legitimization of minority claims be applied in practice? My view is that this would involve nothing less than promoting the development of minority publics of the type that Fraser (1997, 81) terms "subaltern counterpublics." It is possible, in my estimation, that such multiple publics become arenas for ethical-political discourses concerning the identities and cultural needs of the respective communities.

The counterpublics that already exist function – as Fraser has shown – as safe spaces where the group's members develop, within a favorable communicative environment, both an awareness of their true interests, as well as the skills needed to defend these interests in public discussions. Furthermore, the so-called "enclave deliberations" are regarded by both their critics and supporters as capable of serving "the larger cause of a fully inclusive public discourse by giving disempowered or marginalized groups an opportunity to develop their own unique perspectives and arguments, which might otherwise be overlooked or ignored" (Karpowitz et al. 2009, 582). Fraser (1997) uses the example of late twentieth century feminist counterpublics to show how such discourses can take place by means of "a variegated array of journals, bookstores, publishing companies, film and video distribution networks, lecture series, research centers, academic programs, conferences, conventions, festivals, and local meeting places." Of course, counterpublics can also function in many other formats – through discourses within the audience of an organization like the European Council for Fatwa and Research ("a transnational institution committed to the elaboration of a Muslim jurisprudence for minorities through the production and dissemination of fatwas for Muslims living in Europe" – Caeiro 2010, 435), or on the pages of minority media outlets (Kaufer and Al-Malki 2009), or within a network of bloggers (Eckert and Chadha 2013), and so forth.

However, there is a significant difference between, on the one hand, the model of minority publics that I propose as a means to overcome the cultural gap in public deliberations concerning minority policies and, on the other, the model followed by the feminist, gay/lesbian, and African-American counterpublics that functions more or less successfully today, especially in the United States. In contrast to the latter model, I regard minority public spheres not as training grounds where people belonging to categories and groups of citizens subject to discrimination can prepare themselves for battle in the public arena, but rather as platforms from which they can demonstrate to the public at large what really matters to them.

Consequently, I do not seek to help the minority publics and the general one find a common language by minimizing the requirements for deliberativeness in public communication, as scholars such as Bohman, Valadez, James, Deveaux and quite a few others do. On the contrary, it is especially important for the model I propose that ethical-political discourses in minority publics take place in such a way that they leave no room for doubt on the part of the general public that they are procedurally correct, that is, that their results are agreed upon in a rational, inclusive, free, and equal manner by all parties affected. It is thereby possible to prevent any suspicion that the minority claims produced by such discourses may result from strategic manipulation by community leaders (or factions), "false consciousness," or other factors that render them unworthy of public recognition.

So, the communicative empowerment of a minority group would ideally amount to the attainment by its members of the ability to conduct an ethical-political discourse concerning its cultural needs that conforms to the most important criteria of public deliberation. In practical terms, the communicative empowerment of a minority community would make it possible for ever-growing numbers of its "rank-and-file" members to participate in public-deliberative debates concerning their cultural needs in relation to the reproduction over time – definition, redefinition, reconstruction, and so forth – of the group's identity. Nowadays the ever accelerating development of internet communication makes such a prospect entirely realistic.

Notes

1 A similar understanding of so-called "external" legitimacy – "we measure external legitimacy as 'the extent to which key actors, decision-makers and the media accept and support the procedure and its outcomes'" – is presented in the article "Deliberative Democracy and Inequality: Two Cheers for Enclave Deliberation among the Disempowered" (Karpowitz et al. 2009, 602). The difference from my approach is that this article concerns a case of enclave deliberation that deals with an issue of general concern, which, as such, involves no element of cultural "intransparency." For this reason, evaluating the procedural correctness of the deliberation is of merely secondary importance in the recognition of the legitimacy of the outcome.
2 In the context of the considerations I set forth here the adjective "political" is misleading, but I prefer not to change Habermas's term in order to avoid bigger misunderstandings.

References

Abu-Nimer, Mohammed. "Framework for Nonviolence and Peacebuilding in Islam." In *Contemporary Islam: Dynamic, not Static* edited by Abdul Said, Mohammed Abu-Nimer, and Meena Sharify-Funk, 131–172. London: Routledge, 2006.

Amiot, Catherine E., Roxane de la Sablonnière, Deborah J. Terry, and Joanne R. Smith. "Integration of Social Identities in the Self: Toward a Cognitive-developmental Model." *Personality and Social Psychology Review* 11 (2007): 364–388.

Barber, Benjamin, *A Place for Us: How to Make Society Civil and Democracy Strong*. New York: Farrar, Straus and Giroux, 1998.

Benhabib, Seyla. "Toward a Deliberative Model of Democratic Legitimacy." In *Democracy and Difference*, edited by Seyla Benhabib, 67–94. Princeton: Princeton University Press, 1996.

Bohman, James. *Public Deliberation*. Cambridge, MA: The MIT Press, 2000.

Caeiro, Alexandre. "The Power of European Fatwas: The Minority Fiqh Project and the Making of an Islamic Counterpublic." *International Journal of Middle East Studies* 42 (2010): 435–449.

Christopherson, Kimberly. "The Positive and Negative Implications of Anonymity in Internet Social Interactions: 'On the Internet, Nobody Knows You're a Dog.'" *Computers in Human Behavior* 23 (2007): 2028–2056.

Cohen, Joshua. "Pluralism and Proceduralism." *Chicago-Kent Law Review* 69 (1994): 589–618.

Cohen, Joshua. "Procedure and Substance in Deliberative Democracy." In *Deliberative Democracy: Essays on Reason and Politics*, edited by James Bohman and William Rehg, 407–438. Cambridge, MA: The MIT Press, 1997.

Dahlberg, Lincoln. "Rethinking the Fragmentation of the Cyberpublic: From Consensus to Contestation." *New Media & Society* 9, no. 5 (2007): 827–847

Eckert, Stine and Kalyani Chadha. "Muslim Bloggers in Germany: An Emerging Counterpublic." *Media, Culture & Society* 35, no. 8 (2013): 926–942.

El-Nawawy, Mohammed and Sahar Khamis. "Collective Identity in the Virtual Islamic Public Sphere. Contemporary Discourses in Two Islamic Websites." *The International Communication Gazette* 72, no. 3 (2010): 229–250.

Fraser, Nancy. 1997. *Justice Interruptus. Critical Reflections on the "Postsocialist Condition."* London: Routledge.

Gambetta, Diego. "Claro! An Essay on Discursive Machismo." In *Deliberative Democracy*, edited by Jon Elster, 19–43. Cambridge, UK: Cambridge University Press, 1998.

Gledhill, James. "Procedure in Substance and Substance in Procedure: Reframing the Rawls–Habermas Debate." In *Habermas and Rawls: Disputing the Political.* Routledge Studies in Contemporary Philosophy 23, edited by James G. Finlayson and Fabian Freyenhagen, London: Routledge, 2011.

Gutmann, Amy. *Identity in Democracy*. Princeton, NJ: Princeton University Press, 2003.

Habermas, Jürgen. "Religious Tolerance – The Pacemaker for Cultural Rights." *Philosophy* 79 (2004): 5–18.

Haslam, Alexander S., Stephen D. Reicher, and Michael J. Platow. *The New Psychology of Leadership: Identity, Influence, and Power.* New York: Psychology Press, 2011.

Haines, Russell, Jill Hough, Lan Cao, Douglas Haines. "Anonymity in Computer-Mediated Communication: More Contrarian Ideas with Less Influence." *Group Decision and Negotiation* 23 (2014): 765–786.

Janis, Irving L. *Groupthink*. Boston: Houghton Mifflin Company, 1982.

Karpowitz, Christopher, Chad Raphael, and Allen S. Hammond. "Deliberative Democracy and Inequality: Two Cheers for Enclave Deliberation among the Disempowered." *Politics & Society* 37, no 4 (2009): 576–615.

Kaufer, David and Amal Mohammed Al-Malki. "The War on Terror through Arab-American Eyes: The Arab-American Press as a Rhetorical Counterpublic." *Rhetoric Review* 28, no. 1 (2009): 47–65.

Kirshner, Alexander S. "Proceduralism and Popular Threats to Democracy." *The Journal of Political Philosophy* 18, no. 4 (2010): 405–424.

Lawrence, Eric, John Sides, and Henry Farrell. "Self-Segregation or Deliberation? Blog Readership, Participation, and Polarization in American Politics." *Perspectives on Politics* 8, no. 1 (2010): 141–157.

Mansbridge, Jane, James Bohman, Simone Chambers, David Estlund, Andreas Føllesdal, Archon Fung, Cristina Lafont, Bernard Manin, and José Luis Martí. "The Place of Self-Interest and the Role of Power in Deliberative Democracy." *The Journal of Political Philosophy* 18, no. 1 (2010): 64–100.

Novoselsky, Valery. "Internet as a Tool of Change and the Role of Roma Virtual Network in a Process of Roma Empowerment." www.romavirtualnetwork.org, accessed December 20, 2015.

Öberg, PerOla and Katrin Uba. "Civil Society Making Political Claims: Outcries, Interest Advocacy, and Deliberative Claims." *Public Administration Review* 74, no. 3 (2014): 413–422.

Roccas, Sonia and Marilynn B. Brewer. "Social Identity Complexity." *Personality and Social Psychology Review* 6 (2002): 88–106.

Settles, Isis H. and Nicole T. Buchanan. "Multiple Groups, Multiple Identities and Intersectionality." In *The Oxford Handbook of Multicultural Identity*, edited by Verónica Benet-Martínez and Ying-yi Hong, 160–180. Oxford: Oxford University Press, 2014.

Simone, Maria. "Deliberative Democracy Online: Bridging Networks with Digital Technologies." *The Communication Review* 13 (2010): 120–139.

Smith, Andrew F. *The Deliberative Impulse: Motivating Discourse in Divided Societies.* Lanham, MD: Lexington Books, 2011.

Sunstein, Cass. *Republic.com*. Princeton, NJ: Princeton University Press, 2001.

Sunstein, Cass R. "The Law of Group Polarization." *The Journal of Political Philosophy* 10, no 2 (2002a): 175–195.

Sunstein, Cass R. "On a Danger of Deliberative Democracy." *Daedalus* 131, no. 4 (2002b): 120–124.

Sunstein, Cass R. "Ideological Amplification." *Constellations* 14, no. 2 (2007): 273–279.

Tajfel, Henri and John Turner. "The Social Identity Theory of Intergroup Behaviour." In *Psychology of Intergroup Relations*, edited by Stephen Worchel and William G. Austin, 7–24. Chicago, IL: Nelson-Hall, 1986.

Conclusion

The subject of this study concerns the protection of minority cultural identities. I proceed from the premise that such identities can be best defended if two conditions are met. On the one hand, protecting a minority cultural identity should make it possible for the members of a given community to live in a manner that is in every way equal to how all other citizens of the country live. On the other, it should contribute in no way to social conflict in any sense of the term.

This study rests on a number of contingencies in order to ensure that it can realistically achieve its objectives. One is that the protection of minority identities is examined within a liberal-democratic social setting, that is, a setting that allows for the functioning of a critical public sphere in which the citizenry is able to exercise "communicative power," to use the Habermasian term. This involves a society where institutions of political power generally take into account public opinion, which, in turn, is formed through public debates regarding the common good and the fairness of social relationships – debates that are largely exempt from manipulation. For example, it is not possible to legitimize public policies that obviously serve private interests at the expense of the common good by means of demagoguery, bribing influential journalists and political analyzers, blackmailing and threatening civil activists, and so forth, because safeguards have been put in place that enable other participants in public communication to expose such abuses without fear of retribution. Another premise is that legislative and political mechanisms have been put into place in order to ensure that the universal rights of minorities are observed to the degree that such issues as discrimination, infringement of the freedom of speech, and the manipulation of elections to the detriment of minorities are no longer a primary concern.

An additional preliminary stipulation is that this study focuses on the possibilities for protecting the cultural identity of minorities in Central and Eastern European countries. We presume that the members of these minorities are characterized by a more or less modern outlook in the sense that they share socio-psychological attitudes and moral values which acknowledge individual autonomy and uphold the ability of individuals to make independent and responsible decisions, base their behavior on universal humanistic standards, and reflect upon their own behavior through the lens of these standards. Consequently, the solutions that this study proposes are not applicable to individuals whose actions are informed by, for example, an unconditional loyalty to a charismatic leader or the conviction that people who do not share their religion do not deserve to be treated as equal human beings.

For such reasons, this study investigates the problems of autochthonous ethnic, religious, and national minorities that possess important historical reasons for placing a value upon their group identity such that they do not nurture the desire to be assimilated into mainstream culture, unlike many immigrants in the countries of Western Europe and North America. Two other important premises are that most of the members of these minorities are reasonably well-educated, and that their communities enjoy a well-functioning public communications infrastructure.

With all of these considerations in mind, what is the specific issue that is at the heart of this study? The first thesis that the study defends is that the protection of the cultural identity of minorities entails more than merely supplementing the observance of universal human rights with the recognition of cultural rights. There are two arguments presented in support of this thesis. The first is that all rights – including cultural rights – are *norms* that, in effect, "homogenize" differences when applied indiscriminately to all of the multifarious issues that are encountered in the life of a minority community. Stated otherwise, the observance of cultural rights alone fails to adequately account for the multiplicity, complexity, and dynamism of minority concerns. The second argument is that such rights can potentially contribute to the fragmentation of societies, particularly when implemented in the form of collective rights, that is, rights which *institutionalize* minority communities to a certain degree. It is thus necessary that the existing system for protecting minority identities be supplemented by instruments that are "fine-tuned" to the specific nature of such issues.

What does "protecting minority identity" mean within the context of the present discussion? This phrase implies, above all, that optimal conditions be created that allow for the reproduction of the cultural identity of minorities over time – in the sense of the *constructionist approach* to identity. Such conditions should foster the realization of cultural identity through educational, mass media, and artistic activities that make it possible for each individual member of a community to identify herself with a cause that transcends the ordinary values of everyday life. This ascribes a special meaning to an individual's existence beyond the mere search for material prosperity. The issues that arise in this regard may at first glance appear to be insignificant and innocuous – what should the language of instruction in school be for the children of ethnic minorities? Is it admissible that localities, rivers, mountains, and so forth, bear two names, one in the official language of the country and another in the local minority language? Is it admissible for Muslim women to wear headscarves in public places? History shows, however, that each of these issues can easily morph into a *casus belli* under certain conditions.

An alternative means for protecting the cultural identity of minority groups that is more flexible than defending cultural rights involves the "empowerment" of minorities by providing opportunities for representatives of minority groups to influence legislative and executive power through participating in the creation and modification of legislative regulations and in the development and implementation of policies that affect minorities. Evaluating the potential of this instrument is a central issue in the present discussion. As modern-day tools of empowerment are overwhelmingly political in nature, this study critically analyzes some of the most common political tools in this regard, such as social internationalism (a phenomenon of the recent past in the countries of Central and Eastern Europe), power sharing (consociational democracy), the politics of presence, and the inclusion of ethnic parties into political life.

One critical argument reveals the danger of combining efforts related to the protection of minority identity with the struggle to gain and affirm political power insofar as such mixing of agendas renders the noble cause of protecting minority cultural identities subordinate to the promotion of private political interests. Another argument highlights the fact that conflating exclusive community solidarity with power relations is a "ticking time-bomb" insofar as power relations can entail the use of force under the pretense of legitimacy.

One viable alternative that this study propounds is the *communicative empowerment* of minorities. This term emanates from the notion of communicative power, which plays a key role in the "two track" model of deliberative politics as developed by Jürgen Habermas and which is best presented in his *Between Facts and Norms*. Communicative empowerment is associated with the influence that minority communities can exert upon public opinion through their publicly legitimized claims, and, consequently, the impact that they can have on the institutions of power through the vehicle of public opinion. The discussion also highlights the fact that communication between minorities and the general public may constitute a significant impediment to communicative empowerment. At the core of this difficulty is the challenge of having to legitimize minority claims to a public that, generally speaking, neither shares the same cultural attitudes, convictions, and values as a given minority, nor is privy to the group dynamics of the minority community in question. This challenge can be further aggravated by the danger that the general public may regard a minority group's claims as an expression of false consciousness on the part of the group that results from the machinations of their leaders, whereby they merit no moral consideration. This constitutes the primary theoretical difficulty that this study was designed to address.

The present discussion puts forward the premise that public deliberation, as a form of public communication that is exempt from manipulation, may provide the proper vehicle for finding a language common to minority communities and the public at large in the societies of Central and Eastern Europe. Moreover, this type of public communication would then be pivotal to the solution of the problem that is being investigated. While this approach proceeds from the Habermasian model of the public sphere, it more generally devolves from the paradigm of *deliberative democracy*. The impediments mentioned above make it impossible for public deliberation to take place directly between a minority group and the general public, but it is worth exploring whether public deliberation could facilitate, albeit more indirectly, a mutual understanding between minorities and mainstream society.

How can this be achieved? What if the intra-group ethical-political discourses in the Habermasian sense, which permit a minority identity to "function" – to be reconstructed, negotiated, renegotiated, and so forth – take place in the format of public deliberation that unfolds "before the eyes" of the public? Could this serve as a guarantee that the claims which come about as a result of such discourses are neither whimsical, nor the results of manipulation or false consciousness but do, in fact, represent the genuine cultural needs of the members of minorities?

If the communication through which the members of a community discuss the external conditions that are necessary for the optimal reproduction of their cultural identity over time is largely exempt from manipulation, this could vouch for the credibility of the claims resulting from this discourse. In this case, the crucial condition helping to overcome the communication barrier between minorities and the general public would be that anyone would be able to see for herself whether or not the public-deliberative parameters of the discourse are at hand in a particular case – namely, rationality, openness (inclusivity), freedom from coercion, and equality of the participants. Even an outside observer would then be able to establish whether or not a discourse displays the characteristics typical of public deliberation.

It goes without saying that the procedural correctness of this type of intra-group discourse requires that the interests of society as a whole are represented as well. Otherwise, the discourse would degenerate into what is known as "enclave deliberation," with all the detrimental consequences that would hold for the credibility of the claims produced. Chapter 8 argues that one way in which to preclude the emergence of enclave deliberation involves opening ethical-political discourse to the participation of all members of the given minority community on the premise that its rank-and-file members – unlike leaders, zealous activists, and claimants to leadership within the group – would not be interested in advancing claims that aim to benefit the minority at the expense of the society as a whole.

In the final analysis, all of the considerations we have raised lead to the conclusion that the communicative empowerment of such minority groups as those typically encountered in the societies of Central and Eastern Europe is possible, provided that it happens in conjunction with the creation of a culture of egalitarian, public-deliberative communication within the groups in question. The explosion of various forms of internet communication in recent years holds certain particularly promising prospects in this regard. Safeguarding the cultural identity of minorities through communicative empowerment may well prove to be complementary to – not competitive with – the more traditional approaches such as the promotion of cultural rights and the political empowerment of minority communities.

Index

For Product Safety Concerns and Information please contact our EU
representative GPSR@taylorandfrancis.com
Taylor & Francis Verlag GmbH, Kaufingerstraße 24, 80331 München, Germany

www.ingramcontent.com/pod-product-compliance
Lightning Source LLC
Chambersburg PA
CBHW050439280326
41932CB00013BA/2170